THE STATE OF GERMANY
The national idea in the making, unmaking and
remaking of a modern nation–state

IN MEMORY OF BILL CARR
Professor William Carr, 1921–91

THE STATE OF GERMANY

The national idea in the making, unmaking and remaking of a modern nation-state

Edited by John Breuilly

Longman
London and New York

Longman Group UK Limited,
Longman House, Burnt Mill,
Harlow, Essex CM20 2JE, England
and Associated Companies throughout the world.

Published in the United States of America
by Longman Publishing, New York

© Longman Group UK Limited 1992

First published 1992

British Library Cataloguing-in-Publication Data

A catalogue record for this book is
available from the British Library

ISBN 0 582 07864 4 CSD
ISBN 0 582 07865 2 PPR

Library of Congress Cataloging in Publication Data
The State of Germany: the national idea in the making, unmaking,
and remaking of a modern nation-state / edited by John Breuilly.
    p.   cm.
  Includes bibliographical references and index.
  ISBN 0-582-07864-4 – ISBN 0-582-07865-2 (pbk.)
  1. Nationalism–Germany.   2. Germany–Politics and government.
I. Breuilly, John, 1946–
DD175.S85   1992
943. 08–dc20

Set by 7 in Bembo 10/12
Produced by Longman Singapore Publishers (Pte) Ltd.
Printed in Singapore

Contents

Contents

Notes on contributors

John Breuilly is Senior Lecturer in History at the University of Manchester. His publications include *Nationalism and the State* (1982); *Joachim Friedrich Martens und die Deutsche Arbeiterbewegung* (1984), and *Labour and liberalism in 19th century Europe* (1992). He is currently involved in a research project on the comparative cultural history of mid–19th-century Hamburg, Lyon and Manchester.

Michael Hughes is Senior Lecturer in History at University College of Wales, Aberystwyth. His publications include *Law and Politics in Eighteenth Century Germany* (1988), *Nationalism and Society: Germany 1800–1945* (1988), and *Early Modern Germany, 1477–1806* (1991).

James J. Sheehan is Dickason Professor in the Humanities and Professor of History at Stanford University. He is the author of *German Liberalism in the Nineteenth Century* (1978), *German History, 1770–1866* (1989), and other studies on modern German history. He is now working on the emergence of the German art museum as a social and cultural institution.

Dieter Langewiesche is Professor of Modern History at the University of Tübingen. His publications include *Liberalismus und Demokratie in Württemberg zwischen Revolution und Reichsgründung* (1974), *Liberalismus in Deutschland* (1988), and *Europa zwischen Restauration und Revolution 1815–1849* (2nd edn, 1989). Books he has edited include *Die deutsche Revolution von 1848/49* (1983), *Liberalismus im 19.Jahrhundert: Deutschland im europäischen Vergleich* (1988), and *Revolution und Krieg. Zur Dynamik historischen Wandels seit dem 18.Jahrhundert* (1989). He is currently engaged in research on Württemberg and Baden during the Third Reich.

William Carr was, until his death in June 1991, Professor Emeritus at the University of Sheffield. His publications include *Schleswig–Holstein,*

1815–1848: a study in national conflict (1963), *History of Germany 1815–1945* (1969, now in its 4th edn), *Arms, Autarky and Aggression* (1972), *Hitler: a study in personality and politics* (1978), *Poland to Pearl Harbour* (1985), and *Origins of the Wars of German Unification* (1991).

Katharine A. Lerman is Lecturer in Modern European History at St David's University College, Lampeter. Her publications include *The Chancellor as Courtier. Bernhard von Bülow and the Governance of Germany 1900–1909* (1990). She is presently working on a study of Bismarck.

William Sheridan Allen is Professor of History at the State University of New York at Buffalo. He is the author of articles on the theories of fascism and totalitarianism, the Holocaust, the German resistance to Hitler, and public opinion in the Third Reich as well as the following books: *The Nazi Seizure of Power* (1965; revised edn, 1984), and *The Infancy of Nazism* (1976).

Michael Burleigh is a Lecturer in International History at the London School of Economics and Political Science. His books include *Prussian Society and the German Order* (1984), *Germany Turns Eastwards: A Study of 'Ostforschung' in the Third Reich* (1988, 2nd edn 1990), (with Wolfgang Wipperman) *The Racial State: Germany 1933–1945* (1991). He is currently researching into the Nazi 'Euthanasia' programme and editing a *History Today* book on Nazi racial and social policy.

Peter Alter is deputy director of the German Historical Institute, London, and Professor of Modern History at the University of Cologne. His publications have been in the areas of Irish, British and German history. They include *The Reluctant Patron: Science and the State in Britain 1850–1920* (1987) and *Nationalism* (1989). He is currently writing on the *German Question and Europe*.

Mary Fulbrook is Reader in German History at University College, London. Her publications include *Piety and Politics: Religion and the rise of absolutism in England, Württemberg and Prussia* (1983), *A Concise History of Germany* (1990), *The Fontana History of Germany 1918–1990: The Divided Nation* (1991), and *The Two Germanies 1945–1990: Problems of Interpretation* (1992). She is joint editor of *German History: the Journal of the German History Society*. Her current research is into elites, dissent, and political culture in East Germany, 1945 to 1990.

Wolf D. Gruner is Professor of European History and European Studies at the University of Hamburg. He is the author of many articles on German, European and regional history and on relations between Germany and other European countries and has edited a book on *Gleichgewicht in Geschichte und Gegenwart*. His books include *Die deutsche Frage. Ein Problem der europäischen Geschichte seit 1800* (1985), *Die Rolle und Funktion von Kleinstaaten im internationalen System 1815–1914* (1985), *Bündische Formen deutscher Staatlichkeit in Geschichte und Gegenwart*, and *Deutschland mitten in Europa* (1991). He is at present writing a book on the German Confederation of 1816 to 1866.

List of abbreviations

CDU	Christlich–Demokratische Union (Christian Democratic Union)
CSU	Christlich–Soziale Union (Christian Social Union)
FDP	Freie Demokratische Partei (Free Democratic Party)
FRG	Federal Republic of Germany
GDR	German Democratic Republic
KPD	Kommunistische Partei Deutschlands (Communist Party of Germany)
NPD	Nationaldemokratische Partei Deutschlands (National Democratic Party of Germany)
NDSAP	Nationalsozialistische Deutsche Arbeiterpartei (National Socialist German Workers' Party)
SA	Sturmabteilung (Storm Troop)
SED	Sozialistische Einheitspartei (Socialist Unity Party)
SPD	Sozialdemokratische Partei Deutschlands (Social Democratic Party of Germany)

Preface

In November 1989 the Berlin Wall came down. By the end of 1990 the two German states had been reunited. Many Germans as well as non-Germans wonder what reunification means. Should one be concerned about the re-emergence of a powerful German nation-state, even if that power is based upon economic rather than military strength? Or should one consider that the changes that have taken place in Germany, in Europe, and in the world of international relations since 1945 mean that such concerns are misplaced, a product of historical preoccupations that have been rendered obsolete?

Much of this debate will focus on contemporary events and views about what is wholly new in Europe and Germany. However, it is important to question the historical perspectives that so often underlie contemporary understanding. When people refer to the 'German question', almost invariably the Germany which serves as a reference point is the unitary nation-state which existed between 1871 and 1945. How one understands the 'question' is then linked to one's view of that nation-state – its internal character, its foreign policy, and its own changing history. However, this perspective is misleading. It excludes the other 'Germanies' of the modern period – the Germany of the Holy Roman Empire, of the Napoleonic period, of the post-1815 Confederation, of the German National Assembly in 1848–9. It often neglects the point that before 1871, between 1871 and 1945, and after 1945 there was never a single, indeed often not even a dominant, idea of what Germany was or should be. Rather there were different, changing and conflicting views. Finally, the perspective can often assume some simple and direct connection between what Germans thought Germany should be like, and what in practice happened in Germany. Yet it may be that the actual nation-state of 1871 or 1919 or 1933 (and 1990?) did not express any 'idea' of Germany at all.

The purpose of this book is to recover something of the plurality, changeability and contingency of the idea of Germany. Most of the chapters – those by Hughes, Sheehan, Carr, Lerman, Burleigh, Fulbrook and Gruner – began life as talks in a series I organised in the academic year 1989–90 under the title of 'The Making and Unmaking of a Nation-State'. I asked each speaker to consider two particular questions. First, for the period and subject under consideration, what was meant by ideas such as German, Germany and nationality? Second, what, if any, were the political consequences of such ideas?

The idea for the series was conceived in the academic session 1988–89 and the speakers and topics fixed upon by the spring of 1989. Only during the course of the talks did the dramatic changes take place in Eastern Europe which led rapidly to German reunification. What had begun as primarily a question of historical understanding suddenly acquired a contemporary significance. It seemed to me that there was a very special merit in turning the talks into a book. There was a danger after November 1989, and especially after unification in 1990, that the flood of books and articles on the German question would be fixated on the present situation. Historical interpretation, insofar as it was introduced into the discussion, would run the danger of being too strictly subordinated to very immediate concerns. The theme of these talks was clearly central to any historical perspective on contemporary German events, but having been worked out before November 1989 had a valuable distance from those events.

There were omissions in the original series of talks which needed to be addressed in the book. The chapters start in the late eighteenth century, when ideas of political reform in 'Germany' were gathering pace. There was, however, a large chronological jump from James Sheehan's study of Napoleonic Germany to William Carr's consideration of German unification under Bismarck. Something on the national question in 1848 was needed, and Dieter Langewiesche agreed to write a chapter on this subject.

Michael Burleigh's fascinating study of a particular branch of academic study – the study of Eastern Europe – casts new light on continuities of national thinking from Weimar, through the Third Reich, to post-1945 Germany. However, it needed to be complemented by a study of the fate of nationalism under the Third Reich in more general terms, and this is undertaken by William Allen. Mary Fulbrook considers the ideas of nationality in the two Germanies which emerged out of the ruins of 1945 and Wolf Gruner looks at the place of Germany in contemporary Europe against a broad historical perspective. However, neither of them had much opportunity to consider the nature and importance of ideas of German nationality in immediate post-1945 Germany. Peter Alter has done this.

Other chronological omissions remain: on the restoration period 1815–48, on the character of Bismarckian Germany between 1871 and 1890, and on the Weimar Republic. However, it is not possible to include everything in a single book. Furthermore, the chapters on the preceding and succeeding periods cast light on these phases. In my Introduction I also try to trace broad continuities and changes for the whole time span covered by this book, and in particular to make points about these relatively neglected periods. Finally, in the Conclusion, in a necessarily speculative way, I turn to the prospects for a united Germany in the immediate future.

What is important is that the general reader, as well as specialists who focus on only one small part of modern German history, should be able to get from this book a sense of the varying, conflicting, changing meanings of terms like Germany, German and nation and an appreciation of the complicated and often surprising connections between such terms and the actual political history of modern Germany.

I would like to thank the contributors to this book. They all coped very well with their editor. I am happy to acknowledge the support of the Department of History at Manchester University which provided some financial support for the original series of talks. Above all, I wish to thank the Goethe Institut in Manchester, and especially its Director, Gerhard Murjahn. For a number of years the Institut has generously supported series of talks on modern German history. Without the Institut there would have been no talks and, therefore, no book. I would like also to thank Ian Kershaw for his advice on the Introduction and Conclusion.

William Carr sent me the final version of his chapter just a couple of weeks before his death on 20 June 1991, aged 70. His loss will be felt greatly by historians of modern Germany. His books, ranging from specialist studies to a very successful textbook on nineteenth- and twentieth-century Germany, have been a major contribution to our understanding of modern German history. He was also a wise and considerate friend of younger historians. This book is dedicated to his memory.

John Breuilly
Manchester
August 1991

CHAPTER ONE

The national idea in modern German history

John Breuilly

I

The history of Germany between 1871 and 1945 has been the subject of intensive study and strong, often violent disagreement. Could unification have taken place in some other way? Could the new nation-state have developed different political structures and pursued other foreign policies? How much of the responsibility for the world wars lay with those outside Germany? Should Hitler and National Socialism be understood as exclusively German phenomena – the culmination of a peculiar national history – or as an extreme version of a politics which could also be found in other parts of Europe? Those are questions which an interested reader can pursue in many other books (see Further Reading). This book has a rather different, though closely related theme: the character of the national idea in German history and its political significance.

Before this theme can be approached properly it is necessary to put aside certain ways in which modern history, especially German history, is commonly understood. The unitary nation-state of 1871–1945 serves as the reference point for our understanding of all modern German history. More generally, the unitary nation-state is commonly regarded, whether for good or bad, as the 'normal' political unit of the modern period. The history of modern Europe is seen as the history of the rise of the nation-state. Older political units were destroyed through this process – both small polities such as city-states, bishoprics, archbishoprics and petty princedoms, and also the large multi-national dynasties. Germany is one example of this process. The Holy Roman Empire, made up of these kinds of political units, was destroyed with the rise of the territorial state, and eventually the most powerful of those states – Prussia – eliminated the remaining small states and expelled the multi-national Habsburg dynasty from Germany in order to construct a nation-state.

That process is one side of the equation – namely the destruction of other kinds of states. The other side of the equation is what makes the new state a *nation*-state. This is generally assumed to be a sense of national identity within the population of the new state. A history of the creation of Germany is, therefore, a history both of the way in which Prussia constructed a new state and of the development and growth of a sense of national identity, most strongly expressed in the form of nationalism. The historians who celebrated the story of unification, known as the *kleindeutsch* (little German, meaning a Germany under Prussian leadership which excluded Austria) or Borussian or Prussian school of history, saw that story in terms of the convergence and eventual joining together of Prussian state power and German national feeling. It is most evident in the unfinished history of nineteenth-century Germany written by Heinrich von Treitschke.[1] In that study chapters alternate between Prussian-centred political history and German-centred cultural history.

This story can also be seen as one specific variant on a general theme in modern history. Many historians begin their narratives of the formation of this or that nation-state by looking at the origins of a sense of national identity and the construction of early nationalist movements, and then go on to connect that to the formation of new states. Conversely, the ways in which the German case is understood have shaped general views of nationalism and state formation. In his influential book *Nationalism* Kedourie starts with the striking sentence:

> Nationalism is a doctrine invented in Europe at the beginning of the nineteenth century.[2]

Germany serves as a major example for Kedourie's argument. In that argument, the history of the formation of a nation-state is the history of how nationalism moves from being a doctrine at the political margins to becoming the central ideology of the modern state. So general views of nationalism and understandings of the history of German nationalism are inextricably linked. It is necessary, therefore, to look critically not only at specific interpretations of German nationalism but also at ways of approaching the subject of modern nationalism generally.

It is easier to criticise the view that the formation of the German nation-state was inevitable, the German variant of a modern pattern, than to replace it. Many criticisms are no more than variations upon that view, arguing for example that the Prusso-German state could

1. H. von Treitschke, *Deutsche Geschichte im 19. Jahrhundert*, 5 vols, (Leipzig, 1879–94; Königstein, 1981). There is a seven-volume English translation (London, 1915–19).
2. E. Kedourie, *Nationalism* (London, 1971), p. 9.

have evolved in a liberal direction or that there is no essential continuity between the national ideas that prevailed in imperial Germany, in the Weimar Republic and in the Third Reich. However, the unitary nation-state still serves as the reference point, only it is now associated with different views about its character or potential. Sometimes one teleology replaces another. Thus those historians who look back to the 'federalism' of the Holy Roman Empire and the German Confederation to find models for how contemporary Germany (and Europe) might evolve; or who focus on the German National Assembly of 1848–9 and the Weimar Republic in order to locate a liberal and parliamentary tradition, can be as guilty of a selective distortion of German history as those who take the unitary, illiberal and expansionist qualities of the German nation-state as its 'essential' features. In this introduction I wish to question this search for an 'essential' Germany, by showing how changeable and contingent were ideas of German nationality. Having argued that, however, I will go on to connect the argument to broader interpretations of nationalism in order to show that one does not have then to go to the opposite extreme of seeing German nationalism and the formation of a German nation-state as historical accidents, whether lucky or unlucky.

II

There must be some special magic in this word 'German'. One can see that each person calls 'German' whatever it suits him and whatever assists his party standpoint. Thus the use of the word changes according to requirements.[3]

So opined Bismarck in 1864, shortly after coming to power as minister-president of Prussia. He was as guilty of this charge as anyone.

The chapter by Michael Hughes demonstrates a variety of meanings for terms such as German and Germany in the last decades of the Holy Roman Empire. For some the terms were deliberately emptied of political content. The passage from Schiller which is quoted by Hughes

---

3. A Bismarck speech of 22 January 1864 before the Prussian *Landtag*. Quoted in W. Mommsen, *Stein, Ranke, Bismarck: ein Beitrag zur politischen und sozialen Bewegung* (Munich, 1954), p. 187. For the full text see *Bismarck: Werke in Auswahl: Vol. 3* (Stuttgart, 1965), pp. 231–8 (231). My translation.

sees in political power a snare and delusion, insisting rather that German greatness be sought outside, even against the world of politics. Even that has to be treated with some scepticism, however, as Schiller expressed this sentiment when French power was already penetrating the German lands. 'Cultural' greatness could perhaps serve as a compensation for political quiescence. What is more, Schiller expressed a form of cultural elitism. Although Schiller, Goethe and others used German as the vehicle for expressing their ideas, their elevated notion of art disabled them from becoming truly popular figures in their own time. Their transformation into literary giants who prepared Germany culturally for a later stage of political greatness was a posthumous construction.

Hughes focuses upon those who sought political reform within the Holy Roman Empire. The great problem here is that the Holy Roman Empire, though clearly 'German' in some sense, appears wholly unfitted politically as a vehicle for nation-state formation, whereas the territorial states of the time, so clearly the political model for the later nation-state, possessed little of that 'German' quality. Hughes shows that we must not measure the Holy Roman Empire against a model of the territorial state into which all sovereignty is concentrated. Nevertheless, he also rightly warns us against the recent trend to argue that the Holy Roman Empire really was capable of reform. With the rejuvenation of French power after 1789 it became increasingly apparent that the sovereign territorial state, resting on some kind of popular legitimacy, would destroy all other kinds of states. It was in the Napoleonic period, which witnessed the destruction of the Holy Roman Empire, that ideas of the sovereign territorial state with clear frontiers and a constitutional relationship to its subjects took hold in the German lands.

This might suggest that the political ideas Hughes discusses had no significance. They were part of the vocabulary of an obsolete and failed political structure. Dalberg, for example, who is considered as a would-be imperial reformer in the 1780s by Hughes, clearly fails when he seeks, by means of collaboration with Napoleon, to continue with a programme of German political reform. Yet one needs to appreciate that Dalberg remained politically significant. Men who had learned their politics in the Holy Roman Empire were involved in drawing up various schemes for the organisation of Germany which were discussed with increased vigour as the defeat of Napoleon moved from the realm of fantasy to that of possibility and then to that of fact. Rather than see German nationalism at this time as an anticipation of a later German nation-state or as one way of expressing some 'essential' German idea, we should therefore regard it as one aspect of a political culture which was fast becoming obsolete.

The reason it was becoming obsolete was because the most important political developments went on at the level of the territorial state, as Sheehan makes abundantly clear in his chapter. The term 'patriot', both in and beyond the German lands, principally meant reformers who wished to create some popular legitimacy for their particular state. Thus it makes sense to call Montgelas a Bavarian patriot, or Stein and Hardenberg Prussian patriots. As Sheehan also makes clear, the reform programmes of these patriots were motivated by the need to strengthen states which had been desperately weakened by French successes. That applied to 'collaborator' states such as Bavaria, Baden and Württemberg which had won new territory as much as it did to 'resister' states such as Austria and Prussia which had lost territory. Indeed, it is the distinction between reforming patriots and their conservative opponents which is more important than that between those who would work with or fight against Napoleon. Most Prussian reformers, for example, saw no alternative to collaboration with Napoleon until the failure of the Russian campaign at the end of 1812. Even Baron Stein, revered as a German patriot who fought unremittingly against Napoleon, helped administer those parts of Hannover Napoleon gave to Prussia in 1805 and spent a large part of his time as Prussian first minister in 1807–8 negotiating a peace settlement with France.

Sheehan focuses on the reforming process within the territorial states which came to dominate the German lands after 1806. Here I would just draw attention to the marginal role any notion of *German* patriotism played during those years. First, there were the nationalist intellectuals. These picked up on the ideas of the German cultural elitists such as Schiller. They also drew upon Herder who had argued that each nation, identified largely by its language, had a unique character and value. Perhaps the best known is Fichte who, in his lectures of 1808, *Addresses to the German Nation*, developed this Herderian notion, arguing that the language needed to be preserved in all its purity and that there should be an organised programme of education to make Germans aware of their national character. Berlin was still occupied by French troops at this stage and the French censor considered it advisable to allow Fichte to lecture, in part because a programme of educational and cultural renewal presented no threat to the French, unlike any advocacy of guerrilla warfare or popular insurrection. Prussia remained almost wholly quiescent under French control, in marked contrast to countries such as Spain and Russia.

There were other German patriots who were closer to political power than these intellectuals and who advocated more immediate resistance. The best known of these is Baron Stein. An imperial knight who had been 'abolished' by Napoleon's reforms, he had also been a long-serving official in the Prussian service. He had risen to ministerial status in the unreformed administration before 1806 and began to counsel reform only in the months immediately following the military defeats of October 1806. These limited reform proposals, and especially the violent manner in which he pressed them upon the king, led to his dismissal for 'insolence' in January 1807. He retired to Nassau where he wrote a famous reform memorandum, the Nassau Denkschrift. This over-praised document focused upon civil reform designed to increase civic participation and reduce government expenditure, but ignored entirely the pressing problems of military expenditure and relations with France. He was appointed chief minister in October 1807 and served for almost exactly a year before being dismissed on Napoleon's insistence.

There was Stein, the patriotic reformer dedicated to strengthening the Prussian state and realistically negotiating with France. There was also the Stein who dreamed of a rising against the French, inspired by the Spanish insurrection of 1808. After his dismissal Stein resided in Austria and advised the government there which declared war on France in 1809. In the propaganda build-up to this war, in which the Austrian government hoped to obtain support from other parts of Germany whose governments were allied with Napoleon, sentiments of German patriotism were invoked. Incidentally, Herder's idea of connecting German patriotism to 'folk' culture had more impact in the Austrian court, where the Empress and others wore 'peasant' costumes at balls, than it did in Berlin which was still much influenced by the Francophile contempt in which Frederick II had held most things German. Thus German patriotism had different meanings at this time, and it is misleading to make much of any particular connection to Prussia.

The war proved short and disastrous for Austria. It brought Metternich to power in Vienna with a policy which insisted on collaboration with Napoleon, a repudiation of patriotic state reform, and an intense suspicion of German national sentiments or ideas of appealing to popular forces beyond the control of the existing government. Stein now removed himself to Russia. As Franco-Russian relations deteriorated after 1810, so Stein became an adviser to Tsar Alexander. In 1812 he was joined by patriots from Prussia who could not accept the military alliance their king had made with Napoleon. Stein was charged with the task of administering occupied areas in Germany after the failure of Napoleon's Russian campaign and the advance of Russian soldiers into central Europe.

It does make sense, therefore, to call Stein a German patriot and, furthermore, one who had considerable political influence. But what kind of patriot was he and what kind of influence did he possess?

In a famous letter of 1812 Stein expressed his patriotic sentiments.

> I have only one fatherland, and that is Germany, and because according to the old constitution I belong to that and not simply to any part of that fatherland, so am I committed to the whole fatherland and not to any one part of it. To me the dynasties at this moment of great developments are a matter of complete indifference. My wish is that Germany will be great and strong, in order that it win back its standing and independence and nationality and assert itself in its position between France and Russia.[4]

The passage repays close attention. At first glance, one might see Stein as being animated by traditional imperial patriotism of the kind analysed by Hughes. The reference to the 'old constitution', his own status as a deposed imperial knight, his intense hatred for the French satellite states which were created out of the destruction of the Holy Roman Empire: all seem to bear this out. But there are contrary indications. Stein was himself one of these collaborators in 1803–6 as Prussia also profited from the destruction of the Holy Roman Empire. One must remember that the letter which is quoted was to Graf Münster, a representative of the old Hannoverian interest, and Münster wished to be assured that Stein no longer served Prussia, a regional rival that might stand in the way of a Hannoverian restoration or that he was too closely tied to Russian interests which had, after all, in 1807 largely confirmed Napoleon's position in Germany.[5] Above all, it was the very exclusion of Stein from state power which led him to German patriotism. The Napoleonic satellite states, Prussia and Austria had all failed – Germany became a substitute idea.

It is also clear that Stein recognised that simple imperial restoration would not suffice; the old Holy Roman Empire was too weak a structure to assert itself between France and Russia. Equally, he was not thinking in terms of the construction of any kind of unitary national state. There is little evidence that Stein saw any close connection be-

4. Stein to Graf Münster, quoted in G. Ritter, *Stein: eine politische Biographie* (Stuttgart, 1981), p. 408. For the full text of the letter see *Freiherr vom Stein: Briefe und amtliche Schriften*, vol. 3 (Stuttgart, 1961), pp. 817–18. My translation.

5. Indeed, this is made clear in the opening of the letter which is usually omitted from quotations in secondary sources. What is more, suspicion of Stein's Russian connections and of his lack of concern with specifically Prussian interests created hostility between Stein and Prussian patriots such as Yorck in 1813–14.

tween language and 'cultural' nationality on the one hand, and citizenship and political loyalty on the other. He defended the inclusion of Poles in the Prussian state on the grounds that the Hohenzollern dynasty could rule in a way that would satisfy both German and Polish speakers. From 1814 when a post-war settlement had to be considered, his main concern seems to have been with the way in which Prussia and Austria as the major (but not the only) German powers could cooperate with one another and the remainder of the German lands to prevent a power vacuum developing.

Arguably this was precisely what was aimed at in the 1814–15 peace settlement, and in particular in the form of the German Confederation. Stein objected to the way in which the Napoleonic creations such as Baden and Bavaria were preserved, but the general idea behind the Confederation fitted in with many of his patriotic ideas.

One can draw a number of conclusions from this. First, German patriotism was marginal in the Napoleonic period. At a popular level loyalties to confession, region, narrow self-interest, and traditional rulers prevented any conception of German identity playing a significant role. Indeed, it was only where such loyalties were even stronger – as in Spain and Russia – that a kind of populist resistance to Napoleon developed. However, it would be quite misleading to see this as having anything in common with modern nationalism, although nationalist myth-makers recruit such resistances to their cause. For modern patriotism, in which state and nation are connected by ideas of culture and constitutionality, one has to turn to France and England at this time. As yet modern political movements in Germany were starting to develop only within the newly forming territorial states formed out of the destruction of the old Germany. At that political level it was the battles between reformers and conservatives within the modernising territorial states which mattered most. German ideas could be used in those battles and in the conflict with Napoleon, but they could be used by Austrians as well as Prussians. Ideas of cultural nationality could also be used by other states, without any implication of a related political programme. In 1808 the Bavarian government invited Goethe to draw up a German *Volksbuch*, intended to make clear the cultural glories of Germany. Goethe declined the invitation, but what is interesting is that the government asked him, seeing no conflict between such an enterprise and the attempt to build up the Bavarian state, a Napoleonic creation and ally. Genuine German patriotism tended to be disassociated from the centres of political power and sometimes took a cultural form which actually implied political quiescence. Where, as with Stein, it had a political focus, it was fluid, changing according to circumstances, and rarely, if ever, thinking about state reform in unitary and national terms.

It is from this perspective that it is valuable to look at the German Confederation established in 1814–15. The Confederation has generally had a bad press. For those historians who look to some longstanding German tradition of 'federalism', it is far inferior to the Holy Roman Empire. It did not last nearly as long. It could appear the instrument of Austria and Prussia, unable to provide liberties and protections for the less powerful as had been – sometimes – the case in the old Empire. For those historians who look forward to modern statehood – unitary, national, rooted in popular sovereignty – the Confederation appears equally deficient.

Neither of these models could have been achieved in 1814–15. The catastrophic failure of the old empire, the destruction of the many small states in the south and west, including the temporal power of the Catholic Church, ruled out restoration. Austria and Prussia, both anxious to check the power of the other, were compelled instead to work with the medium-sized states which Napoleon had created. There were exceptions. The 'pure' satellite states of Westphalia and Berg, ruled by relatives or cronies of Napoleon, were abolished; the British interest required the restoration of Hannover; the need to compensate Prussia in Germany for loss of Polish territory, combined with the failure of Saxony to abandon Napoleon before the Battle of Leipzig in October 1813, led to the transfer of northern Saxony to Prussia. But the major Napoleonic creations in southern Germany – Baden, Bavaria and Württemberg – ruled by native German princes, were preserved.

Precisely the same forces prevented anything other than a confederal arrangement. Hardly anyone with political power thought of, let alone wanted, a unitary nation-state or modern constitutional arrangements. It would have raised institutional and boundary questions which many statesmen would not have understood, let alone answered. Neither, however, did they think purely in terms of a system of totally independent states in the German lands. The failure of the Confederation to develop powerful confederal institutions has led historians to underestimate the 'restoration' intentions at work in 1814–15. Statesmen then did not think, as we do, of states as territorially compact concentrates of sovereignty. Their political culture was of the kind described by Michael Hughes. Notions such as a confederal army, confederal courts, constitutional 'harmonisation' in which central governments would be reined in by estate assemblies, and the retention of special political privileges by some of the casualties of the

Napoleonic transformation, such as the imperial knights – all made sense within this political culture. They also made sense to those who were concerned that lack of coordination between the German states could create a dangerous power vacuum, and that vesting too much power into the hands of central government, even if this took the form of bureaucracy commanded by monarchy, might promote some of the levelling purposes of the French Revolution.

Many of these intentions came to nought. The individual states did increasingly become the centres of power. This was most obvious in the way the Confederation came to be used by Austria and Prussia as an instrument for interference in the affairs of other states. But, less obviously, the fact that Austria and Prussia *had* to interfere in this way, through the use of political power rather than by means of constitutional conventions as in the old Empire, also showed that these other states were strengthening their central institutions. Finally, Austro-Prussian conflict on such matters as a confederal army prevented any practical achievements. The fact that the institutions which created this territorial state-power were bureaucratic rather than parliamentary has often meant that historians whose criteria of modernity are liberal as well as national have failed to see the modernising character of the Confederation and its individual members.

The changes introduced in 1814–15 altered the political meaning of the idea of German nationality. Older political idioms drawing upon imperial traditions, sometimes newly flavoured with romantic or Catholic ingredients, came to seem more and more irrelevant, taking on an increasingly precious and reactionary character. Individual states, especially the Bavarian monarchy, promoted values of cultural Germandom, but did not see this as in any way charged with political implications that would threaten them.

Where German nationality did take on a new political significance was in relation to the development of modern state power. In a positive way, above all in Prussia, German nationality could be seen as an ally to state interest. Prussia had become a much more 'German' power in 1814–15 – losing Polish territories, acquiring new lands in central and western Germany, and facing the problem of a territorial division between her two western provinces and the rest of the state. Austria, by contrast, had opted in 1814–15 to exercise her influence in Germany by 'indirect' means and had made her major territorial gains elsewhere.

The national idea was also taken up by some opposed to modernising but illiberal states. Liberal opponents of many of the smaller princes, for example, found that they were blocked as much by Confederal

interference as by their own ruler. This led them towards a programme of national as well as state reform and also encouraged contacts between like- minded opponents in the various states. Increased
literacy, the growth of a 'public opinion' which modernising states
inadvertently created even as they also practised censorship, the multi-
plication of contacts across regions and states – all this gave a cultural
underpinning to elite liberal nationalism.

There were other kinds of oppositions. For example, the construction of larger states created religious minorities. Rhenish Catholics had
become an important minority within Prussia, adding their numbers to
those of Catholic Germans in provinces such as Silesia; Protestants in
Franconia and in the Palatinate constituted a large minority in Bavaria.
To the old conflicts between the confessions were added new conflicts
as a modernising, increasingly secular state sought powers in such areas
as education and marriage. Very often such minorities saw in more
powerful national institutions a means of reducing the interference of
the individual state. The same was true of artisans and peasants, vil-
lagers and townspeople, who rejected many of the innovations imposed upon them from the state capital.

This made the national idea a widespread, even a popular one by
1848, yet an idea which was unclear and to which people subscribed
for diverse and even contradictory reasons. Dieter Langewiesche shows
in his chapter how many of the illusions associated with the idea of
nationality were exposed in 1848–9, and how the 'springtime of nations' turned into a winter of discontent and national conflict. At the
same time, the German National Assembly clearly steered the national
idea in a liberal and modernist direction. It became increasingly clear
that a national state would have to be a sovereign and territorial state;
plans for some other way of sharing power were discredited. That in
turn meant that clear views were required as to the institutional features and boundaries of such a state. It also became clear in 1848–9
that Austria as a multi-national dynasty could never accept such a state.
However, it was not clear that Prussia, a dual nationality dynasty,
could be much more positive.

Thus a convergence between liberal nationalism and the Prussian
state was by no means inevitable. Clearly, however, 1848–9 had made
any other possible convergence between state power and nationality
unrealistic. The advocates of *Realpolitik* who argued the national role
of Prussia did so, therefore, by bolstering the negative point that no
other solution was possible with the argument that 'progress', understood as a kind of unstoppable historical force, would compel a convergence between Prussian power and German nationality. Many

liberal nationalists, both within and outside Prussia, did not believe that Prussia could play a positive role in creating a nation-state until she herself liberalised, and saw such liberalisation coming about as a consequence of economic and social progress. Many conservative Prussians also believed that a national Prussia would also be a liberal Prussia, and therefore opposed any abandonment of the dualist partnership with Austria.

The way in which Bismarck managed to overcome this political division is described by William Carr in his chapter and need not be considered further here. I would only add that a unique feature of Bismarck's thinking was that he accepted much of the case put forward by the liberal *Realpolitiker*. If and when Prussia 'went forth'[6] into Germany she would eventually have to concede constitutionalism and cooperate with progressive social and economic interests. However, he believed also that this could be done on terms which would preserve much of the old order, though conservatism would have to re-found itself in modern conditions.

What is also clear from Carr's chapter is how risky was Bismarck's course and how easily it might have failed. Neither the arguments of inevitability nor of Bismarck's diplomatic genius should obscure that basic point. Furthermore, there was no groundswell of national feeling in 1866–7 to support Bismarck. What also needs to be stressed is that the achievements of 1866–7 could, from a 'national' perspective, be better described as a *division* rather than a unification. The Confederation was destroyed; Austria was excluded from contacts with other German states; the south German states were tied militarily and economically to Prussia but struggled against further political connections; and in northern Germany a 'greater Prussia' was created as most of the new territories were annexed as new provinces. No wonder many nationalists opposed what Bismarck had done.

The 'completion' of unity in 1870–1 stands in a complicated relationship to what had been created in 1866–7. On the one hand, the Second Empire was more German and less Prussian. The war of 1870–1 had been one between nations, unlike the 'civil war' of 1866. The south German states were not annexed to Prussia but preserved, and this required the creation of more powerful 'German' institutions through which they could be connected to Prussia. However, the state was accordingly less unitary than the greater Prussia of 1867, its 'constitution' taking the form of a treaty between states rather than formu-

---

6. Frederick Willian IV in March 1848 had declared that Prussia would 'go forth' into Germany.

lating the desired relationship between a state and its citizens. Consequently the federalism of the Second Empire took the form of tolerating different kinds of governments, rather than devolving power from the centre on a uniform basis.

As a consequence, a major tension within the new state concerned how far the national idea should be associated with reform and change designed to create a more unitary and uniform state and society. The problem for those conservatives at the centre of power was that their desire to defend the status quo conflicted with the need to undertake reform in order to preserve or enhance the power of the new state. The national idea was taken up by reformers to justify the erosion of state rights, and the concentration of greater powers into national institutions. National liberals were the principal spokesmen for such a programme, but their arguments could also be taken up by radicals and even socialists who could see in this a way of undermining a state-based conservatism. However, precisely this kind of pressure could force national liberals into an increasingly illiberal definition of their programme – for example, deprecating parliament as a cockpit of factions which would undermine national unity. By the 1880s the national idea had been shorn of much of its liberal, reformist character and was used instead as a call to the defence of existing institutions, above all the army and the monarchy. New institutions, for example the navy, were supported only where their authoritarian character ensured they would not fall prey to 'factions', that is the popular parties which opposed the liberals. Indeed, it would not be going too far to say that national arguments in defence of the status quo had increasingly become the central component of national liberal as well as conservative ideology. This could obscure the national commitment of their political opponents.

National institutions acquired greater powers thereafter not so much because this was seen as ideologically desirable by those in power, but rather because it was a practical necessity. Innovations in such fields as welfare and warfare (health insurance, navy-building) could be undertaken only by the central state, and so new agencies had to be set up to carry out these tasks. As Kathy Lerman makes clear in her chapter on Chancellor Bülow, this presented insoluble problems to a conservative who both took up the national idea as a rallying cry and as a programme of military and colonial assertion, and yet at the same time tried to practise a 'do-nothing' conservatism.

The result was incoherence. One can see this at the level of national symbols. The symbols of the nineteenth-century nationalist movement – the colours of black-red-gold, a unitary constitution, a

national hymn or anthem: this all came into conflict with the federalist, state-rights, monarchist traditions which the German Empire tried
to preserve. The result was a flag which uneasily combined German
with Prussian colours, the lack of an official national anthem until
1922, and a 'pragmatic' constitution which was placed over the constitutions of individual states, was never revised, and which could not, therefore, take proper account of the increasing power of national institutions.

Yet that increased power had to find some expression in political
consciousness. Political regionalism declined in the Second Empire. By
1914 political opposition, be it Catholic or socialist or radical, was
largely focused on Berlin and organised by nationwide bodies. Participation in the state increased – measured by voting, membership of
political parties and other organisations, those affected by national welfare and educational policies, or those serving in the armed forces.
More generally, industrial and urban growth, and mass literacy had
created a sphere of public opinion which governments could not ignore. Many of these new participants did not like the way national
institutions functioned. By 1912 most voters voted for parties opposed
to existing arrangements. Specifically nationalist policies on such matters as
colonies and navy-building were as vehemently opposed as they were
supported. Right-wing nationalism was itself riven by the tensions between energetic and populist imperialism and defence of the status quo.

Nevertheless, the mere existence of Germany as a powerful and in
many respects successful state transformed the scope and character of
the national idea. There were two aspects to this. First, at the institutional level it was clear by 1914 that political habits had been created
by people who had known nothing other than the Second Empire.
Arguably 'political identity' should be understood as the assumptions
which accompany such political habits, rather than a separate set of
reflections which are deliberately communicated to the population.
Second, it was in the last decades before 1914 that a genuinely industrial society was created and which made possible, in a linguistically
and ethnically fairly homogeneous society, the development of 'standard national culture'.[7]

As a consequence, by 1914 few German speakers in the German
Empire thought of Germany as anything other than the territory of
that Empire, and of themselves as anything other than national members of that state. This was the basis of a latent sense of national identity which extended beneath the level of everyday political conflict.
The extent of this was made clear in August 1914 when Germans of

7. See E. Gellner, *Nations and Nationalism* (Oxford, 1983) for this idea and how it is
connected to industrialism.

all political persuasions rallied to the country. Although many of the internal political divisions had re-emerged by 1918, at the same time the war constituted a national experience far beyond any earlier event.

The problem was how to give this strong sense of national identity political expression after the war. The images of the Weimar Republic are so frequently those of division and weakness, that it is necessary to emphasise the strengths and agreements which were also important. The Weimar Republic was, by twentieth-century standards, a more 'national' state than the Second Empire. It was federalist, granting large powers to the constituent states. However, this was constitutional federalism which devolved that power in a systematic and uniform way, quite unlike the federalism of the Second Empire. Sovereignty now resided with an elected parliament, a national institution in a way in which the Hohenzollern monarchy never had been. There was an official national anthem and the adoption of the black-red-gold national colours.[8] Although some writers have seen Weimar continuing traditions of federalism from earlier centuries, I would rather stress that this was in many ways the first unitary nation-state in German history.

Furthermore, there was a significant, if limited and often implicit political consensus. Few wished to return to the monarchical order. The Second Empire, by losing the war, had discredited itself. Few accepted the justice of the Versailles peace settlement – the difference was rather between those who believed there was no choice but to accept the settlement and then to seek gradual revision and those who advocated rejection of the settlement. William Allen in his chapter draws attention to the widespread acceptance of the nation-state and national identity, even extending to the German Communist Party. What is more, one must bear in mind how Weimar survived major crises – the immediate post-war turmoil, the multiple crises of 1923, and for nearly four years the greatest depression known to modern capitalism, although of course that ultimately was the major cause of the downfall of the republic. Its institutions survived longer than those of liberal democracy in post-war Italy. Its fate was not exceptional: east of the Rhine, only one liberal democracy created at the Versailles settlement still survived by 1938 – namely Czechoslovakia. The 'failure' of Weimar has to be put in that perspective.

All that said, it is also clear that Weimar suffered from grave weak-

---

8. Furthermore, the declaration of the national colours is presented as an end in itself at the beginning of the constitution (Article 3). In the constitution of 1871 the adoption of the colours black-white-red are presented as a technical consequence of having a 'German' navy and merchant marine, coming in Article 55 in a section on shipping and navigation.

nesses. Many could not accept its legitimacy, viewing it as the product of defeat, the work of those who had collaborated with Germany's wartime enemies. The range and depth of political divisions made it impossible to create stable parliamentary government in which power alternated between parties or groups of parties which all accepted the constitution. Much power remained out of the control of public authorities – in the hands of big business, the army, the bureaucracy, and these groups in turn felt no commitment to the republic. Few accepted the boundaries of the state as final and legitimate, although the extent as well as the character of boundary revision was a matter of dispute. So although a territorial, sovereign national state, the territory, the sovereign institutions, and even the claim to patriotism were all matters of bitter dispute.

What this meant was that in times of crisis the national idea – an idea which was almost universally accepted in some form or another – could be turned into a weapon against government and parliament. The national idea meant unity whereas parliament meant division; it meant strength whereas the republic was weak. How it came about that Hitler and the National Socialist movement were best able to exploit the national idea in these ways is something which cannot be considered here. It is a complex story on which there is a mass of literature. (See Further Reading.) I would stress only two points. First, Hitler's success was predicated on the basis of a near universal acceptance of the nation-state as the political norm, coupled with a widespread rejection of the Weimar Republic as the legitimate form of that nation-state. Second, for most Germans the attraction of Hitler lay in the novel and energetic way in which he subscribed to that national consensus. It was not the specifically Nazi components of his ideology (anti-Semitism, race-centred nationalism, the drive for living space in the east) which appealed so much as the belief that he and his party had a better chance than most (and at least deserved an opportunity) of creating strong government which would tackle the problems besetting Germany.

The problem for the historian of the national idea in the Third Reich is, therefore, to relate this 'mainstream' nationalism (which itself had conservative, liberal and radical variants) to the specifically Nazi components of nationalism. In a particularly illuminating way this is what Michael Burleigh does, showing how right-wing nationalists of Weimar could, through a combination of ideological shifts and opportunist adjustments, make the transition to Nazi ideas of blood and race. This is important for the light it casts upon the relationship between more traditional forms of nationalism and the radical nationalism of National Socialism.

How far most Germans ever came to accept distinctively national socialist ideas is a difficult and contentious subject. Clearly foreign policy successes which did not merely undo Versailles but went further (e.g. the Anschluß with Austria) could evoke some popular response. This might be taken to mean that for many Germans the idea of Germany extended beyond the Germany of 1871, let alone that of 1919. On the other hand, it might be taken to mean that the citizens of a country which identify with it as their nation will normally accept increases in its power and territory if these do not appear to involve great sacrifice on their part. Indeed, William Allen goes further and argues that the fear that such sacrifices might be called for far outweighed pleasure in the triumphs.

I think one has to make some distinctions between these various phases of foreign policy and domestic responses. The Austrian enthusiasm for the Anschluß, for example, should be regarded less as the expression of a long-standing desire to be a part of Germany than as another bitter response to the defeat of 1914–18 and the internal crises which beset Austria in the 1930s. After all, the pan-German movement of Schönerer before 1914 had never commanded widespread support. The anti-Semitism of Austria in 1938 could in turn be linked to the feelings of crisis in the country. Certainly it was far stronger in Vienna than in Berlin. It was, after all, in Vienna that Hitler had learnt his anti-Semitism. Very different appears to be the response of Reich Germans, who were much cooler towards the union and took much less active a role in anti-Semitic actions.[9] This has an important implication. 'National' identity was bound up with political habits and institutions: Reich Germans had a different identity from Austrian Germans. The experience of war and defeat rapidly undermined Austrian enthusiasm for membership of a greater Germany. Yet it would be superficial to say that Austrians then conveniently 'forgot' that enthusiasm; their political traditions and experiences did indeed make them very different kinds of Germans from those who had grown up in the Reich. How a separate national identity was, on that basis, developed after 1945 is beyond the scope of this book.[10]

Again, one has to be discriminating about the popular response to other foreign policy achievements. The repudiation of Versailles (its

9. Willian Allen argues this very strongly. So far as 'Crystal Night' in 1938 is concerned, it seems to me that much of the distaste was for the lawless and violent nature of anti-Semitic action, rather than a principled antipathy to anti-Semitism as such.

10. See Robert Knight's contribution to 'Panel Discussion: Responses to the Question – "What has been the driving force behind German unifications and reunifications – cultural identity, power politics, or economic necessity?" ' *German History: Journal of the German History Society.* 9/2 (1991), pp 158–63

arms limitations, the demilitarised Rhineland) would naturally evoke widespread support because there had been a national consensus opposing Versailles. Nevertheless, this was always tinged by fear of war. I would not go quite as far as William Allen in depicting popular opinion as negative in response to the defeat of Poland in 1939 and France in 1940, but it appears to be the case that it was *after* the victory, and partly in response to the ease of such victories, that enthusiasm was expressed. Again, most Germans in principle had no objection to defeating Russia, but insofar as one can judge from the very guarded responses people offered in public, there was a feeling that it was unwise to embark on war on a second front. And as soon as the war clearly started to go wrong, certainly from the time when the defeat at Stalingrad had become common knowledge, the popularity of Hitler and the regime sank quickly. How far and how quickly this led to anti-nationalism along the lines argued by William Allen, or rather to a return to a more moderate and traditional nationalism, is a matter for debate.

It is also difficult to ascertain the extent to which the Third Reich actually did succeed in overcoming the internal divisions which beset the Weimar Republic. The regime preached the message of 'national community' (*Volksgemeinschaft*) and abolished many of the bodies which institutionalised internal conflict (parliament, trade unions, a free press), replacing them with institutions supposed to express national unity. How far that also abolished identification with 'sub-communities', and how far the new institutions actually managed to nurture a new sense of national identity is more debatable.[11] The key argument in William Allen's chapter is that the actual nationalist actions of the Third Reich not only went against 'mainstream' currents of national thinking, but also had the effect of gradually destroying all forms of nationalism. The assertion of national power brought with it war and defeat and occupation; the persecution of internal 'enemies' brought with it state terrorism and the destruction of the rule of law and the fear that you might be next on the list; the policy of a *Volksgemeinschaft* failed in fact to eliminate social divisions and was often seen as an opportunity for corrupt Nazis to enrich themselves. More generally one might argue that the descent into cultural barbarism undermined a sense of national identity which was based upon Germany's cultural as well as political and economic achievements.

Arguably there were also positive responses to some of these

11. Allen used the notion of 'subcommunities' in an essay comparing Italian fascism and National Socialism when in opposition. W.S. Allen, 'The appeal of fascism and the problem of national disintegration', in H. Turner (ed.) *Reappraisals of Fascism* (New York, 1975).

measures – for example, conventional middle-class values could support measures against the left, against trade unions, and against ethnic and other minorities, though naturally there would be an equally negative response from the working class, the left, liberals, and many committed Christians. Furthermore, responses could vary over time. Many Germans after 1945 recalled the years 1933 to 1939 as the best of their lives and replied affirmatively to the statement that Hitler would have been one of the greatest Germans but for the war. There are, of course, problems in interpreting such testimony, but it does point to a nuanced picture. Generally, however, the scholarly consensus has come to stress the failings rather than the successes of *Volksgemeinschaft* ideologies and policies in the Third Reich.

The year 1945 was as close as is possible in a modern society to a new beginning. Clearly Germans had to bring to their new situation some sense of what they were as Germans. As Peter Alter makes clear, physical survival was the overwhelming preoccupation and most Germans had little time to concern themselves with the issue of 'national' survival. Partly this was because the extremely harsh situation left little time for any other concerns. But partly it relates to William Allen's point that Hitler had discredited *every* kind of national sentiment.

The Allies were not committed to a division of Germany, once Austria had been restored and boundary changes made to take account of the interests of states such as Poland and Czechoslovakia. Partition emerged more as a consequence of the new Cold War divisions than as a deliberate policy to keep Germany weak. As Mary Fulbrook makes clear, it was in committing themselves to one or other side in that Cold War, that the political elites of West and East Germany came to construct new states. Only gradually, and in the case of the German Democratic Republic (GDR) somewhat later, did the states which developed out of this *de facto* partition seek national legitimacy. It was the commitment to the 'West' or to the 'East', and incorporation within an international bloc which mattered most. Any idea of national legitimacy was subordinated to that broader commitment. Adenauer's fear that a united Germany might lead the Federal Republic to abandon that Western orientation led him to look with grave suspicion on most ideas of reunification. German conservatives in the Federal Republic sought to combine the cultivation of a sense of national identity with this clear Western commitment.

By the 1960s opinion polls showed that in the Federal Republic a generation which had grown up since the war had little regard for national unity and regarded the GDR as a foreign place. Indeed, the increasingly strident manner in which conservatives talked of the need to create a sense of 'national identity' by the 1980s points to the decline of such a sense, replaced rather with a commitment to the institutions of the successful Federal Republic and integration into broader western institutions.

Mary Fulbrook also argues that similar developments were taking place in the GDR, though of course the lack of political freedom, of opinion polls and electoral contests between independent political parties makes it much more difficult to demonstrate. Certainly it would appear to be the case that any lack of 'legitimacy' (and the events of 1989–90 surely demonstrate how far the GDR regime lacked such legitimacy) was *not* related to a sense that the country was deficient as a *national* state. Indeed, the cultivation of national history from the 1970s points to the fact that the regime actually felt it necessary to try to manufacture support in that area. This policy failed along with the rest of its policies. More to the point – the sheer existence of a stable system for forty years was bound to shape the values, attitudes and habits of those who had never lived under any other system (even if they could imagine what that might be like).

By 1989 very few Germans in either state regarded national unification as an important, or likely prospect. Unification came about less as a result of a strong commitment to the idea of a united Germany than because of the power vacuum created by the collapse of communist power in East Germany. The role of 'nationalism' in 1989 was important – both in the sense of the commitment of the Federal Republic to the ideal of unification (a commitment which Chancellor Kohl then proceeded to act upon in a very decisive way) and of the desire of most East Germans to gain access to the West through unification. But its importance was principally in conditioning responses to a crisis that originated for other reasons. Furthermore, its own ambiguities are now becoming increasingly apparent. I will take up these points at greater length in the Conclusion.

That is why the creation of a reunified Germany can so easily coexist with a sincere commitment to European federalism and even to a disavowal of international power politics. (One thinks of the criticisms of Germany for not being prepared to act like a 'real' power during the Gulf War, and the rather feeble argument that the Basic Law of 1949 forbade Germany from acting any differently.) The case for linking German unification with European integration, and for stressing the complementarity of national and European identities, is strongly put by Wolf Gruner in his chapter. This case is not merely to check foreign fears or nationalist tendencies, but rather expresses the way political values have developed in Germany since 1945.

In 1871, 1919 and 1945 changes in the borders and institutions of Germany were associated with war. In 1933 and the years up to 1939 they were associated with the rise of an extremist nationalist movement to power and the use of state violence both at home and abroad. In 1989–90 change came about peacefully, guided by moderate political forces. The national idea, having entrenched itself as a 'natural' identity since 1871, was essential to that change. East Germans could only look to West Germany as the state they wished to join on the grounds of common nationality; no other East European state has such an opportunity open to it (though Jews can look to Israel as their true home). West Germans felt a moral obligation to the commitment to reunification enshrined in the Basic Law of 1949 and adhered to in all subsequent diplomatic undertakings, again because of this assumption of a common national identity.

That 'natural' sense of national identity goes back to the 'mainstream' national sentiment established between about 1890 and 1933. Before then any sense of national identity was usually confined to minorities and had varying political, often anti-political characteristics. That mainstream national sense was destroyed as an active political sentiment between 1933 and 1945 and has only played a part in the transformation of 1989–90 because of crises caused by many other factors.

III

Thus the meanings to be attributed to such terms as German, nationality and nation-state have varied greatly in content and significance between the late eighteenth century and today. One also has to view these meanings against a broader background. National histories tend to take the nation for granted. Historians are often suspicious of general theories, preferring to look at the 'facts' before them and on that basis telling a story 'in its own terms'. Without considering the general problems with this view, it is clear that the emergence of national consciousness and the formation of nation-states are general features of modern history. So it is worth asking if the case of Germany is but a specific variant of a general theme.

The general theme is the convergence of nationality and state to form nation-states. One obvious way of explaining this convergence is to see one of these as cause and the other as effect. Nationalist histo-

rians see the history of nation-state formation in terms of the rise of
national awareness among both elites and at a popular level. Politics
eventually has to follow the pressure of this sense of national identity
and so nation-states are formed. Other historians have seen nationalism
as little more than an ideological fig-leaf used by states and other interests to justify the expansion of their power both to their subjects and
to outsiders.

Such accounts are unsatisfactory. It is clear that a unified Germany
was created long before nationalism was a strong and active political
sentiment, certainly before it was a widespread and popular feeling.
Equally, however, it is clear that Bismarck would not have appealed to
the idea of Germany unless in his view it had possessed some independent political significance.

The idea of a 'convergence' between national feeling and the Prussian state is also deeply flawed. I have already argued that the idea of
German nationality had many, changing and often conflicting
meanings, so it can hardly be seen as a constant or growing element
which at some point 'combines' with state power. Furthermore, this
idea of changing meanings can also be applied to the idea of the Prussian state. Prussia constantly changed her territories, her institutions
and her relationships with her subjects and other states. What is more,
the very idea of what it meant for a state to expand her power and
territory changed. When Frederick the Great annexed new territories
after a successful war, he did not invoke the idea of Germany or issue
a constitution. Instead, for example in the case of Silesia, he agreed to
respect the customs and traditions of the new acquisition provided its
inhabitants transferred their allegiance to him. The policy of creating
uniform institutions was first pursued, rather fitfully, in post–1815
Prussia. The decision to take this further and to extend it to constitutional as well as administrative arrangements came only in 1848. It is
not a coincidence either that the description of Prussia as *a* state was
only first officially used in its first constitution, that of December 1848.
By 1866 it had become 'obvious' that Prussia could legitimise the extension of her power in Germany, power acquired in the first instance
through war, only by constructing a constitutional state. Clearly a
modern notion of the Prussian state needs to be related to a modern
notion of German nationality. In order to do this we need to return
to the era of the French Revolution and Napoleon.

The Revolution, especially with the outbreak of war between
France and much of the rest of Europe in 1792, transformed and
brought together the ideas of state and nation. The state was no longer
understood as a dynastic construct, legitimised by tradition, its mission

as guardian of the Christian faith and protector of the customs and laws of its subjects. Even before 1789 this understanding had been questioned by those who saw the monarch as a secular and reforming figure, the purpose of whose rule was to maintain and increase the happiness of his subjects. However, the break of 1789–92 made the shift to a new understanding quite clear.

The state was now an instrument, not in itself a sacred institution. But whose instrument? It was the instrument of its subjects. To effect this change, those subjects had to become citizens. Citizens were equals; therefore the distinctions of privilege had to be abolished. In principle this was a project which did not ask questions about the language or customs or history of the subject-citizen. In practice, in the midst of war against other states as well as against internal rebellions, the successive governments of France fused the idea of nation as the body of the citizens with the idea of the nation as the French.

This affected other parts of Europe in various ways. In part it stimulated a similar sort of patriotic resistance. However, without the prior internal changes of the kind that had taken place in France, this was of limited importance. Usually what is regarded as 'nationalism' turns out on closer inspection to be either the response of marginal elites – as in Germany – or a populism stimulated by very traditional institutions and sentiments – as in Spain.

At the level of individual states it produced patriots, who recognised the need to reform governments and their relations to their subjects in order to survive, whether as collaborators or opponents of Napoleon. What is important is that this reform process did not come to an end in 1814–15, even if the explicitly political, liberal side of it was severely set back. With the growth of market economies, of a more complex civil society which could not be simply ignored or controlled by governments, there also developed an enlarged sphere of 'public opinion'.

In these circumstances the idea of 'Germany' could acquire new significance in a variety of ways. First, in terms of the balance of power, it was clearly necessary to try to ensure that the German lands did not once again lapse into so decentralised and weak a situation as to create a power vacuum. Austro-Prussian dualism, rather than the realisation of federalist principles laid down in 1814–15, served this purpose. Once the principal rivalry came to be that *between* Austria and Prussia, clearly the working definition of Germany provided by their dualism would no longer suffice. Both states would then appeal to alternative notions of Germany to justify their own policies.

Second, and this relates to general views of nationalism, changes in the relationship between state and society conferred a new significance upon ideas of 'political identity'. The secular, territorial state made larger claims upon its subjects and yet, with the development of market economies, an enlarged public opinion, and a greater and more diverse subject population, there was a decline in the controls associated with churches, nobilities, guilds and monarchies – that is a society based upon a web of privileges. This was why states considered it so necessary to issue constitutions, to build up a favourable public image. It was necessary to find new, 'public' ways of controlling subjects and eliciting their cooperation and support. As we have seen in the case of the Bavarian monarchy, part of such an enterprise could consist of cultivating notions of German cultural nationality.

There was a long-standing sense of such notions, seen in the use of words such as '*deutsch*' and '*Germania*'. Generally, however, such terms had had little direct political significance before the late eighteenth century. Now both governments and oppositions to governments began to invest them with political significance. The idea of politics being about *representation* – of classes, of citizens, of the general interest – constantly pressed those active in politics to say *who* they represented. To refer to the sentiments, language, traditions, customs – in short, the *culture* – of those who were ruled, was one, increasingly important way of answering this question.

What is more, 'culture' in this sense acquired an increasing autonomy. The growth of communications, the increased importance of schooling, the need to find common terms to address larger audiences for newspapers and journals and books – all this enhanced the role of teachers, journalists and authors. They operated these specialised cultural institutions through the medium of language, and so the idea of nationality as cultural and a matter of language became more significant. This was not peculiar to Germany and considerations of these kinds have been central to some general interpretations of the development of modern national consciousness.[12]

One should not take the argument too far. As 1848–9 revealed, the idea of German nationality was still politically fluid and could lead to conflict, and was also something which had not really penetrated much below elite level. Nevertheless, those elites mattered. When the Prussian government came to pursue a policy of confrontation with Austria within Germany, it had to take account of those elites.

Bismarck did not really do much in this way before 1866. Until then his policy was largely one of Prussian aggrandisement and he

---

12. See, above all, Gellner, *Nations and Nationalism*; and B. Anderson, *Imagined Communities: Reflections on the Origins and Spread of Nationalism* (London, 1983).

ignored, even opposed, the liberal sentiments which dominated nationalism. Part of his genius, however, consisted in his recognition that the enlarged Prussian state needed the cooperation of the 'political nation', and this could be obtained only by constitutionalism and the acceptance of many liberal policies. State-formation under modern conditions, even if achieved by means of successful war in the first instance, could no longer take the traditional form of adding to the property of the monarch.

Placing unification, therefore, within a broader context of the development of the modern territorial state, a market economy, and an increasingly autonomous culture, enables us both to understand the German case better and to relate it to general approaches to the rise of the nation-state.

In the early years of the Second Empire there was little in the way of a 'national consensus'. Regional, political and religious differences still mattered more to most Germans than did the nationality they had in common. For many, a German nation-state could not be regarded as complete if it excluded Austria. For others, the central role of the authoritarian Hohenzollern monarchy led them to reject the idea of the new state as a German and national one.

Nevertheless, the 'nation-state' itself can extend and consolidate this sense of national identity. Given that most of the inhabitants of the new state were native speakers of German; that participation in government did increase; that national institutions touched people's lives in more and more ways; and that generally the power and prosperity of the country increased between 1871 and 1914 – given all that, it is no wonder that the Second Empire established itself, territorially if not institutionally, as the normal idea of Germany. Again, historians of other 'nation-states' in western and central Europe have argued that the creation of national consensus and identity at a popular level first became significant only in the three or four decades before the First World War.

I would argue that the idea of Germany which was formed in those decades has continued to be the 'normal' idea of Germany. In the optimistic period at the beginning of the First World War, politicians on the right could lay claim to an expanded view of Germany; as they were to do again in their critique of Versailles; and also in the Third Reich. Many Austrians welcomed the 'return' to Germany in 1938, and Reich Germans accepted that and other additions to Germany's territory and power. But these were exceptional sentiments and periods, soon undermined by defeat. In any case, the desire to exercise control over other peoples does not display any peculiarly German nationalist sentiment: it is quite clear that the British or the French were not averse to imperial power. What has endured, however, is the sense that the two German states (but not Austria) really do share a common national identity. That has often been a rather latent sense, not one which informed practical politics for much of the period between 1945 and 1989 and which did not set itself against broader forms of internationalism or increased acceptance of one's own 'partial' German state as legitimate and complete.

A sense of nationality, therefore, is very closely bound up with the fortunes of the modern territorial state. In the cases not only of Germany, but also of Britain and France, it was arguably in the period 1890–1914 that such a sense was created at a mass level. That did not, of course, preclude bitter divisions, but such divisions tended to be about the form rather than the fact of the nation-state. Furthermore, the simultaneous development of such national sentiments in other states worked in a mutually reinforcing way.

However, the bitter divisions within post-1919 Germany made it difficult, then impossible, to find political institutions which could command a national consensus. The politicians of Weimar tried to embody the idea of a nation-state in political institutions, but they were rejected. The Third Reich took flight from institutional solutions into the idea of the 'leader' state and imperialist expansion. The politicians of the immediate post-war years were preoccupied with adjusting to the pressures exerted by their former enemies, leading to division as those enemies themselves came into conflict and treated their sphere of Germany as a client. The success of the Federal Republic of Germany from the 1950s finally provided an alternative and stable political identity to that of *kleindeutsch* Germany, despite the efforts of some to maintain a commitment to that latter Germany. As with the Second Empire, a key element in this achievement has been simple survival and economic growth. But unlike the Second Empire, it has also been the product of a democratic constitution which has positively integrated most citizens into the institutions of the state. That success story not only made West Germans uninterested in 'old-style' nationalism, but also turned their state and society into a beacon of hope for the inhabitants of East Germany. For much of the post-war period, hope has taken the form of escape to the west or aid from the west. The German Democratic Republic did undoubtedly create a stable political structure and addressed some of the issues of 'political integration'. It did not survive merely by coercion. Nevertheless, it did not have the strength that a democratic constitution and a high standard of living created in West Germany. Moreover, the mere fact that East Germans could look to West Germany as a model weakened the GDR. It was the bankruptcy and collapse of the German Democratic Republic that brought about reunification rather than any strong commitment to an earlier model of Germany. Once again, one has to see the idea of nationality as important, but not all-important and also as taking a different form in this situation from the forms it had taken in earlier decisive moments of state-formation in Germany.

Obviously, the making, unmaking and remaking of a German nation-state is a unique history. Something of that history will be considered in the chapters in this book. Yet at the same time it is one 'national' history among many, and needs to be seen in that context. It also has to be seen as one element within a broader process of modernisation.

SUGGESTIONS FOR FURTHER READING

The best general survey of nineteenth- and twentieth-century German history is W. Carr, *A History of Germany 1815–1945* (1st edn., 1969), now due to come out in a fourth edition extended to take account of the events of 1989–90. Generally on the role of nationalism and of national identity in German history see M. Hughes, *Nationalism and Society: Germany 1800–1945* (London, 1988); and the interesting, though in my view misleading, argument presented in H. James, *A German Identity 1770–1990* (London, 1989).

More detailed for the earlier part of the period is J. Sheehan, *German History 1770–1866* (Oxford, 1990). We lack anything really up-to-date in English for the 1866–1900 period. Interesting is H.-U. Wehler, *The German Empire 1871–1918* (Leamington Spa, 1985) but this is a translation of a book which first appeared in 1973. Wehler's approach, treating the new nation-state as in some ways defective, has been criticised in D. Blackbourn and G. Eley, *The Peculiarities of German History* (Oxford, 1984). Generally for post-1900 German history see V. Berghahn, *Modern Germany: Society, Economy and Politics in the Twentieth Century* (Cambridge, 1987, 2nd edn.).

Weimar Germany, its collapse and the Third Reich have generated an enormous historical literature. On Weimar and its collapse see now I. Kershaw (ed.) *Weimar: Why did German Democracy Fail?* (London, 1990). For problems of interpreting the Third Reich see I. Kershaw,

The Nazi Dictatorship: Problems and Perspectives of Interpretation (London, 1989, 2nd edn.). Alter and Fulbrook provide guidance to further reading on post-1945 Germany.

For a general treatment of nationalism I would refer to J. Breuilly, *Nationalism and the State* (Manchester, 1985) which includes a treatment of nationalism in the periods of German unification and of National Socialism. Other general works I have found illuminating are E. Gellner, *Nations and Nationalism* (Oxford, 1983); B. Anderson, *Imagined Communities: Reflections on the Origins and Spread of Nationalism* (London, 1983); and A.D. Smith, *National Identity* (London, 1991).

CHAPTER TWO

Fiat justitia, pereat Germania? The imperial supreme jurisdiction and imperial reform in the later Holy Roman Empire

Michael Hughes

The recent reopening of the 'German question', with the rapid achievement of reunification, accelerating progress towards European political union, and the 'historians' dispute' (*Historikerstreit*) has revived debates about German identity, different forms of national unity and Germany's place in Europe. No new conclusions have been reached but a lot of old questions have been re-asked in stimulating ways. The 'nation-state' of 1871–1945 is no longer the only model of Germany available, although it has proved remarkably resilient. This led, for example, to a long neglect by German historians of the tradition of federalism and its equation with particularism and reaction. Loose federative political structures like the Holy Roman Empire and *Mitteleuropa* are again interesting. After a decade of concentration on Germany's recent past, the focus of historical attention has widened, with growing attention on the pre-unification period and even the later Holy Roman Empire.[1]

Historical judgements of the Holy Roman Empire have in the past too often been based on inappropriate or anachronistic models. Its image has also changed with the prevailing political climate. The concentration of many German historians on the process of state creation (*Staatsbildung*) has also distorted the picture. The growth of the individual German states interfered with the growth of the Empire as a state, while the fact that the Empire and its institutions continued to

1. R.A. Fletcher, 'History from below comes to Germany: the new history movement in the Federal Republic of Germany', *Journal of Modern History*, 60 (1988), pp. 557–68; G. Strauss, 'The Holy Roman Empire revisited', *Central European History*, 11 (1978), pp. 290-301.

exercise functions of government prevented the states possessing total and undivided sovereignty. Dismissive views of it were common in the later nineteenth century, after the unification of 1871, portrayed in nationalist historiography as the end of German weakness symbolised by the Old Reich.

In recent years the view of the later Holy Roman Empire among historians has changed and become much more positive. The Reich is no longer just a *Doktorfrage* but is becoming a very popular choice of subject for a *Doktorarbeit*. The latest substantial textbooks on the later Empire reflect this new approach.[2] Perhaps the pendulum has swung too far; there is some danger now of a new form of anachronism, a new *Reichsromantik* or *Reichspathos*, with the Holy Roman Empire being portrayed as a combination of the European Court of Human Rights, the United Nations and the European Community. The fact that the Empire was, at least in part, devoted to peace, freedom and justice derived as much from external factors as from a conscious choice of its inhabitants. This idealisation of the old Reich is itself part of the 'new nationalism' seen recently in Germany. What the new work has clearly shown is that the imperial institutions, traditionally written off as moribund, were active long after 1648. In recent years there has been a minor boom in studies of one of these, the imperial cameral court (*Reichskammergericht*).[3]

Though pre-modern in essence, the Reich did show evidence of growth, vitality and progress and can no longer be seen as a nation in aspic. The looseness of the German constitution provided opportunities for a great variety of different evolutions and there was nothing inevitable about developments. The post-1648 German political system was a mixture of different features, the geological record of successive accretions: the relics of a unitary German monarchy, important survivals of a feudal political structure, the skeletal remains of an aristocratic limited monarchy and distinct traces of federal elements. Tension between the old *Lehensordnung* (the feudal bond between lord and vassal) and the evolving federative structure continued to affect the Empire until its end. The relative weight of imperial power, or its substantial vestiges, the *Reservatrechte* (the residual powers that remained with imperial institutions) and the 'liberty', or power, of the Estates of the Empire changed with the political situation inside and outside

---

2. H. Schilling, *Höfe und Allianzen: Deutschland 1648–1763* (Berlin, 1989) and H. Möller, *Fürstenstaat oder Bürgernation: Deutschland 1763–1815* (Berlin, 1989) emphasise the need to appreciate the *Rechts- Freiheits- und Friedenstraditionen* which the Empire embodied, even if its form was bizarre to modern eyes.

3. V.Preß, *Das Reichskammergericht in der deutschen Geschichte* (Wetzlar, 1987).

Germany. The first was strengthened by Austrian influence in the Reich, the attachment of the small states to the Emperor and patriotic enthusiasm, especially in war and most especially after victories; the second was fuelled by *raison d'état*, the need for self–help and disillusionment with the Empire (*Reichsmüdigkeit*).

This chapter, originally delivered as a talk in a series entitled *The Making and Unmaking of a Nation-State*, deals with one aspect of the development of German national sentiment in the eighteenth century. It will focus upon imperial consciousness (*der Reichsgedanke*), in particular upon support for the system of superior imperial or federal jurisdiction, exercised after 1497 through the two courts of the Empire, the *Reichskammergericht* and the *Reichshofrat*. The title chosen, 'Let there be justice, even if Germany perishes!', was the motto for Germany suggested by the young Hegel in his 1802 draft *The German Constitution* (*Die Verfassung des Deutschen Reiches*), in which he wrote of Germany as a shadow state, a state of the imagination, which existed only in its rights, laws and judicial system.[4] Other commentators were less pessimistic. The notion of a Reich of the spirit – the idea that Germans, because of their intellectual and cultural superiority, did not need a political framework – is familiar. It was expressed by Schiller in the often–quoted statement of 1804:

> The German Empire and the German nation are two different things. The glory of the Germans has never been based upon the power of its princes. Separated from the political sphere, Germans have established their own values. Political defeats could not undermine those values.[5]

This chapter will argue that, in a similar way, the survival of imperial jurisdiction, symbolised in the proverb *Reichsvecht bricht Landesrecht* – imperial law takes precedence over state law – represented a kind of Reich of the law, the Reich as a *Justizstaat* , abstract but nonetheless important. This jurisdiction enjoyed support from an important section of German intellectual opinion *and* a much wider public opinion from the fifteenth century until the end of the Empire in 1806 and even after 1806. Furthermore, a revitalisation of imperial jurisdiction was one of the aims of the movements for reform of the constitution of the Empire from the fifteenth century to the eighteenth century,

---

4. The draft was not published until 1893: G.W.F. Hegel, *Politische Schriften*, vol. 1 (Frankfurt, 1966), pp. 29ff. It is analysed in S. Avineri, *Hegel's Theory of the Modern State* (London, 1972), and there is a translation in T.M. Knox (ed.) *Hegel's Political Writings* (Oxford, 1964).

5. Quoted in T. Schieder, 'Friedrich der Große – eine Integrationsfigur des deutschen Nationalbewußtseins im 18. Jahrhundert', in O. Dann, (ed.) *Nationalismus und sozialer Wandel* (Munich, 1986), pp. 113–27.

known as *Reichsreform*. Its main manifestations were found in the writings known collectively as *Reichspublizistik*.[6] *Reichspublizistik* was not 'publicity' but the study of German public law (*Staatsrecht*), the nature of political authority and the distribution of power in the Empire. Knowledge of imperial law and history continued to be seen as important; academic lawyers were often employed as diplomats, administrators and advisers by governments, and university law faculties were often approached by governments for their opinions on unclear legal points. The importance of the debate among theorists and writers in forming public opinion was shown by the great importance the Emperor and the German princes attached to having in their employment writers of legal and historical polemics, versed in the law and constitution of the Empire. A new four-year training course for administrators instituted in 1780 at Vienna included in its curriculum German legal history, German constitutional law and imperial law. The university at Göttingen, the best university in eighteenth-century Germany, was a major centre for their study.[7]

The *Reichspublizistik* had two main aspects: analysis of the nature of the imperial constitution and proposals for its improvement and change. It was produced from the fifteenth to the early nineteenth century, with marked clusterings in the late fifteenth and early sixteenth centuries, the years after 1648 and in the last decades of the eighteenth century. There was a lively debate on the imperial constitution and attempts to find a new intellectual basis for what, during centuries of development when different forces had pulled it in contradictory directions, had developed into an exotic hybrid. The debate still goes on. At the twenty-eighth annual congress of German historians at Cologne in April 1970 there was a lively discussion of the question 'What was the Reich?'. Professor Wandruszka reached the interesting conclusion that it was 'a possibility'.

Speculation about the German constitution and its improvement seemed to become particularly intense in periods of instability, war or post-war adjustment. For example, the religious troubles of the 1530s produced a lively debate on the issue of the German states' right of resistance against the Emperor, which expanded into considerations of the nature of the imperial constitution. The periods after the religious peace of 1555 and the Thirty Years' War saw similar peaks. The

6. The Max Planck Institute in Göttingen has a collection of over 10,000 items of *Reichspublizistik*. The best survey in English is H. Gross, *Empire and Sovereignty: A History of the Public Law Literature in the Holy Roman Empire 1559–1804* (London and Chicago, 1973; repr. 1975).

7. C.E. McClelland, *State, Society and University in Germany 1700–1914* (Cambridge, 1980), pp. 43ff.

treaties of Westphalia included provisions for major changes in the imperial constitution but these were not put into effect. After 1648 friction between the Emperor and the princes, between princes and their subjects and between factions in the free cities all increased. The relationship between the confessions was still uncertain and the smaller states in particular were aware of their vulnerability. All this contributed to a lively interest in the nature of the Reich. Polemicists, often sponsored by the German governments, especially the Protestants, mobilised arguments drawn from history, political theory and law to attack or defend the position of the Emperor, the Electors, the princes and the free cities. Opponents of imperial authority usually had as their target not the existence of the Empire but the supposed ambition of the Emperor to subvert the constitution and establish a despotism.

Reform proposals formed the other main aspect of *Reichspublizistik*. The most common recipe to deal with the problems of the German constitution was a decisive recognition of the federal nature of the Empire and its institutional expression. In spite of their obvious weaknesses, objections to their mode of operation and campaigns by the German princes to restrict their competence in support of claims that their governmental functions (*Landeshoheit*) should include total judicial sovereignty,[8] the function of the imperial courts in resolving conflicts betwen governments and between rulers and subjects was seen by commentators as one of the best aspects of the Reich constitution. The *Landfrieden*, the acceptance that peace should be the normal condition of society and that disputes should be resolved by judicial means, became increasingly important in the fifteenth century. Banning all measures of violent self-help, the *Fehde*, the private war fought under *Faustrecht* (the 'right of the fist') and laying down what could and could not be properly undertaken by individuals and governments in pursuit of their rights, the peace was an essential guarantee of order in a very complex political, religious, economic and social structure. By implication, an imperial supreme tribunal was an essential corollary of it. At first only geographically and chronologically limited *Landfrieden* were enacted and the activity of the king's supreme court was intermittent. A peace covering the whole Empire (*Reichslandfrieden*) was first proclaimed at the Mainz *Reichstag* in 1235 and a temporary one-year *Landfrieden* was issued in 1467, involving an absolute ban on *Faustrecht*. There was an aulic tribunal (*Hofgericht*) attached to the royal court, though it is not clear how wide was its competence or how

8. M. Hughes, *Law and Politics in 18th-Century Germany* (Woodbridge, 1988), pp. 44ff.

consistent its activity. The same is true of the short-lived cameral court (*Kammergericht*) in the court of Frederick III.

More consistent progress was made in the last decades of the fifteenth century. There was near unanimity in the reform literature of the time on the need for a revival of imperial authority in the Reich, in particular the establishment of effective imperial jurisdiction with a permanent court in a fixed location in the Empire. The diets of 1486 and 1487 refused to provide the Emperor with the financial help he requested in order to compel him to agree to the establishment of a permanent court. The first universal permanent general peace for the whole Empire was proclaimed at the Worms diet in 1495 and the first permanent imperial court, the imperial chamber court (*Reichskammergericht*), was set up to administer it in the same year, to be followed two years later by the imperial aulic council (*Reichshofrat*). The establishment of the Circles and the Ordinance of Execution of 1555 completed the structure.

The conviction that an effective imperial jurisdiction was beneficial to Germany was not restricted to academic and political opinion, but was deeply rooted in popular feeling. Images of the Hohenstaufens Frederick I and Frederick II as powerful rulers and of the Interregnum of 1250 to 1275 as the anarchic 'terrible time without an Emperor' were sharply etched in popular memory. Enhanced imperial jurisdiction figured in many of the millenarian and apocalyptic works of the late fifteenth and early sixteenth centuries, such as the anonymous *Reformation Kaiser Sigismunds* and *Reformation Kaiser Friedrichs II* (attributed to the named Emperors and dated 1435 and 1441 but in reality written in the early 1520s) and the *Book of the Hundred Chapters*. The notion of the Emperor as a judicial *deus ex machina* was a common feature, seen for example in the Kyffhäuser legend of the sleeping Emperor waiting to return to save Germany. Such ideas also became prominent during the peasant risings of the late fifteenth and early sixteenth centuries. The peasant 'parliament' at Heilbronn in 1525 considered a plan put foward by the former Mainz official Friedrich Weigandt for a fundamental reform involving the Emperor taking back to himself all his lost powers and establishing a centralised state with a hierarchy of imperial courts.

In the seventeenth century such plans were put forward, among others, by Pufendorf, Hippolitus a Lapide and Leibniz. Many of these schemes shared common features, a standing imperial executive, a permanent treasury and a standing army, as well as a German national law code. These would unify Germany and enable her to fulfil her function as a barrier against the establishment of the French universal monarchy which threatened the whole of Europe. Leibniz called for the codification of all imperial law in a new *Codex Leopoldinus*. Even the extreme anti-imperialist Hippolitus a Lapide's plan for a conversion of the Reich into a princely republic contained a proposal for a tribunal to deal with disputes between the princes who were to share sovereignty in it.

The period after the Seven Years' War saw another peak in the output of *Reichsreform* literature. The war intensified the debate on government, administration, the law and constitutions, as had the Thirty Years' War. Like that war it was in some respects a German civil war: during it the army of the Empire was mobilised and defeated by Prussia. It involved a suspension of the imperial constitution, threw into stark relief the problem of the relationship between the two German great powers and the rest of the Empire, and threatened to re-open old political and religious divisions. During the war Prussia's anti-Habsburg propaganda raked up all the old charges that Austria aimed at establishing a Catholic absolutist despotism in Germany and religious friction continued to trouble the *Reichstag* after 1763. It added to Germany's identity problems: many Germans admired Frederick II while realising that his actions threatened the stability of the Empire. There was a rash of works on what it meant to be German in the 1760s.[9] The war showed up the inadequacies of existing administrative systems and produced a vigorous reform effort in individual German states, large and small, reinforced by economic problems experienced after the war in some states where the stability of the coinage had been undermined and inflation was high. As a result of these and other factors the whole relationship of the state and society came under examination.[10]

The war also roused expectations of change; a period of instability, which had lasted since 1740, seemed to have come to an end in 1763. Strangely for the 'Age of Reason' there was in the 1760s a millenarian atmosphere in some quarters with predictions of a coming great spiritual revolution, the greatest overturning since the Reformation, which would sweep away ignorance and allow a victory of Reason. The war was followed by a pause in the struggle between Prussia and Austria,

9. W. Sheldon, 'Patriotismus bei Justus Möser', in R. Vierhaus (ed.) *Deutsche patriotische und gemeinnützige Gesellschaften* (Munich, 1980), pp. 31–49, especially p. 31.

10. E. Weis, 'Absolute Monarchie und Reform in Deutschland des späten 18. und des frühen 19. Jahrhunderts', in F. Kopitzsch (ed.) *Aufklärung, Absolutismus und Bürgertum in Deutschland* (Munich, 1976), pp. 192–219; K. Epstein, *The Genesis of German Conservatism* (Princeton, NJ, 1966), pp. 237ff; G. Parry, 'Enlightened government and its critics in 18th century Germany', *Historical Journal*, 6 (1963), pp. 178–92.

which was to become serious again only in the late 1770s as a result of Joseph II's policies. The year 1764 saw the election and coronation of Joseph as king of the Romans, that is automatic successor as Emperor to his father Francis I, whose failing health was the main reason for the election. This event, attended by considerable pomp and ceremonial, was widely seen as a new beginning for the Reich and a symbol of its new unity. Joseph was the first king or Emperor elected by all the electors without dissent and no new restrictions were placed on him in his capitulation of election. These facts were commented on by contemporaries as an optimistic sign for the future.

The optimism was soon disappointed. The Reich faced a number of new problems and old ones soon reappeared. For example, religious conversions meant that in 1763 there were seven Catholic and only two Protestant electors and there was a continuing pressure from some of the princes for a reduction in the dominant position of the electors. Joseph's attitude to the Reich was practical, unsentimental and insensitive. He paid lip-service to the imperial idea: in April 1787 he wrote to the coadjutor of Mainz, Dalberg, assuring him of his concern for the 'general welfare of Germany, our common fatherland . . . because I love it and am proud to be a German', but his marginal comments on memoranda on reform of the Empire written by Dalberg in 1787 included: 'I don't understand what this idiocy is all about' and 'This is pure fantasy'.[11] Joseph viewed the Empire as a source of possible advantage to Austria and little more. Long-standing Habsburg ambitions to acquire Bavaria in exchange for more remote territories were revived. Reform of the Catholic Church in Austria was undertaken, which involved infringements on the rights of German prelates. In the 1780s Joseph tried to revive lapsed imperial rights of presentation to benefices in imperial abbeys and foundations, of which there were almost 300 in the Reich, using the aulic council for this purpose. This did nothing to add to the Emperor's popularity in the German Catholic Church. Joseph also proposed a reform of the imperial courts, ignoring the rights of the princes in this matter. The reform was suspected to be a cover for attempts to ensure that the verdicts of the *Reichshofrat* were more uniformly in Austria's political interest and the suspicion was well-founded.

Such actions raised questions about the role of the Emperor. One expression of growing disquiet was a revival of the notion of *Drittes Deutschland*, the Third Germany, also known as trialism, the idea that the states which made up Germany without Austria and Prussia should

11. Quoted by R. Vierhaus ' "Patriotismus" – Begriff und Realität einer moralisch-politischen Haltung', in Vierhaus (ed.) op.cit., p. 15.

come together to defend their independence against the two German great powers. National feeling also expressed itself in calls for a strengthening of the Reich against the larger states, especially Prussia and Austria, which seemed ready to sacrifice the smaller states for their own narrow interests. The partition of Poland was seen as a dreadful warning of what could happen in the Reich. This was the origin of the *Fürstenbund* (League of Princes) of 1785, itself a symptom of a growing constitutional crisis. It began as a movement among some of the medium-sized princes to build a union of Third Germany and it was only later taken over by Prussia for its own ends, when its original purpose was abandoned. Its stated aim was to preserve the status quo in the German constitution and Article 4 of its Act of Association committed its members to seek a reform of the imperial supreme courts and to defend them against imperial encroachments. The establishment of the *Fürstenbund* added to the constitutional debates and new questions were asked about the relationship of the Emperor to the Empire. Disenchantment with the situation was typified in an anonymous pamphlet of 1787, which asked *Warum soll Deutschland einen Kaiser haben?* (*Does Germany need an Emperor?*) and concluded that the office was now redundant as the whole Empire was against the tide of the times.

Such a view was unusual. Politically informed Germans looking at their country in the later eighteenth century found much to bemoan but also much to praise. Some reacted with resignation, others with a desire to change things; very few thought in terms of sweeping away the Reich and replacing it with something else. For one thing, it was difficult to define acceptable alternatives. For most commentators the Holy Roman Empire was the ideal German community, in spite of its obvious flaws. There was a widespread view that Germans were singularly fortunate in the constitution of their country, which allowed a wide measure of freedom to the individual states and to individual Germans, while protecting certain basic rights against encroachments. Imperial law guaranteed to all subjects freedom to practise one of three legal religions somewhere in the Empire, freedom of movement within the Empire to all who were not *glebae ascriptus* (those tied to the soil under tenancies which placed legal restrictions upon them), the right to inherit property anywhere in the Empire, the right to justice in properly conducted courts and the right to security of person and property under the law. Already in the second half of the eighteenth century the modern notion of freedom as something to be enjoyed by the individual was beginning to grow up alongside the older tradition of liberties as privileges possessed by particular groups; in the eyes of many commentators the imperial constitution was flexible enough to accommodate and protect both.[12]

As a result there was a widespread belief that any political arrangement for the German nation must combine unity and diversity in correctly balanced proportions. There was also a conviction that the end of the Empire would be a catastrophe and real fears of a great cataclysm (*Umwälzung*) if the structure of the imperial constitution was disturbed. The preservation of the Empire as a loose framework was held to be in the interest of Europe and the individual German states. At the same time the old medieval universalist view, which had seen the Reich as the leading state of Christendom and the Emperor as its secular head, was passing away and was being replaced by a new universalism more in tune with the enlightened spirit of the age, a combination of patriotism and cosmopolitanism which saw the advancement of Germany as beneficial to the whole of humanity.[13]

There are, of course, inherent difficulties in assessing how representative or influential the views of a small educated elite were and how far they were in advance of political and social realities and how far lagging behind them. German public opinion was real in the late eighteenth century though far from united; a distinction must be drawn between the views of the educated, a small group in which there were widely differing opinions, and those of the mass of the people whose horizons were narrow and to whom the idea of Germany was very remote. That said, there is growing agreement that German national sentiment existed as a growing force in the later eighteenth century.

A recent important study of the French Revolution[14] has drawn attention to the great intensity and mobilising power of a new form of patriotism which emerged in France after the Seven Years' War. This produced a new concept of citizenship which took precedence over regional, class or group loyalties, taught that all patriotic citizens had a duty to involve themselves in state affairs and began to break down the walls between the state and private spheres so typical of the *ancien régime*. While various factors produced a more restrained situation in Germany, it is clear that something similar existed there in the later

12. For a basic introduction to the increasing importance of a concept of the individual see K. Epstein, *The Genesis of German Conservatism* (Princeton, NJ, 1966), pp. 29ff; and for a fuller treatment, M. Berman, *The Politics of Authenticity* (London, 1971).

13. Vierhaus, 'Deutschland im 18. Jahrhundert: soziales Gefüge, politische Verfassung, geistige Bewegung', in F. Kopitzsch (ed), *Aufklärung, Absolutismus und Bürgertum in Deutschland* (Munich, 1976), pp. 173–91, especially pp. 176–7. See also F. Meinecke, *Cosmopolitanism and the National State* (Princeton, NJ, 1970).

14. S. Schama, *Citizens* (London, 1989).

eighteenth century. Although it was still very much a minority movement, the numbers of those who saw themselves as patriots or *Vater-
landsfreunde* were increasing. Access to university education and the
emergence of the concept of the all-round education (*Bildung*) contributed to growing pride in middle-class achievement. Another factor
was the rise of an all-German middle class, a group of mobile, educated and professional people, including academics, students, officials,
officers, diplomats, musicians and projectors[15] whose links with their
enges Vaterland (narrow fatherland) weakened as they moved around
the Reich[16]. The press, though censored in many states and small, was
expanding, particularly the periodical press, and this acted as a unifying
force, as did the expanding network of clubs, reading circles and Ma-
sonic lodges.[17] One feature of all this was a growing knowledge of
and interest in the history of Germany and a better appreciation of
how it had developed to its present 'monstrous' state.

   The concept of the good citizen or patriot was political, social and
moral: he was seen as having a duty to act as a model in his personal
life, to involve himself in *die gemeine Sache* (the general or common
interest) and to work for the common good of the fatherland, rising
above the narrow class, occupational, religious or regional group to
which he belonged. F.C. Moser defined a patriot as follows:

> A true patriot is . . . a godly, honest, steady, patient, courageous and wise
> man, with a thorough knowledge of the laws and the constitution, of the
> causes of prosperity and defects in his fatherland, which he uses to find
> the best help and the most enduring improvements. He seeks this at all
> times, motivated by a true love of mankind, without consideration of
> party or person, or serving his own interests.[18]

15. 'Projectors': people who went round hawking wonderful projects to solve,
usually at a stroke, the economic problems of a state. Some were alchemists, some were
of the John Law type. The term (in German *Projector* or *Projektmacher*) was widely used
in the seventeenth and eighteenth centuries.
16. W. Ruppert, *Bürgerlicher Wandel* (Frankfurt and New York, 1981), pp. 137f.,
185f. U.A.J. Becher, *Politische Gesellschaft: Studien zur Genese bürgerlicher Öffentlichkeit in
Deutschland* (Göttingen, 1980), pp. 216–18. H. West, 'Göttingen and Weimar', *Central
European History*, 11 (1978), pp. 150–61, has material on the growing recognition of the
importance of travel and mobility.
17. Möller, op.cit., pp. 496ff; R. Vierhaus, 'Deutschland im 18 Jahrhundert'; in
R.Vierhaus (ed.) *Deutsche patriotische und gemeinnützige Gesellschaften* (Munich, 1980), pp.
187–8; J. Van Horn Melton, 'From enlightenment to revolution', *Central European
History*, 12 (1979), pp. 103–23, especially p. 11 on the massive expansion in the output
of periodicals after the Seven Years' War. The largest 'political' journal, Schlözer's
Statsanzeigen, printed about 4,500 copies.
18. Quoted by N. Hammerstein, 'Das politische Denken Friedrich Carl von Mosers', *Historische Zeitschrift*, 212 (1971), pp. 316–38 (332). There is some material on the Patriots in M.
Lindemann, *Patriots and Paupers: Hamburg, 1712–1830* (Oxford & New York, 1990), pp. 5ff.

The Patriot movement represented a kind of political 'third way' between the corporative state of Estates, regarded as reactionary, and the enlightened absolute monarchy, and a middle culture between the Frenchified courts and nobility and the traditional regional *altständisch* (old estate or corporate) culture. It was based on the involvement of the people, by which was understood the middle classes, in the state and in that lay the roots of popular sovereignty, democracy and modern nationalism.

In Germany the issue was complicated by the fact that every German had two states, the territorial state and the Reich. 'Fatherland' could mean either of these or the German nation as an abstract cultural entity without borders. German patriotism was therefore innately ambivalent; it could lead to support for the untrammelled freedom of the individual states (*Staatssouveränität*) to liberate the reforming urges of progressive rulers, or for a revitalisation of the imperial constitution as a barrier against the despotism of an unenlightened prince.

A majority of the German Patriots accepted that the essence of a good political system was one in which the only limits on freedom were those made necessary by the common good and in which there was some mechanism to restrain or moderate the exercise of power. This could include enlightened public opinion, written constitutions or law codes, creating the state based on law (*Rechtsstaat*), intermediate powers, such as parliamentary institutions, or the imperial laws and tribunals.

The Empire was far from ideal as a political organisation, but it was held to be capable of reform which would bring it closer to such an ideal. There was also a general acceptance that the Empire had ceased to be a unitary monarchical state in anything but a symbolic sense and had evolved into a federative state. To enable it to exercise its vestigial state-like functions the Reich needed appropriate federal institutions, including a high court to act as an ultimate tribunal of appeal, to set standards of law and to arbitrate in disputes. Although it had ceased to be a power structure, it was still an organisation based on law, a structure capable of preserving peace and order. The principles implicit in absolutism, *la loi c'est moi, le droit c'est moi*, the unfettered right of the ruler to legislate, did not apply in the Holy Roman Empire. There rulers were held to be restrained by godly law, natural law, the fundamental laws of their state and the laws of the Empire. Imperial jurisdiction represented an independent judicature in the terms of Montesquieu's division of powers. The governments of the German states were subject to restraints on their freedom of action which were universally knowable in the form of imperial law. The behaviour of governments was itself subject to external standards of what was right, including minimum standards in the dispensing of justice. In all such matters the imperial courts exercised a supervisory, interpretative and enforcing role.

All these factors contributed to a wave of *Reichsreform* literature of enormous proportions in the later eighteenth century. The overwhelming bulk of the output was quite impractical and Utopian and much was anonymous or by obscure authors. It was produced by academics, *literati*, administrators of states large and small, historians and journalists. The authors, in a manner typical of the time, often combined academic and official functions.[19] Catalogues of names are tedious but examples will illustrate the wide interest in the German constitution and the great variety of the reform schemes put forward. These included a general secularisation, the elimination of the small states, trialism, institutional reform, the establishment of a genuinely representative *Reichstag* and a strengthening of imperial jurisdiction.

There was no unity among the advocates of *Reichsreform* though there are dangers in exaggerating the differences between them and in assigning the various publicists to hermetically self-contained categories. Interestingly, all shades of opinion saw something positive in the constitution of the Empire, at least as the framework for a political renewal of Germany. The reform movement had 'enlightened' and 'traditionalist' schools within it. Some like J.J. Moser were conservatives or legal positivists, concerned primarily with describing the German constitution and law as they had developed historically over centuries.[20] They were not concerned with measuring the constitution against some abstract rational model and their remedy for the obvious problems was a universal observance of imperial law as it stood rather than reform of it. Moser and others assigned to the constitutional law of the Empire the function assigned by Bodin and Hobbes to the sovereign, to act as an impartial agent for the maintenance of peace in a society threatened by internal dissolution. Justus Möser, another kind of 'traditionalist', was a powerful defender of the rights of Estates and corporations and strongly supported the Empire as guarantor of those rights.[21]

19. U.A.J. Becher, *Politische Gesellschaft*, op.cit., pp. 12–15.
20. Mack Walker, *Johann Jakob Moser* (Chapel Hill, NC, 1981).
21. Some notion of his assessment of success of the *Reichsreform* movement can be seen in the title of one of his works: *Ein sehr großer Vorschlag, der nicht ausgeführt werden wird* (*A very ambitious proposal which will not be put into practice*). J.B. Knudsen, *Justus Möser and the German Enlightenment* (Cambridge, 1986), includes (pp. 99ff) material on imperial reform literature.

The reform schemes put forward by J.J. Moser's son, Friedrich Karl Moser, in the 1750s and 1760s, in a number of pamphlets and books, especially his anonymously published *Von dem deutschen Nationalgeist* (*On the German National Spirit*) (1765) and *Patriotische Briefe* (*Patriotic Letters*) are better known. Moser, like his father, was a practical administrator and politician, as well as an academic commentator. He was chief minister of Hesse-Darmstadt and a member of the imperial aulic council in the years 1767 to 1770 and 1780 to 1798. He saw the revival of the court as the starting-point in his scheme for a patriotic revival of Germany.

Other writers were more progressive. Karl Friedrich Häberlin (1756–1808), an academic lawyer, a practitioner in the *Reichskammergericht* and a diplomat in the service of Brunswick, was a leading advocate of *Reichsreform*. He regarded the imperial courts as the last barrier against despotic government and praised the imperial system for giving Germans a measure of freedom and security, the like of which was enjoyed only by the English. A.L. von Schlözer, one of the fathers of German liberalism, was a pioneer of political journalism in Germany as well as an academic historian and his journal *Staatsanzeigen* had the largest circulation of any such publication in Germany. Otto Heinrich Freiherr von Gemmingen (1755–1836), a diplomat, playwright and author, while Badenese envoy in Vienna, published a pamphlet *Ich bin ein Deutscher und will ein Deutscher bleiben* (*I am German and wish to remain German*). Wilhelm Ludwig Wekhrlin (1739–92) was a bold and active journalist of advanced views and publisher of a number of magazines, the most famous of which was *Das graue Ungeheuer* (*The Grey Monster*). In November 1783 Wilhelm von Edelsheim, chief minister of Baden, put forward a scheme for a union of the Third Germany, excluding the two great powers, plus an institutional reform of the Reich. One of the best-known advocates of *Reichsrefor* including a thoroughgoing modernisation of the judicial system, was Karl Theodor von Dalberg, the last elector of Mainz.[22] Other examples were Johann H.G. von Justi, a Prussian officer, professor of *Cameralwissenschaft* (the 'science of administration') in Vienna and supervisor of the Prussian glass and steel works, Wiguläus F.A. Kreitmayr, chancellor of Bavaria in the 1760s and a noted commentator on imperial law, and Gerlach

22. After 1803 von Dalberg played an important role in the reorganisation of Germany by the French, with whom he cooperated willingly. He probably believed it would be possible to enlist Napoleon as a genuine protector of German interests, to retain something of the imperial constitution and to defend the smaller states. He was mistaken on every count. Neither Napoleon nor the larger German rulers intended the League of the Rhine to be a genuine union.

A. von Münchhausen, prime minister of Hannover and a prominent legal and constitutional theorist.

Support for a powerful federal jurisdiction reappeared during the troubled last years of the Reich and after its end in 1806.[23] There is still dispute among historians whether the French period, 1792 to 1814, saw a rapid modernisation, the catching-up of a Germany previously sunk in lethargy and stagnation, or brought to an end an established process of political change.[24] During it major steps were taken to turn Germany into a confederation of sovereign states. Mediatisation swept away hundreds of 'sovereign' entities. Many of the German states began substantial internal reform and this often involved a sustained assault on the rights of privileged corporations, which had earlier looked to the imperial courts to preserve their position. For such groups the virtues of the mediating and conserving imperial structure became more obvious when it had disappeared.

Napoleon originally planned to establish a federal supreme court in the Confederation of the Rhine (*Rheinbund*) established in July 1806. A draft constitution was drawn up in February 1806 but this did not come into effect. The powerful member states were unhappy about any diminution of their sovereignty.

Attempts were made to resurrect something of the institutional framework of the Holy Roman Empire during the negotiations at the Vienna Congress in 1814 and 1815 and there was a lively debate on the advantages and disadvantages of the old imperial constitution. There were many calls, especially from the mediatised and smaller states, for the restoration of the office of Emperor hereditary in the house of Austria and for a revival of at least the legal protective framework of the Empire in the form of the supreme court. Twenty-nine governments, later joined by five more, argued that they were not bound by the Treaty of Paris, under which a Germanic confederation was to be established, not having been signatories to it, and that, in calling for the restoration of a modernised Empire, they spoke for the majority of Germans. This early plea for national self-determination was not to come to anything, mainly because of the unwillingness of

23. See the list of reform proposals in H. Schulz for the period 1797 to 1806 in his 1926 Gießen dissertation *Vorschläge zur Reichsreform in der Publizistik von 1800–1806*. See also R. Berney, 'Reichstradition und Nationalstaatsgedanke (1789–1815)', *Historische Zeitschrift*, 140 (1929), pp. 57–86; and W. Mommsen, 'Zur Bedeutung des Reichsgedankens', *Historische Zeitschrift*, 174 (1952), pp. 385–415.

24. R. Vierhaus, 'Politisches Bewußtsein in Deutschland vor 1789', *Der Staat*, 6 (1967), pp. 175–96. See also H.-U. Wehler, *Deutsche Gesellschaftsgeschichte: vol. I. 1700–1815* (Munich,1987).

the larger states to tolerate anything which infringed their sovereignty, but it was the subject of lively discussion.[25] Prussian draft constitutions for the Confederation, W. von Humboldt's *Denkschrift über die deutsche Verfassung* (*Memorandum on the German constitution*) (1813) and Hardenberg's draft of 13 September 1814, contained provision for a federal court to act as a tribunal of first instance in disputes between member states. Under another article subjects were to be allowed access to this court under certain circumstances.

There was a skeletal superior jurisdiction in the 1815 Confederation but it did not develop. The built-in anomaly between the claims of the member states to total sovereignty and the *Bund*'s powers of supervision and intervention was never resolved.[26] There was no supreme court in the Confederation though it was laid down in the Act of Association that each member state had to have a proper independent judicial system with three separate instances and Article 53 of the Vienna Final Act gave the *Bund* limited rights of intervention to deal with differences between member states and in defence of subjects' rights.

In addition, the Federal Diet did, on occasion, operate as an informal judicial tribunal, reproducing some of the functions of the old imperial courts. This quasi-judicial authority was possible under Article 13 of the Act of Confederation, which laid down that all member states had to have constitutions based on Estates. The restoration of Estates constitutions was to lead to political battles in a number of states, as the nobility and other privileged groups tried to use this as a means of undoing modernisation measures, for example the abolition of privileges, carried through during the Napoleonic period. In 1816 the liberal Grand Duke of Saxe-Weimar asked the Federal Assembly to guarantee the constitution he had just negotiated with his subjects and specifically requested it to enforce verdicts of the Saxe-Weimar supreme court against grand-ducal officials if the Estates brought successful cases against them and a future Grand-Duke refused to carry out the verdict. In spite of considerable opposition from Metternich the Diet agreed to this. During the debate the representative of the Saxon

25. H. Ullmann, 'Zur Entstehung der Kaisernote der 29 Kleinstaaten vom 16.November 1814', *Historische Zeitschrift*, 116 (1916), pp. 459–83; H. Durchardt, 'Reichsritterschaft und Reichskammergericht', *Zeitschrift für historische Forschung*, 5 (1978), pp. 315–37 (especially p. 337); and H.R. Feller, *Die Bedeutung des Reichs und seiner Verfassung für die mittelbaren Untertanen und die Landstände im Jahrhundert nach dem Westfälischen Frieden* (Marburg dissertation, 1953), p. 180, note 78. Generally for diplomacy in 1814–15 see E.E. Kraehe, *Metternich's German Policy* 2 vols (Princeton, NJ, 1963–84), vol.2.

26. F. Hartung, *Deutsche Verfassungsgeschichte*, pp. 176–77. See now D. Grimm, *Deutsche Verfassungsgeschichte 1776–1866* (Frankfurt, 1988), pp. 65–68.

states said that it was necessary to avoid the impression that the only aim of the Confederation was to secure the sovereign rights of the states while denying subjects the rights they had enjoyed, as least in theory, under the previous imperial constitution. The Federal Assembly also involved itself in constitutional disputes in Württemberg (1817) and Lippe-Detmold (1819–1838), in the latter case establishing a mediation commission, but it refused attempts by representatives of more liberal governments to make it a general constitutional court of appeal. During the French period constitutions had become firmly established as part of the German political scene and there had been a clear change of attitude on how the exercise of power was to be restrained. The nineteenth century liberal notion of the *Rechtsstaat* as a guarantee against abuses of government power found its strongest expression in Germany in the idea of an independent judicial system and the right to impeach ministers, rather than other barriers against tyranny, such as the division of powers or a right of resistance deriving from an implied contract. But Rotteck and Welcker's *Staatslexikon* (1845–8) praised the imperial courts as ornaments of the old imperial system and expressed the view that their revival would be greeted with enthusiasm in the Germany of the 1840s. The 1848 German constitution proposed in §125 a *Reichsgericht* as a supreme court of cassation and a constitutional court.[27]

Some historians argue that imperial jurisdiction had a negative side: the availability of litigation to subjects suffering oppression weakened the Germans' self-help instincts and strengthened their tendency to look for help and reform from above. Some see the existence of the imperial courts as a barrier to modernisation; by defending the Estates, based as they were on corporate liberties and privileges, they prevented the introduction of reforms like equality before the law and the abolition of tax exemptions.[28] It is possible to exaggerate the immobility of the Empire and the glacial nature of change in it. The basic concern of the imperial courts was indeed to maintain the legal status quo, to preserve existing rights against encroachment, but they did, for example, intervene actively in constitutional disputes in a number of states and free cities to protect the subject or to mediate new constitutions. They did not act simply to preserve the power of traditional elites; their main function was the maintenance of public order and

27. See E. Hucko (ed.) *The Democratic Tradition: Four German Constitutions* (Leamington Spa, 1987), pp. 102–4.
28. G. Strauss, 'The Holy Roman Empire Revisited', p. 292; the Empire was " a structure that guaranteed status, privilege and property by acting as a barrier against change."

observance of the law. In his 1802 draft on the German constitution Hegel recognised this in his description of the German Reich as 'a system of the most comprehensive justice' ('*ein System der durchgeführtesten Gerechtigkeit*').

SUGGESTIONS FOR FURTHER READING

K. O. v. Aretin, *Heiliges Römisches Reich 1776 bis 1806: Reichsverfassung und Staatssouveranität*, 2 vols (Wiesbaden, 1967).

T.C.W. Blanning, *Reform and Revolution in Mainz* (Cambridge, 1974).

J. Gagliardo, *Reich and Nation: The Holy Roman Empire as Idea and as Reality 1763–1806* (Bloomington, Ind. and London, 1980).

H. Gross, *Empire and Sovereignty: A History of the Public Law Literature in the Holy Roman Empire* (Chicago and London, 1973).

M. Hughes, *Law and Politics in Eighteenth-Century Germany* (Woodbridge, 1988).

Journal of Modern History, 58 (1961), Supplement, 'Politics and Society in the Holy Roman Empire 1500–1806'.

H. Möller, *Fürstenstaat oder Bürgernation: Deutschland 1763–1815* (Berlin, 1989).

B. Roeck, *Reichssytem und Reichsherkommen. Die Diskussion über die Staatlichkeit des Reiches in der politischen Publizistik des 17. und 18. Jahrhunderts* (Stuttgart, 1984).

H. Schilling, *Höfe und Allianzen: Deutschland 1648–1763* (Berlin, 1989)

H. Schulz, *Vorschläge zur Reichsreform in der Publizistik von 1800–1806* (Diss., University of Gießen, 1926).

J.J. Sheehan, *German History 1770–1866* (Oxford, 1989).

G. Strauss, 'The Holy Roman Empire revisited', *Central European History*, 11 (1978), pp. 290–301.

J.A. Vann, *The Swabian Kreis: Institutional Growth in the Holy Roman Empire 1648–1715* (Brussels, 1975).

J.A. Vann and S. Rowan (eds) *The Old Reich* (Brussels, 1974).

M. Walker, *Johann Jakob Moser and the Holy Roman Empire of the German Nation* (Chapel Hill, NC, 1980).

CHAPTER THREE

State and nationality in the Napoleonic period

James J. Sheehan

In order to establish its identity, every nation must seek to create a national history. As official versions of the nation's origins, these histories forge a nation's links to its past, provide justifications for its present, and establish guidelines for its future. Because national histories tell the story of how a nation had to become what it is, they are all both deterministic and teleological. However many distractions and defeats a nation might suffer on its path to nationhood, the path itself was set, the national journey planned, the final destination unavoidable. Of course there are often those who attempt to delay the nation's formation: foreign enemies, who are frightened or envious of the nation's power, and – even worse – domestic opponents, who cannot or will not accept the nation's true destiny. Characteristically, national histories describe how the representatives of true nationhood eventually triumph over their foes at home and abroad in a struggle that continues to resonate in the contemporary political world, where international enmity and internal discontents still test the nation's resolve.

Germany is the *locus classicus* of national history. Nowhere else in Europe were historians so deeply engaged in the political process of nation-building, nowhere was history a more powerful weapon in the battle for national identity, and nowhere did an official version of the national past triumph so completely over its rivals. By the middle decades of the nineteenth century, the advocates of a Prussian-led German nation-state had begun to formulate an account of the German past that bolstered Prussia's claims. After 1866, when Prussia's military victories opened the way for her political hegemony, this account became – and in many ways remains – 'German history'. Central to this account is a dual process of self-awareness: it is essentially the story of how the German folk became aware of their identity as Germans and of how the Prussian state became aware of its mission to create a German nation-state. Bismarck, the architect of German national unification, brought these two stories together in a series of military and

47

political triumphs. The result was the Germany that had to be, the Germany created between 1866 and 1871.[1]

In this version of the national past, the revolutionary period has an especially important part. In 1842–3 Johann Gustav Droysen, one of the founders of the Prussian (or *kleindeutsch*) school of German history, interrupted his work on the Hellenistic period to deliver a series of lectures on what he called 'the age of the wars of liberation', which were published three years later. Although Droysen discussed developments from 1770 to 1815, the culmination of his story was those 'unforgettable years . . . in which for the first time in centuries, the German *Volk*, together and with a deep sense of unity, struggled and won'. But for Droysen, and for the generations who followed him, the wars of liberation involved not only a mobilization of the *Volk*, but also a recognition on the part of the Prussian state that it had a historic mission to fulfil. 'From then on,' Droysen wrote, 'it belonged to the true character of the state to be national, and to the true character of the *Volk* to have a state'.[2]

In this chapter I offer a critique of this traditional view of state and nation in the revolutionary period. I shall argue that the most important impact of the French conquest was not on German national identity, but rather on the politics of the various states, that among the German states the Prussian experience was not exceptional, but rather part of a larger pattern of reform and reorganization, and finally, that the impact of nationalism during the so-called 'wars of liberation' was limited to a small minority of Germans, especially German intellectuals, whose memoirs and historical accounts helped to create a mythic image of the national past.

STATES AND REVOLUTION

The period with which we are concerned was one of the most turbulent in modern European history. Between the storming of the Bastille

1. For more on these issues, see J. Sheehan, 'What is German history? Reflections on the role of the nation in German history and historiography', *Journal of Modern History*, 53/1 (1981), pp 1–23, W. Hardtwig, 'Von Preussens Aufgabe in Deutschland zu Deutschlands Aufgabe in der Welt', *Historische Zeitschrift*, 231/2 (1980), pp. 265–324, and the essays in O. Büsch and J. Sheehan (eds) *Die Rolle der Nation in der Deutschen Geschichte und Gegenwart* (Berlin, 1985).

2. Droysen, *Vorlesungen über das Zeitalter der Freiheitskriege* (Gotha, 1886, 2nd edn.), vol. 1, p. 3 and vol. 2, p. 457.

in 1789 and Napoleon's final defeat at Waterloo in 1815, war and rebellion raged across the continent, sometimes spilling over into Europe's colonial extensions. Ancient institutions crumbled, kings toppled from their thrones, territories changed hands with bewildering speed. From the Iberian peninsula to the heart of imperial Russia, statesmen struggled to survive while ordinary men and women felt the power of political change and paid the price for political conflict. Like the years between 1914 and 1945, the only other modern period with which it might be compared, the revolutionary era was characterized by a reciprocally reinforcing collapse of both the domestic and international orders. Within France itself, the war that began in the spring of 1792 'revolutionized the revolution' as the new government desperately sought to mobilize the nation's social and political energies, first just to survive, then to sustain an ever-widening circle of conquest. At the same time, the victorious French armies brought revolutionary change with them, to the lands annexed to France, to the satellite states established along France's frontiers, and, most important of all, to those states that tried to imitate French methods in order to stop French expansion. As a result of almost a quarter of a century of continued upheaval, the style, scope and stakes of politics were permanently transformed.[3]

This transformation was particularly significant for the history of German Europe, that diverse and politically fragmented collection of states, independent cities and semi-sovereign territories, which in 1789 was still loosely knit together by the Holy Roman Empire. Almost from the start, the reverberations within France were felt by the old-fashioned regimes along the Empire's western border. In 1792 and 1793 French forces conquered, were driven from, and finally reconquered German territory on both sides of the Rhine. By the end of the decade, the revolutionary armies, now under the inspired military leadership of Napoleon Bonaparte, had pushed deep into German Europe. After a series of stunning victories against the major German states, Napoleon established a system of allies and satellites in order to provide a buffer between France and potential enemies in the east. In 1806 he collected these polities in the Rhenish Confederation, a French-sponsored league that replaced the old Empire, which passed virtually unmourned from the historical stage. But because they were never enough to satisfy his apparently insatiable lust for power and

---

3. On the relationship between domestic change and international conflict, see T.C.W. Blanning, *The Origins of the French Revolution Wars* (London and New York, 1986) and G. Best, *War and Society in Revolutionary Europe* (New York and Oxford, 1986).

glory, Napoleon's conquests did not bring stability. Finally, after his disastrous defeat in Russia in 1812, his former allies edged away and his old enemies recovered their will to resist him. In October 1813 a multi-national force defeated Napoleon at Leipzig and within a few months, his domination over central Europe was broken. But long after the Emperor himself had reached his final exile, the effects of his rule remained.

Although the geographical shape and political order of almost every German state changed between 1789 and 1815, the intensity of change varied: it was greatest in the areas on the west bank of the Rhine that were directly annexed by France, weakest in a few of the middle-sized northern and central states that somehow managed to stay out of the path of the French juggernaut. But with few exceptions, every German polity had to bear the extraordinary costs of war – costs that were hardly less punishing for France's supposed allies than for her would-be antagonists. Moreover, many states had to come to terms with a radical redefinition of their territorial identity: at one time or another, almost 60 per cent of the German population changed rulers in this period. Taken together, the fiscal burdens of war and the political task of state building required that governments find new ways to mobilize the social, economic and spiritual resources of their populations. Whether they wanted to or not, German statesmen had to follow the French example: We must create, the Prussian reformer Hardenberg wrote,

> a revolution in the positive sense . . . to be made not through violent impulses from below or outside, but through the wisdom of the government . . . Democratic principles in a monarchical government – that seems to me to be the appropriate form for the spirit of our age.[4]

Among the most durable political creations of the revolutionary era were the so-called *Mittelstaaten*, the medium-sized states in south-western Germany that Napoleon assembled from the scattered fragments of the old Empire. In the following brief summary of German politics, I shall concentrate on the most important of these states – Baden, Württemberg and Bavaria – whose development I shall then compare with the situation in Prussia.

Napoleon's decision to establish the *Mittelstaaten* was dictated by French national interests: the Emperor wanted a band of states large enough to stabilize his eastern frontier, but not powerful enough to challenge France. With this in mind, he provided cooperative dynasties

---

4. P. Thielen, *Karl August von Hardenberg, 1750–1822* (Cologne and Berlin, 1967), p. 207.

with former free cities, ecclesiastical principalities, and other minor imperial territories. Relatively speaking, the biggest beneficiary from this apparent largesse was the Margrave of Baden-Durlach, who, in addition to becoming a Grand Duke, greatly expanded his modest holdings with the former bishoprics of Constance, Basel, Strassburg and Speyer, as well as part of the Palatinate, including the cities of Mannheim and Heidelberg. The Duke of Württemberg received a royal title as well as substantial territories. The Elector of Bavaria, also a newly minted king, now ruled over the most important of the new states, which comprised the rich lands once held by bishops and independent city-states.

Of course polities had always grown and declined, added territories after victory, lost them after defeats. In the past, however, when a territory changed hands it was often simply grafted on to its new owner, usually joined through dynastic ties and military force; only gradually, if at all, were these new lands fused with the conqueror's social and political order. Such an arrangement could not work in the revolutionary period. In the first place, in the course of the eighteenth century statesmen had developed a new sense of what states should be like: no longer just conglomerates of varied pieces, states should have unified laws and common institutions, through which they could be uniformly governed and centrally controlled. Moreover – and more important than these still largely theoretical aspirations – the old methods simply could not have worked given the scale of state-building the new governments faced. In a state like Baden, for example, which had to absorb extensive new possessions with diverse institutions and loyalties, conglomeration would have produced chaos. And chaos was just what the French patrons of the new states wanted to avoid. Instead they wanted stability and support – money, resources and manpower to feed the limitless appetites of the imperial war machine. To provide these things, the governments of the *Mittelstaaten* had to organize and control their recent acquisitions.

Except in Württemberg, where King Frederick played an important political role, the direction of reform in the *Mittelstaaten* was in the hands of civil servants, who used the special opportunities offered by the revolution to impose their own vision on their states. Most of these men had held important positions under the old regime; many, such as Count Montgelas in Bavaria or Karl von Hardenberg in Prussia, came from aristocratic families with European connections. Not surprisingly, the reformers' first task was to create a well-ordered and responsive administrative apparatus. Everywhere the jumble of overlapping jurisdictions that had limited the effectiveness of pre-revolution-

ary bureaucracies was replaced by ministries with well-defined respon-
sibilities for particular governmental functions. At the same time, lines
of command between the central government and the localities were
sharpened, new administrative districts were created, and the relationship between state authority and traditional institutions was clarified.
Several states also instituted new regulations governing the recruit-
ment, promotion and conduct of state employees, who were thereby
protected from unwarranted interference by the monarch. In effect,
the new administrative arrangements increased civil servants' power
over their societies as well as over their own institutions.

Reform also involved social emancipation. This meant the removal
of traditional restraints on people's mobility, property and labour. For
instance, guilds lost most of their power to limit the number of those
who could practise a particular trade; cities lost the right to control
who could reside within their walls. Jews, whose ability to work and
live where they wished was tightly restrained, were given greater – but
by no means total – social and economic freedom. Peasants were freed
from many of their dues and services that tied them to their landlords.
All in all, emancipation was supposed to release the productive forces
in society and thereby encourage economic growth and social progress. But at the same time, it cleared the institutional ground between
the individual and the state by cutting away that web of traditional
bodies that had once surrounded – and sometimes protected – most
Germans. In this sense, emancipation was closely tied to the growth of
bureaucratic power, indeed the two were different sides of the same
historical movement.

We can see the connection between bureaucratization and emancipation in the constitutions that were introduced into most of the *Mittelstaaten* in the final stages of the reform era. On the one hand, these
constitutions set legal limits on governmental power and provided
guarantees for individuals' civil rights. On the other hand, however,
they also affirmed the central importance of the civil servant for the
political and social order. Constitution and administration – *Verfassung*
and *Verwaltung* – were not opposing developments, but integral parts
of the process of state-building: Baden, for instance, had both the
strongest constitution and the most firmly entrenched bureaucracy of
any German state.

While the French victories were creating the newly enlarged states
of the south and west, the kingdom of Prussia had remained on the
sidelines. From 1795, when Prussia had signed a peace treaty with the
French in order to concentrate on getting its share of the disintegrat-
ing Polish state, until 1806, the Prussian government had tried to pur-

sue a policy of self-serving neutrality. During this period, some progressive elements within the civil service had tried to press for reform, but their efforts were frustrated by the indecisiveness of the king and the power of the old elites at court, in the army, and in local government. But in Prussia, as in the *Mittelstaaten*, foreign affairs created the possibility for domestic reform: in 1806, King Frederick William allowed himself to be drawn into a war with Napoleon at a most inopportune moment. The result was the twin military disasters of Jena and Auerstädt and the dismemberment of the kingdom. There seemed good reason to believe that Prussia's long and difficult climb to great power status had come to end.

In the period of crisis that followed defeat, the Prussian reformers got their chance. Led first by Baron vom Stein, then by Hardenberg, a new government introduced many of the same measures that were being adopted throughout the German lands. The bureaucracy was reconstituted, ministries formed, local administration redesigned. Serfdom, which was more onerous in Prussia's eastern provinces than in most of the southern and western states, was abolished. The authority of the guilds and local communities – weaker to begin with than in many states – was further limited. Moreover, the king, prompted by his reform-minded advisers, promised that he would grant his subjects a constitution that would guarantee their basic rights and introduce representative institutions.

Both the origins and structure of the Prussian reforms strongly resembled developments in the *Mittelstaaten*: in all of these states, external pressures were decisive; in all of them, civil servants played key roles and administrative reform had a special place; everywhere, emancipatory measures struck down traditional privileges and encouraged mobility and growth. There was not, as Prussia's scholarly admirers once argued, anything inauthentic about the changes introduced in the south and west, nor was there anything unique about the process in Prussia. If anything, the Prussian reforms were more limited in scope and qualified in accomplishment than their counterparts in Bavaria, Baden or Württemberg. In large measure this was because Prussia, unlike these smaller states, was able to rebuild its army and regain a place among the major powers: on the basis of these foreign political achievements, the king recovered the will and the ability to set limits on reform, broke his promise of a constitution, and reinstated some of the privileges of the old elites. Ironically, the same foreign political successes that opened the way to reaction after 1815, later became the basis for Prussia's claim to leadership of the German national movement.

STATES AND THE NATION

Before following the second strand of our story during the Napoleonic period, it is necessary to say a few words about the *nation* as a historical category. In the national histories that I mentioned at the beginning of this chapter, the existence of the nation is assumed. National histories show how people become conscious of the nationality they already possess, how states realize their national mission, how nation-states take their true form. Not surprisingly, the language of national history is filled with organic imagery: nationalism has deep 'roots' in the past, ideas provide the 'seeds' of nationhood, nations 'grow' and 'mature'. The message of these metaphors is clear: nationality is an essential element of human identity, nations are the most important focus for public loyalties, the nation-state is the most natural unit of political organization. In fact, when seen against the broad sweep of European history, all of these propositions are dubious: the triumph of nationalism and the nation-state was short-lived and incomplete, the always problematic product of a particular set of historical circumstances. Of course for centuries people had thought of themselves as French, or German, or English, but these national identities were almost always less important than their religion, region, immediate community and kin. For most of Europe's past, therefore, nationality ranked fairly low among people's various loyalties and a fusion of national identity and political organization would have seemed neither necessary nor possible.[5]

During the eighteenth century some Germans became aware of their nationality's importance. To an intellectual like J.G. Herder, for example, all authentic cultures had a national base: a people's art and literature drew its strength and character from the language, mores and past experiences of the collectivity that Herder called the *Volk*. At a time when Germans were creating a national literature, this insistence on the cultural nationality seemed to make a great deal of sense. Moreover, to educated men and women – the readers and writers who made this national literature possible – German culture, that is *their* culture, seemed clearly superior to the Frenchified culture of the aristocracy and courts. German national consciousness, therefore, was

5. Among the many theoretical works on nationalism, I find those by Ernest Gellner especially useful: see his *Nations and Nationalism* (Ithaca, NY, and London, 1983). See also J. Breuilly's broadly based and carefully argued insistence on the centrality of politics for understanding nations and nationalism: *Nationalism and the State* (Manchester, 1982).

inseparable from a cultural struggle against foreign and especially against French influences. But virtually no one believed that this cultural struggle had to do with politics as we understand it. Nationality had little or nothing to do with states.

After their initial enthusiasm for the French Revolution had passed, most German intellectuals viewed what was happening west of the Rhine in terms of this cultural antagonism between Germans and Frenchmen. Now, however, the enemy was not a superficial and materialistic court culture, but a shallow and mechanistic rationalism that threatened deeper, more authentic German values.

We can see this shift with particular clarity in the career of Joseph Görres. Born in 1776, Görres grew up in Koblenz where he witnessed the upheavals following the French invasion. Originally, Görres viewed the invaders as the instruments of enlightenment ideals and historical progress; in 1798 he laid his essay on 'Universal Peace' at 'the altar of the fatherland', by which he meant the French republic. But when he went to Paris a year later, he was shocked by what he found. The French, he discovered, might be quicker and wittier than the Germans, but they were also unreliable and shallow; the Germans were slow, but persistent and deep. Eventually he recognized that the divisions between the two nations were profound; France was his fatherland no longer.[6]

At first, Görres's hostility towards the French had no political implications. But in late 1812 and 1813, as Napoleon's military fortunes began to decline, Görres began to talk about a national uprising against the tyrant, an uprising that would be 'the destiny of the species for many generations'. Soon he became a leading ideologist for the 'war of liberation', whose sacred mission he celebrated in an influential journal, *Der Rheinische Merkur*. Together with a number of other prominent intellectuals who were inspired by this last great struggle against the French, Görres now argued that national culture had to have a political basis: the identity of the *Volk* and their lands, he believed, required common institutions and a common constitution. Although these advocates of a united Germany were often uncertain about its precise shape and divided about what kind of institutions it should have, they did see — as a thinker like Herder had not — that nationality was a political as well as a cultural phenomenon.

The nationalist intellectuals' prominence was greatly enhanced by their relationship with the political leaders of the anti-French campaign. In the course of 1813 and 1814, Görres and other self-ap-

6. On Görres's development, see Sheehan, *German History, 1770–1866* (Oxford, 1989), pp. 374ff.

pointed spokesmen for the *Volk* were taken up by the leaders of Russia and Prussia, who subsidized their publications and apparently endorsed their ideas. Although national historians have made a great deal of this cooperation, it is important to bear in mind how very brief and instrumental it was. Understandably enough, Napoleon's enemies recognized the potential advantage of having public support for their efforts. Moreover, they wanted to put pressure on those German princes still allied to France by threatening to mobilize their populations against them. Nevertheless, as soon they could, most governments withdrew their always tentative endorsement of national enthusiasms. With Napoleon safely out of the way, Görres, for example, found himself without official support. Before long, the authorities closed his journal, censored his writings, and eventually forced him into exile.

It is also important not to lose sight of the fact that the popular appeal of nationalist propaganda was very limited. Even among intellectuals, the group most susceptible to nationalist feelings, there were many who looked upon the war with hostility and suspicion. Goethe, for example, never approved of patriotic posturing, while the philosopher Hegel retained his admiration for Napoleon until the very end. There were, to be sure, a number of young people who donned what they regarded as authentic Germanic outfits and performed gymnastics under the leadership of *Turnvater* Jahn on Berlin's Hasenheide. Some students rushed to the colours in 1813 and fought valiantly in Freiherr von Lützow's Free Corps. Theodor Körner, a young poet who died while serving with Lützow, left behind some stirring verses celebrating the joys of comradeship and the thrill of combat:

> As brothers we are all together
> Which makes our courage grow,
> Joined by language's holy bond,
> By one God and one Fatherland,
> Faithful, German blood.

But patriotic youngsters like Körner were a small minority in 1813 – even, as it turns out, among Lützow's volunteers, who were mainly craftsmen and labourers, not the idealistic students whose legendary exploits have been celebrated again and again in the histories of national liberation.[7]

We have no way of knowing how deeply nationalist feelings pene-

---

7. H. Zimmer, *Auf dem Altar des Vaterlandes: Religion und Patriotismus in der deutschen Kriegslyrik des 19. Jahrhunderts* (Frankfurt, 1971), p. 35. On the social composition of the Free Corps, see the data gathered by R. Ibbeken, *Preussen, 1807–1813* (Cologne and Berlin, 1970).

trated into German society. There is some evidence that most people remained unmoved by the struggle against France, probably because they were preoccupied, as they had every reason to be, with the harsh necessities of everyday life. The strongest opposition to France seems to have been caused less by the new national ideals than by more traditional sources of antagonism: the opposition of devout Christians towards French religious policies, the hostility of those who suffered from French taxes or economic competition, the resentment of tightly knit communities towards strangers. Significantly, the only popular German rising against France (which in fact began as a rebellion against another German state) took place in the Tyrol, a region that was socially and culturally far removed from national ideology. Overall, therefore, the role of the *Volk* in their own liberation was limited. Napoleon was defeated and driven out of German Europe by an alliance of states, whose regular armies defeated him in the field. The victors at Waterloo were those dogged defenders of the old regime, the Duke of Wellington and General von Blücher.

By forcing it into the mould of national history, conventional historiography has not only distorted the details but also obscured the real significance of the revolutionary period for German developments. This significance had less do with creating the national future than with destroying the past: by sweeping away the Holy Roman Empire, most of the free imperial cities, the lands of the imperial nobility, the ecclesiastical principalities, and scores of other small polities, the forces of war and revolution cleared the social and political landscape of a thicket of traditional institutions that had ordered German public life for centuries. The immediate beneficiaries of this process were the states. Their triumph was, first of all, a matter of political geography; from the hundreds of entities that were scattered across German Europe in 1789, only about two dozen remained, the most prominent and important of which were those medium-sized states whose imprint has still not totally disappeared from the political map. But as important as the states' geographical pre-eminence was the triumph of the principles upon which state power rested, the principles of political sovereignty, integration and cohesion. From this perspective, we can see the revolutionary era as the culmination of the bureaucratic state's prolonged struggle against traditional limitations on its power.

But is it unreasonable to ask if this triumph is not itself part of the nation-building process? After all, wasn't the map of central Europe in 1815 one step closer to national unification than the kaleidoscopic landscape of the old Empire? The answer is yes, but only if the maps are set within the narrative frame of national history. Outside this frame, it is equally possible to argue that the *Mittelstaaten* formed after 1800 were impediments to nation-building since they were surely more willing and better able to defend their independence than most of the territories they absorbed.

But in two important ways the revolutionary period did help prepare the way for German unification under Prussian leadership.

First, Prussia emerged from this period substantially strengthened, in part by the reforms introduced in her political and military institutions, but much more by the addition of new territories in the west. The possession of substantial parts of the Rhineland and Westphalia provided the Hohenzollern with a bridge of influence across north-central Europe. Furthermore, the acquisition of the rich resources of the Ruhr (whose potential was unrecognized in 1815) helped provide the basis for Prussia's industrial and military power in the second half of the century. The coal and iron of the Ruhr had much more to do with the settlement of the German question in 1866 than the nationalist rhetoric of patriotic intellectuals and the youthful enthusiasm of the student volunteers. Ironically, the loss of a great deal of Polish territory in the east, against which Prussia had protested so vigorously in 1815, also enhanced her potential as a leader of the national cause.

Second, the story of the revolutionary period took on a significance of its own, important less for what happened than for what people thought had happened. In memoirs, history books, novels, and paintings, the 'wars of liberation' were shaped to fit an unfolding narrative of nation-building, in which the *Volk*'s historic rising became at once prologue and precondition of the nation's ultimate triumph. And like all authentic national myths, this saga was written and rewritten to fit the needs of different historical moments, from the early days of Bismarck's Reich, when Treitschke celebrated the reformers in his great history of the nineteenth century, to the closing days of Hitler's, when Goebbels tried to inspire patriotic fervor with a film about the heroic defence of Kolberg against the French. As historians, it is our task to view the myths of national history with critical detachment without ever losing sight of their power and persistence.[8]

8. The most suggestive work in English on the evolution of national myths is by George Mosse. See especially his *The Nationalization of the Masses* (New York, 1975). The most recent treatment of these issues is M. Hughes, *Nationalism and Society: Germany, 1800–1945* (London, 1988).

SUGGESTIONS FOR FURTHER READING

A complete guide to documents and source materials can be found in K. Müller (ed.) *Absolutismus und Zeitalter der französischen Revolution (1715–1815)* (Darmstadt, 1982). Among the recent works in German the best are T. Nipperdey's *Deutsche Geschichte, 1800–1866: Bürgerwelt und starker Staat* (Munich, 1983) and H. U. Wehler's *Deutsche Gesellschaftsgeschichte*, vols 1 and 2 (Munich, 1987). Wehler's extensive footnotes cite the most important literature, with particular emphasis on social and economic developments.

The most complete treatment of the period in English is J. Sheehan, *German History, 1770–1866* (Oxford, 1989). On the revolution's impact in particular regions, see T.C.W. Blanning's *The French Revolution in Germany: Occupation and Resistance in the Rhineland, 1792–1802* (Oxford, 1983) and M. Walker, *German Home Towns: Community, State, General Estate, 1648–1871* (Ithaca, NY, 1971). Three older works are still useful for the evolution of political ideas: E.N. Anderson, *Nationalism and the Cultural Crisis in Prussia, 1806–1815* (New York, 1939), R. Aris, *History of Political Thought in Germany from 1789 to 1815* (London, 1936) and G.P. Gooch, *Germany and the French Revolution* (London, 1920).

CHAPTER FOUR

Germany and the national question in 1848

Dieter Langewiesche

THE GERMAN CONFEDERATION AS A MULTI-NATIONAL LEAGUE OF STATES

No German national state was established in the territorial reordering of Europe which took place at the Congress of Vienna. The German Confederation which in 1815 replaced the Holy Roman Empire of the German nation was a league of states. Its establishment may have dashed the national hopes of many Germans but it fulfilled the wishes of European monarchs for a new international system in which no one state was dominant. The German Confederation was a mixture of the weaknesses and strengths which existed in central Europe. It bound forty-one states together so loosely that there was never any chance that they could pursue a common and active foreign policy. At the same time its existence acted as a constraint upon Russian or French attempts to achieve predominance in Europe.

The Confederation appeared unlikely to provide the basis of any moves towards a national state for a number of reasons. First, three foreign monarchs were connected to the Confederation through personal union: the English King as king of Hannover (until 1837); the Danish king as Duke of Holstein and Lauenburg (until 1864); and the King of the Netherlands as Grand Duke of Luxemburg and, from 1837, Duke of Limburg (until 1867). Second, Austria especially, but also Prussia, the two leading powers within the Confederation, were semi-detached members. The Prussian provinces of West and East Prussia, as well as its possession, the Grand Duchy of Posen, were not included within the Confederation. Austria, the old German imperial power, was a multi-national monarchy. Its Polish, Hungarian and Italian possessions also were not included in the Confederation. However, in those territories that were included, there lived nearly 6 million people of non-German nationality – Czechs and Slovenes,

Poles and Croats and Magyars, as well as more than 400,000 Italians. In various parts of the Habsburg monarchy which did belong to the Confederation, non-Germans predominated, as in Bohemia, Moravia, Silesia, Carinthia, Gorizia and Trieste. There were more Poles than Germans in the Grand Duchy of Posen as well. Thus within the Confederation and the closely connected Habsburg dynasty there lived just about every European nationality which did not yet possess its own nation-state. The Confederation was in danger of being plunged into nationality conflicts as soon as nationalism began to develop among these stateless nations. Every attempt to turn the Confederation into a German national-state must conflict with the interests of other nationalities, and every attempt by any of those nationalities to establish their own states must end up clashing with the German national movement. When revolution broke out in 1848 these latent problems were brought out into the open.

THE DREAM OF THE 'SPRINGTIME OF PEOPLES' AND ITS EARLY END

In 1848, for the first and last time a revolution covered the greater part of the continent – from France over the German and Italian states, throughout the territories of the Habsburg dynasty into Moldavia and Wallachia, Balkan possessions of the Ottoman Empire. Other states did not go unscathed. Reforms were speeded up in the Scandinavian countries, Belgium, the Netherlands and Switzerland. There were attempts at uprisings in Ireland, Spain, Greece and even in England. These all failed as did hope of radical change in Russia. This was a truly European revolution, but one which was to turn the various nations against one another.

The revolution began in February and March accompanied by the hope that this would see the 'springtime of the peoples', as this dream was called by contemporaries. It was a dream of a Europe in which the brotherhood of peoples would replace the self-seeking diplomacy of the old powers, inaugurating an era of a peaceful Europe made up of nations with equal rights organised into democratic states. Many writings, speeches and images testified to this belief that men stood on the edge of a new age, an age of independent and democratic nations.

The dream soon melted away. The idea of the nation did indeed come to be the strongest tie holding men together within the revolutionary movements, men who pursued very different goals within their different societies. But this same powerful ideal also led nations and nationalities against each other and into alliances which contradicted their democratic and liberal objectives. This was a general phenomenon: there was nothing special about the German national movement in this regard.

HALYCON DAYS OF REVOLUTION IN THE HABSBURG DYNASTY

We can begin our tour of the European nationality conflicts which undermined the attempt to establish a German national state with the observations of a shrewd contemporary who himself experienced and suffered through the dramatic evolution from solidarity to conflict. The report was that of a student from Cernowice, the largest town in Bohemia, who was living in Vienna, perhaps the best vantage point from which to see these changes. The Habsburg dynasty was more affected than any other state by the claims to equal treatment made by the various nationalities and Vienna was the dynasty's seismographic centre. When a constitution was promised, the student wrote to his parents in Cernowice in mid-April 1848 that

> the most touching scenes took place. While mounted soldiers, greeted everywhere with applause, rode through the city announcing the news, one could see Poles and Germans, Italians and Bohemians, Hungarians and Tyroleans link arms and solemnly promise to reject every kind of national hatred. Citizens embraced students with tears of joy. One cannot describe how happy people were. In the evening there was a procession. The National Guard marched from the university along the street to the castle carrying before them a picture of the Emperor. Cries of 'Long live his Majesty!' continued through the whole night.[1]

These happy days of revolutionary harmony did not last long. Only three months later, in July, the same witness, a committed democrat, member of the Academic Legion (an independent part of the National Guard made up of students) which had played a key role in the early

---

1. P. Frank-Döfering, *Die Donner der Revolution über Wien: Ein Student aus Czernowitz erlebt 1848* (Vienna, 1988), p. 41.

stages of the revolution, described very different scenes when writing to his father. When the Hungarians 'praise their nobility', the Germans react with contempt.

> For isn't it the case, dear father, that the Hungarians never loved our Emperor as we German Bukowiner [inhabitants of the Duchy of Bukovina] do. It seems very odd to me the way in which the entire Italian contingent within the student body gradually no longer take up their posts, and there is a rumour that they have gone to help the Piedmontese. Now they fight against the dynasty and one hears that they would like to press on into the Tyrol.

Just as he wrote, another student burst into his room and jubilantly announced:

> the great victory of our general Radetzsky in Italy [the battle of Custozza on 25 July in which the Piedmontese army was defeated] . . . That removes the danger from the south to our country for the time being. But it brings with it a strange feeling when one thinks back to just a few months ago to the sense of brotherhood and the promises that were made of lasting friendship. That had a very short life. Now everyone has gone to the other extreme. It seems that those scenes, which I saw with my own eyes, have disappeared in the gunpowder smoke of the battlefield. Isn't it often the case, dear father, that one man's freedom leads to the oppression of another? Thus the cause in Italy is about the freedom of Italians but it also threatens us Germans in the Tyrol. Such questions of politics and philosophy drive one to despair. What appears good in philosophy, can be cruelly disfigured in the vicious world of politics.[2]

This student saw the nationality conflict from the perspective of someone who had hoped to see the creation of a democratised dynasty under German leadership. If he had had better contacts with the different non–German nationalities in Vienna he would have been able to recognise, even at the beginning of the revolution, that the dream of a 'springtime of peoples' could become a nightmare of nationalities. That could be seen more clearly and earlier in Vienna than anywhere else. By the end of March delegations of all the Slav nations – Slovaks, Serbians, Croatians, Czechs, Poles – appeared in Vienna to put their demands to the central government. They held festivals of brotherhood in Vienna. On one occasion 3,000 people took part. A participant reported:

> a national celebration of a like never before experienced. Slavs demonstrated harmony and mutual respect. Harmony, the lack of which

2. Ibid., pp. 104–5.

has always been our great weakness and the cause of all our unhappiness, is now becoming a reality.[3]

This hope for harmony among the Slav nations was also soon dashed. There was only negative unity – against German demands such as the claims made by the German National Assembly to Bohemia, Moravia and Habsburg Silesia and against the Magyar claims to domination in transleithelan Hungary. That was the limit of practical agreement of Austro-Slavism which sought national autonomy against the larger and more powerful Germans and the Magyars and also against the ideas of Russian Pan-Slavism. In view of the threats from the Germans and Magyars the aim of Austro-Slavism in 1848 was not only to preserve the multi-national Habsburg dynasty, but also to reform it in order to create and protect rights of national self-determination. One might understand this as a rather modern idea, anticipating some of the projects of European integration of our own time which envisage autonomous nations under a supra-national umbrella. However, this would be misleading. The national movements in 1848, in the Habsburg Empire as elsewhere, sought to wrest freedom in both their internal and external affairs from the control of those who had held power over them. However, when these movements came into conflict with one another, they did not hesitate to form alliances with the old power-holders. Precisely because they could not resolve conflicts between themselves, these movements looked to the idea of a monarchical authority to do that for them. The illusion that it would be possible to use the old dynastic power structure to promote the cause of national liberation can be observed in all the areas where in 1848 national issues reached a crisis.

ILLUSIONS OF POWER IN FRANKFURT

In the German National Assembly meeting in Frankfurt there was an alarming expression of imperial wishes. Deputies talked of German hegemony from the North Sea and the Baltic to the Adriatic and the Black Sea. Money was collected in all German states for a navy which would project German strength into the wider world. This extravagant

3. Cited in R.G. Plaschka, *Nationalismus, Staatsgewalt, Widerstand: Aspekte nationaler und sozialer Entwicklung in Ostmittel - und Südosteuropa* (Munich, 1985), p. 154.

nationalism found support on the left as well as the right. Deputies looked to the past to justify visions of great power. Varnhagen von Ense appreciated acutely the problems of justifying the boundaries of a German nation state in historical terms:

> A union of Germans, unity for Germany – for some time these words have sounded sweet to the lovers of the nation. Unfortunately the actual issue is difficult, and we never seem to be able to pin it down. It is hard to determine precisely what nationality means because it has changed constantly from the earliest times. Franks and Anglo-Saxons left their homes, mixed with other nationalities, and in this way achieved greatness and freedom. Lombards and Vandals similarly lost their distinctive nationality when they moved to distant lands. Switzerland broke away from Germany, Slav Bohemia and Gallic Belgium joined Germany, and Alsace and Lorraine were given up. How can we decide what we should claim for Germany? There is no satisfactory solution to be had to this mixture of nationalities. We should be satisfied if we come even close to such a solution. In any case, nationality is not the sole, not even the most important basis on which to form states. Shared laws and freedoms are undoubtedly much more important than ethnic ties, especially when these ties have been broken and obscured.[4]

Eventually the majority of the National Assembly came round to this sensible point of view. Imperial rhetoric was confined to the domain of wishful thinking which the euphoria of revolution had spawned. It would, therefore, be unfair to judge the National Assembly of 1848–49 only by that rhetoric. Nevertheless, the assembly was no more prepared voluntarily to abandon national claims than any other nationality which sought a nation-state in those years.

VAIN HOPES FOR THE RESTORATION OF POLAND

How quickly oaths of solidarity between nations could turn into national rivalries is shown in the abortive attempts to create a Polish state. Since the failure of the Polish rising of 1831 the aim of Polish restoration had been taken up by all European freedom movements. Even within the German Confederation there were set up Polish associations which offered financial and moral support to Polish refugees.

---

4. V. von Ense, *Kommentare zum Zeitgeschehen. Publizistik, Briefe, Dokumente 1813–1858*, ed. W. Greiling (Leipzig, 1984), p. 172.

In March 1848 it appeared that revolution had once again placed the restoration of Poland on the agenda. The new Prussian government declared its support for 'national reorganisation' in the Grand Duchy of Posen, which had a Polish majority. The foreign minister von Arnim hoped for French help against Russia in order to restore Poland. This policy failed, partly because the French government and the Prussian king both rejected it, but also because the German and Polish national movements came into conflict with one another as soon as they moved from the pre-revolutionary expression of sentiments to concrete political action. It proved impossible to divide Posen into a German and a Polish area in a way which would satisfy everyone. Poles and Germans were geographically too mixed. There would have been harsh decisions whatever decisions had been taken. What was actually decided was particularly harsh for the Poles. The German National Assembly, in conjunction with the Prussian government, shifted the demarcation line to such an extent that there were more Poles living in the German territory which was intended to form part of the German nation-state than there were living in the Polish residue of Posen. Even this residue would remain under Prussian government if the Prussian National Assembly could have its way. So the German and Prussian National Assemblies, along with the Prussian government, had united together against the policy of restoring a Polish state. Against that united front the Polish national movement had no chance. Its militia was inferior to the Prussian army. It could expect no help from the major powers. In the great debate on Poland in July 1848 some left-wing members of the German National Assembly did try once more to press back German claims in favour of Polish ones. However, this attempt to restore some balance between the nations was voted down by 341 to 31.[5]

GERMAN–CZECH CONFLICTS

Another source of tension which the German national movement could not avoid was to be found in the Habsburg regions of Bohemia,

5. The parliamentary debates on the national problems are described in detail in G. Wollstein, *Das 'Großdeutschland' der Paulskirche: Nationale Ziele in der bürgerlichen Revolution von 1848/49* (Düsseldorf, 1977). A short but well-informed survey is provided by H.H. Brandt, 'The revolution of 1848 and the problem of central European nationalities', in H. Schulze (ed.) *National-Building in Central Europe* (Leamington Spa, 1987).

Moravia and Silesia. These belonged to the German Confederation but only a minority of the population were German. Only some of those Germans took part in the elections to the German National Assembly. The Czechs, and Poles in Silesia, boycotted the elections. There were, however, important differences between the three areas. In Bohemia a strong Czech movement had already emerged with the aim of bringing the three areas under a single political authority with a high degree of autonomy, although within a continuing Habsburg dynasty. This plan not only was resisted by the Germans of the whole region (about 2.4 million) but also was rejected by parliaments in Moravia and Silesia.

There was a lively debate in the German National Assembly on the subject of Bohemia where about 1.7 million Germans lived alongside some 2.6 million Czechs. No one was prepared to admit the option of giving up the territory, but equally there was no majority support for the view that German claims should be defended by war if necessary. The issue of whether to compromise did not divide Germans along left and right lines. The majority of the assembly were more reticent on this issue than they were on those of Posen or Schleswig. They did not offer any territorial concessions, but they did, almost unanimously, declare the need to provide guarantees of the rights of national minorities. Otherwise they left the problem to the Habsburg monarchy. It came up with a military 'solution'.

At the beginning of June 1848 a Slav congress met in Prague, intended as a public reply to the German National Assembly. However, the united front of Slavs which was desired did not come about. The problems and interests of the various Slav nations diverged too much from one another. The Czech national movement reached its climax with the congress, but also started now to go into decline. The Prague insurrection, which followed in the middle of June, had devastating consequences. First, it revealed the social divisions within the Czech camp and had the effect of pushing the political spokesmen of the movement rightwards. Second, the Germans of Bohemia, Moravia and Silesia now began to organise themselves as a political force. Third, the repression of the insurrection by Habsburg soldiers under the command of Prince Windischgrätz showed that the old order had recovered some of its power. What is more, in using that power it received support from other nationalities, in particular the Germans and the Magyars. Of those Germans who expressed their views on the subject, only a very few regarded the defeat of the Czech insurgents as a victory for the counter-revolution rather than for German interests. Varnhagen von Ense was one of that minority. Immediately after the events in Prague he wrote:

> Regrettably many Germans have allowed their sense of nationality to make them arrogant and unjust. They raise themselves above the Slavs and blindly deny them the rights of freedom and independence. But what is the situation of the Germans? Can we be so confident about our own affairs?...I consider this failure to acknowledge the rights of other nationalities as a threat to our own rights . . .In any case, in Prague it was not the cause of the Germans which triumphed over that of the Czechs, but rather it was military power which struck down citizens.[6]

Generally those who subscribed to the German cause, whether they lived in Vienna, Prague or Berlin saw the matter differently. The Bohemian Germans regarded the Prague insurrection primarily as an anti-German protest. Some sent votes of thanks to Windischgrätz. It was this man, a symbol of reaction, who was raised up to the status of the saviour of Germans in Bohemia. Furthermore, the Prague insurrection had a European significance. For the first time in 1848 the superior power of regular soldiers was made clear. The myth of the barricade which had begun in Paris in February was now destroyed by soldiers' guns: first in Prague, then more spectacularly in Paris later in June; and again in Vienna in October. Only where the revolutionary national movement had formed its own army or could get support from some of the existing troops was there effective resistance to the old elites who were quickly regaining confidence. This happened to a degree in Italy and above all in Hungary. By contrast the German revolutionary movement depended upon Prussian or Austrian soldiers to enforce its national claims against other nationalities. Only a few recognised that such national victories strengthened the counter-revolution. This was what happened in Italy.

ITALY AND THE GERMAN NATIONAL MOVEMENT

Until 1848 a liberal Italian nation-state had been one of the aims of the German national and liberal movement. The aim was not given up during 1848, but there was unwillingness to give up German claims to those parts of northern Italy which belonged to the German Confederation. The German National Assembly declared, specifically in relation to the Tyrol, that 'no portion of sacred German soil can be

6. V. von Ense, op.cit., pp. 169f.

surrendered'.[7] Against this the Italians demanded the immediate separation of the Italian lands of Trient and Roveroto from the German Tyrol. A majority of the German National Assembly rejected this demand, although there was a clear language boundary which could have been drawn. At most the assembly was prepared to offer legal guarantees to national minorities. The assembly did not wish to surrender Trieste, where 8,000 Germans lived among 44,000 Italians and 25,000 Slovenes. In its debate on Italy in August the assembly left it to the German national government (the provisional authority created by the assembly with the Habsburg Archduke John at its head) to negotiate with the Austrian government on the matter. It was obvious to everyone what this would involve. By this time Austria had already embarked upon military action against the Italian movement, having its first significant success at the battle of Custozza on 25 July. As with Windischgrätz in Prague, now was Radetzsky celebrated as a defender of German interests. That was clear from the letters of the student in Vienna already quoted. It is also clear from many newspaper articles. The *Grenzboten*, still worth reading as a source of revolutionary opinion, declared that 'it would require rather more than cosmopolitan self-denial to resist celebrating the brilliance and courage of the Austrian army'. It added that 'it will do us no harm, if foreigners learn to respect our weapons as well as the humanism of our extreme left-wing philosophers'.[8] Admittedly the German National Assembly avoided making decisions about the Italian question, but its sentiments were made clear in the speeches of many deputies. Like a magnet, the future German nation-state should draw other nations to it. From this perspective they wished to avoid any weakening of the Habsburg Empire because they saw it as a German power – led by Germans politically, shaped by German culture, a part of German history, and a German outpost in Italy and the multi-national region of south-east Europe.

7. Cited in Wollstein, op.cit., p. 228. See especially P. Burian, *Die Nationalitäten in 'Cisleithanien' und das Wahlrecht der Märzrevolution 1848/49: Zur Problematik des Parlamentarismus im alten österreich* (Graz and Cologne, 1962), pp. 161–74.

8. *Die Grenzboten* 7/3 (1848), p. 279. For reports on articles in various German newspapers, see Wollstein, op.cit., pp. 238ff.

THE SCHLESWIG-HOLSTEIN CONFLICT: EUROPEAN AND GERMAN TURNING POINT

The conflict between Denmark and the German nation in the duchies of Schleswig and Holstein has a unique character among the nationality problems of 1848. No other conflict aroused such emotions among Germans as this one; no other conflict brought a general European war so close; and no other conflict made as clear as this one the interaction between national and revolutionary developments.

The upsurge of the German national movement in the 1840s was closely linked to the disputes between Germans and Danes over Schleswig. Should Schleswig be incorporated into Denmark, should it retain its traditional ties to Holstein which was part of the German Confederation, or should it be brought itself into the Confederation? These were the questions. The answer of the German national movement was clear: the two duchies must remain indivisible and must be German. The Danish minority in Schleswig must accept that. When the Danish government decided on 22 March 1848 to incorporate Schleswig into the Danish state, the Germans immediately began to resist the decision. They set up a provisional government which was recognised by the *Bundestag*, the supreme body within the German Confederation. Schleswig participated in the elections to the German national assembly although not part of the Confederation. Prussian soldiers occupied Schleswig at the request of the provisional government and with the approval of the Confederation. When, thanks to British mediation, Prussian troops were pulled back to southern Schleswig, there was a storm of protest and indignation throughout Germany. Hardly anyone disassociated themselves from this feeling. Even Varnhagen von Ense, who counselled moderation in all other disputes in order to balance and reconcile other nations, had no doubts on this question. 'Our war against Denmark is a just war' and 'opinion in England' was 'quite unfairly' 'very much against us'.[9]

The German National Assembly declared that the Schleswig-Holstein question had become a matter of national honour. But it had also become a problem for European diplomacy and a question of power within Germany.

For the European powers a German national state represented a challenge, a threat to the balance of power which had been restored following Napoleon's defeat. Nevertheless, historical research has

9. V. von Ense, op.cit., p. 163.

shown that the powers had not deliberately opposed German unity. France played only a subordinate role in European questions in 1848. Even in the Schleswig-Holstein dispute she was fairly marginal so far as Britain and Russia were concerned. The Russian Czar rejected all revolutions but was only likely to intervene if and when the revolution overturned a German prince — which did not happen; or if it forcibly took over foreign territory — which did seem likely in Schleswig. The British attitude was less clear cut. The British government was not prepared to put any military obstacles in the way of a German nation-state provided it did not expand the territory of Germany.[10] The British even launched an initiative to divide Schleswig along a language boundary but this was rejected by both the Danes and the Germans. Both did so on the basis not of national self-determination but in order to retain lands which both claimed by historical right. Denmark was the weaker militarily but it had a strong diplomatic position. It was defending what it already possessed, while it was the Germans who wished to expand. What is more, they wished to expand into a key strategic area, the 'Bosphorus of the North'. This was something neither Britain nor Russia could permit. Their pressure forced Prussia to conclude an armistice at Malmö on 26 August 1848. In effect that meant giving up German claims. Germans were outraged, and the National Assembly rejected the armistice. The assembly wanted the Prussian army to enforce the national claim upon Schleswig even at risk of a European war. Only the refusal of the Prussian king prevented that policy being adopted.

The majority of the German National Assembly came to terms with this 'capitulation' by Prussia. Yet the German national movement, especially its left wing, felt itself betrayed. The left preached the idea of achieving German freedom, both within and internationally, by means of a national war. The republicans took this idea up particularly vociferously and pushed it to extremes. They could see that to accept the Malmö armistice meant not only to give way to international pressure but also to concede the impotence of the revolution and its newly created institutions against the old order within Germany. Everyone could now see that without the Prussian army the German national assembly and government could achieve nothing. The nation and its

---

10. See two recent studies with extensive bibliography: G. Heydemann, 'The "Crazy Year" 1848: The revolution in Germany and Palmerston's policy', in Schulze (ed.) op. cit., pp. 167–82, and K. Bourne, 'Nationsbildung und britische Politik: Das Kabinett zwischen 1846 und 1852', in A.M. Birke and G. Heydemann (eds) *Die Herausforderung des europäischen Staatensystems: Nationale Ideologie und Imperialismus* (Göttingen and Zürich, 1989), pp. 96–118.

new institutions had brandished the sword, but the Prussian king retained a firm control over it. Many now recognised what Varnhagen von Ense expressed forcefully:

> The Danish war and the armistice are clear humiliations for us, a slap in the face for the arrogant loudmouths who wanted to make out that a nation that is yet to be born was a conquering nation.[11]

Power lay with the Prussian military which stood behind the Prussian king. Recognising the Malmö armistice, which the Prussian king had agreed without consulting the National Assembly, meant placing the fate of the new nation-state in the hands of a king, indeed a king who was soon to reject with contempt the imperial title that that assembly was to offer him. Thus as early as August 1848 the German national revolution had lost the leader to which it looked. Without this leader it was not possible for the National Assembly and the revolutionary movement to complete the task of internal political reform which it had set itself. The subsequent acceptance of the armistice meant placing the German national revolution into the hands of the Prussian king. The left did not wish that. Therefore they had to insist on a continuation of the war. They also hoped that a national war would set off a new wave of revolutions. In Germany they would be able to sweep away the monarchies, and in Europe bring the nations together in a war against Tsarist Russia, the bastion of reaction. The alternatives were seen as either ending the Danish war and avoiding the threat of European war or renewing revolution in Germany and Europe. The German national movement showed its capacity to compromise by backing down on its national claims and coming to terms with the decision in favour of peace.

National German historiography has always portrayed this decision as a betrayal of the national cause. 'Left' historians have seen it as a betrayal of the revolution. The culmination of this nationalist tradition can be seen in the historiography of the German Democratic Republic where publications right up to the end of that state displayed no appreciation of the dilemma which confronted nationalists at the time: defence of the revolution against the resurgent old elites of Germany or preservation of peace with Britain, Russia, and possibly also France.

---

11. V. von Ense, op.cit., p. 183.

CONCEPTIONS OF THE NATION-STATE IN GERMANY

It was only in France that revolution in 1848 replaced monarchy with a republic. (The cases of Rome and Venice are rather more limited in scope and importance.) Everywhere else the revolution stopped at the foot of the throne. This meant in Germany that a national state could be established only as a federation with a monarchical head. The demand for a unitary republic which a section of extreme left-wing opinion pressed stood no chance, not least because it went against a federal tradition. The two risings in Baden in 1848 in support of a republic did not find popular support anywhere in Germany, indicating that a 'silent majority' were opposed to the idea of a republican nation-state. Furthermore, there was no political centre in Germany comparable to Paris, London or Brussels. The German National Assembly was a focus for national politics but it was rivalled by the Prussian National Assembly in Berlin and the Austrian *Reichstag* in Vienna. The other German states also had their own parliaments, often newly elected, and their governments included men out of the pre-1848 liberal opposition. This influx of new men worked to strengthen the capacity of the various states to resist any unitary tendencies. New princes did come to the throne in Bavaria and Austria, but this worked to stabilise government and dynasty. Consequently there was no question of establishing a centralised state along French lines. Furthermore, if monarchy survived in the individual states, then any national state that was created would also have to have a monarchical head. The self-esteem, power and standing of the German princes meant it was unthinkable that they might accept the leadership of an elected President.

The head of any future national state, rather like the Emperor drawn from the Habsburg line in the Holy Roman Empire, would need to be a considerable ruler in his own right. Once again Varnhagen von Ense was perceptive:

> The power of the Imperial Administrator [*Reichsverweser*] has no foundation, just as with some earlier Emperors who had no great dynastic standing. Such Emperors came to depend upon the Empire for support, which meant they could do little of value for the Empire.[12]

The Austrian Archduke Johann, whom the German National Assembly had named as provisional Imperial Administrator on 29 June 1848, was popularly known as 'Johann the Landless'.

12. Ibid., p. 175

The soldiers he uses to enforce his decisions are lent to him and can always be recalled; the money he needs for his government comes in the form of grants which can be cut off any day. His ministers, even the civil servants who apply his laws, are on temporary loan. [The] newly created imperial power [had] no roots.

Von Ense concluded that such an imperial role needed, as a matter of urgency, to be filled by a ruler of a strong state who could overcome 'the lack of power in German unity'.[13]

For von Ense there was only one possible candidate for this role: the King of Prussia. Admittedly he misjudged Frederick William IV, wrongly believing that the king was prepared to do a deal with democratic forces in Prussia and Germany.[14] He did recognise that Austria could not take the leadership role in Germany. A whole series of problems stood in the way.

The current fragmentation of Austria, the wars which beset her non-German lands, the uncertain future which she faces, [above all the fact that] Slavs and other non-German peoples make up a majority of her inhabitants.[15]

The German National Assembly and the national movement throughout Germany debated these problems at length and in detail. There appeared to be two possibilities: a greater German (*großdeutsch*) or a smaller German (*kleindeutsch*) nation-state. The *großdeutsch* solution entailed dividing the Habsburg territories into a German and a non-German part, these joined together merely by a personal union. Only the German portion would belong to the new nation-state. Such a nation-state would have had generally the same territories as the German Confederation, perhaps with some losses in the south and south-east borderlands where the majority of inhabitants were non-German. Given the territorial continuity with the Confederation, such a nation-state could have been fitted into the European arrangements worked out in 1814–15. That would mean that this solution might be acceptable to the other European powers. However, it would mean the division of the Habsburg dynasty. We can only speculate what that would have meant both for Austria and Europe. Perhaps it would have divided power between Germans and Hungarians in a way reminiscent of what happened within the Habsburg dynasty in 1867 in reaction to the emergence of the *kleindeutsch* solution. Perhaps it would have led

13. Ibid., pp. 176f.
14. W. Bußmann, *Zwischen Preußen und Deutschland: Friedrich Wilhelm IV – Eine Biographie* (Berlin, 1990).
15. V. von Ense, op.cit., p. 177

to the emergence of nation-states along the lines of what was to happen after the First World War.

The majority of the National Assembly and of the national movement wanted to see the *großdeutsch* nation-state. There were a variety of motives. Some saw it in terms of the German imperial tradition. Many Catholics were concerned that without Austria, a German state would be dominated by Protestantism. South German democrats and liberals feared a Prussianised Germany. Some considered that the individual states would have real autonomy in a greater Germany, whereas the removal of Austria would tip the balance too much towards the one major state of Prussia and undermine any genuine federalism.

The *großdeutsch* solution required Austrian agreement, whether voluntary or compelled. However, by October at the latest when imperial troops regained control of Vienna, the counter-revolution was firmly entrenched. The old elites who had regained power rejected any proposal to divide the monarchy and were prepared to risk war to avoid that happening. Opinion outside Austria was not prepared to go that far. Given that, a bare majority of the National Assembly decided on 27 and 28 March 1849 in favour of the *kleindeutsch* nation-state and offered the Emperorship of Germany to the King of Prussia. Most of those who supported this did so only because they could see no way forward without excluding Austria. Many hoped that at least a Habsburg Empire dominated by Germans would be a natural ally of the German state.

No one can know if the Habsburg Emperor would have been prepared to accept this exclusion of Austria without a war. He was never put to the test because the Prussian king sharply rejected the crown offered to him by the National Assembly. This was just a matter of Frederick William's own inclination and will. He was also rejecting the idea of parliamentary monarchy which the imperial constitution laid down not only for the nation-state but also for all the member states. He was rejecting, therefore, not only the imperial title, but also the constitutional control of the crown and its essential support, the royal army. In this Frederick was at one with the Habsburg Emperor and his decision also secured the loyalty of the old elites.

The refusal of the King of Prussia to become head of a German nation-state completely undermined the work of the National Assembly. It wanted to bring about political revolution in Germany, but only by means of reform. The whole strategy of the assembly was based upon securing agreements with the various German princes and their governments. When the Prussian king refused his agreement, then the National Assembly and most of the national movement gave up their constitutional projects. They were not prepared to use force to try to take the matter any further. Some have condemned this as a betrayal of the revolution. But such a judgement fails to understand the basic character of the German revolution of 1848–9. Only a minority of the national movement wanted a radical break with the past which included the monarchy. Most of the rest of the national movement also wanted a democratised Germany. When the reform alliance with the Prussian monarchy broke down, it destroyed the basis of the German national revolution. Within the national movement there was a very great diversity of conflicting views about the political and social character which a future Germany should have. These disagreements were held in check only by a common wish for a German national state. Once the reform strategy had failed in 1849, the national movement broke up into its conflicting elements. The last phase of the revolution confirmed what had long been obvious. There was a majority within the population for creating a nation-state in agreement with the monarchies, but not for a national revolution opposed to the monarchies. One major reason was the fear that a political and national revolution which was not held in check within the monarchical framework might turn into a social revolution.

In addition to the *großdeutsch* and *kleindeutsch* ideas which were discussed within the National Assembly and the national movement, there were further proposals made by the Austrian and Prussian governments which were intended both to end but also to continue the revolution. These alternatives brought the two German powers in conflict with the National Assembly and each other.[16] Both alternatives would have altered the constitutional work of the National Assembly in a conservative direction. However, the Prussian plan was closer to that of the National Assembly and did at least aim to establish a national state. Prussia proposed the creation of a *kleindeutsch* and federal state with a common constitution and an elected parliament and linked to Austria within a broader Confederation. Basically Prussia offered Germans and the German princes a conservative version of the nation-state which the National Assembly had proposed. The Prussian plan failed because some of the German princes rejected it, and above all because it encountered fierce opposition from Austria. Austria was able to use the renewal of crisis in Schleswig-Holstein in 1849–50 to isolate Prussia internationally. With the possibility of war in which Russia would take Austria's side, Prussia gave up its German plans in November 1850.

16. See especially A. Doering-Manteuffel, 'Der Ornungszwang des Staatensystems: zu den Mitteleuropa-Konzeptionen in der österreich-preußischen Rivalität 1849–1851', in A.M. Birke and G. Heydemann (eds), op.cit., pp. 119–40.

Austria's German policy also failed. In 1849 the Austrian minister-president, Prince Schwarzenberg, had demanded the incorporation of the entire empire within the new German state. This would have meant the creation of an empire with 70 million people, bringing together central Europe, northern Italy and much of south-east Europe within one giant federal state. It would have destroyed the territorial arrangements worked out in 1814-15 and upset the balance of power. Consequently the British and French governments, along with the Russian Tsar, worked to persuade Austria to give up this idea. The plan would probably have failed because of resistance from German princes, but pressure from the European powers ensured that it was given up before that issue arose.

A *kleindeutsch* Germany with a monarchical head would not have encountered such opposition from the other powers. Probably they would not have rejected a *großdeutsch* Germany either, although they would not have welcomed this because it would have weakened the stabilising role of the Habsburg dynasty in the multi-national regions of central and south-east Europe. But a federal state which combined a greater Germany with a greater Austria was completely unacceptable. What the other powers most preferred was the restoration of the old order. This was what happened at the Dresden Conference of May 1851. Given the absence of any other practical options, the German Confederation was restored by all the German states. That brought to an end the governmental sequel to the 1848 revolution. But it did not end the demands for a German nation-state: 1848 had made clear that the smaller Germany was the most acceptable option. In this sense the experience of 1848 prepared the ground for the foundation of a smaller Germany between 1866 and 1871, although of course it did not make that foundation inevitable.

INTERNATIONALISM OF THE GREAT POWERS – RIVALRY OF NATIONS

The revolution began with the dream of a 'springtime of peoples'; it ended with the reality of counter-revolutionary solidarity among states. It was not the nationalists who had managed to work together, but rather the Great Powers. Despite their own mutual rivalries and political values, the major powers had made common cause against the revolution. France, the motherland of revolution, did not try to export her revolution or even provide military support, as in Belgium in 1830, for a new nation-state borne out of revolution. Indeed, France helped in the repression of the revolutionary Roman Republic.

Prussia took on that repressive role in Germany. In July 1849 she used military force to crush the revolution in Saxony, Baden and the Palatinate. Russia, the bulwark of reaction which had not been directly affected by revolution in 1848, provided military assistance to Austria in August 1849 to crush the Hungarian Revolution. With that achieved Austria was able to go on to compel Venetia to surrender. That brought the revolution in Italy to an end and also left Austria free to turn back to German affairs and to oppose the Prussian *kleindeutsch* policy. Even Britain, a model for many European liberals, both by diplomatic means and by a very clear policy of non-intervention, helped Austria to defend her position in Italy and Hungary.

Great Power internationalism faced only two opponents. There was an insignificant pacifist movement which reached across national boundaries. There was also some ineffective cooperation among a few revolutionaries who vainly hoped to spark off internationalist activity among various nationalities. Instead, nationalism led to nationality conflicts. National movements were prepared to cooperate with counter-revolution in order to advance their interests against those of other nations. This was a general pattern in 1848, not something confined to Germany. Probably little fundamental would have been been different if the revolutionary movements of Germany and Hungary had been able to cooperate. Many had hoped that such an alliance might have broken the international solidarity of counter-revolution. Perhaps the German revolution might have developed in a different way if the Hungarian army had obstructed the repression of revolution in Vienna in October 1848. However, that would not have solved the great problem of conflicting national claims. Neither the German nor the Hungarian national movements showed any willingness to make concessions to other nationalities. A successful alliance between the German and Hungarian national movements would not have been enough to sustain a 'springtime of peoples' in Europe.

SUGGESTIONS FOR FURTHER READING

The best general treatment of 1848 in Germany is W. Siemann, *Die deutsche Revolution von 1848/1849* (Frankfurt am Main, 1985). There are good shorter general accounts in T. Nipperdey, *Deutsche Geschichte 1800–1866* (Munich, 1983), and J. Sheehan, *German History 1770– 1866* (Oxford, 1990).

For a survey of the revolution in Europe generally see P.N. Stearns, *The Revolutions of 1848* (London, 1974); for shorter studies see R. Price, *The Revolutions of 1848* (London, 1988), and D. Langewiesche, *Europa zwischen Restauration und Revolution 1815–1849* (Munich, 1989).

Specifically on the national problems see H. Lutz, *Zwischen Habsburg und Preußen. Deutschland 1815–1866* (Berlin, 1985); H. Schulze (ed.) *Nation-Building in Central Europe* (Leamington Spa, Hamburg and New York, 1987); A. Sked, *The Decline and Fall of the Habsburg Empire* (London, 1989); H. Rumpler (ed.) *Deutscher Bund und deutsche Frage 1815–1866* (Vienna and Munich, 1990).

On the national debates in the German National Assembly there is the detailed, somewhat descriptive account by G. Wollstein, *Das 'Großdeutschland' der Paulskirche: Nationale Ziele in der bürgerlichen Revolution 1848/49* (Düsseldorf, 1977); shorter and analytical is Wollstein, 'Mitteleuropa und Großdeutschland – Visionen der Revolution 1848/49', in *Die deutsche Revolution von 1848/49*, D. Langewiesche (ed.) (Darmstadt, 1983), pp. 237–57.

CHAPTER FIVE
The unification of Germany

William Carr

Until the winter of 1989–90 the division of Germany into two sovereign states, the legacy of the first Cold War in the late 1940s, seemed an immutable feature of the international landscape, unlikely to be altered in our lifetime. Since November 1989 the situation has been utterly transformed in a bewildering succession of dramatic events: the breaching of the Berlin Wall; the fall of Erich Honecker; the abandonment by the Socialist Unity Party of its monopoly of power; the holding in March 1990 of the first free elections since 1933 – which though massively influenced by West German parties reduced the Communists to a small and discredited rump in the new *Volkskammer*, monetary union between the two Germanies in July; formal union between them in October; and all-German elections in December. In one tumultuous year the forty-year division of Germany had been overcome.

The jubilant scenes as the Berlin Wall was torn down and the enthusiastic declarations of leading political figures in both states testify to the desire of ordinary Germans for reunification of their country, even if the initial euphoria was subsequently diminished by growing awareness of the heavy financial costs and general consequences of the marriage between two disparate social and economic systems. Similarly in the 1860s the desire of the articulate sections of the German public for a united nation played an immensely important role in the final outcome. Nevertheless, it would be a misunderstanding of a complex historical process to imagine that national feeling was the principal factor bringing about the creation of the German Reich in 1871 any more than it has been in the reunification of the two Germanies in 1989–90. In recent months a number of factors have come together to transform the shape of Europe: the changes in the Soviet Union associated with Mikhail Gorbachev; the peaceful revolutions taking place in central and eastern Europe (with the tragic exceptions of Romania and civil war in Yugoslavia) as the Russians relaxed their grip over these countries; the desire both in Washington and Moscow to reduce the crippling burden of armaments for sound economic reasons; and, in consequence, the diminishing military importance of a divided Germany as a strategic buffer between the rival NATO and Warsaw Pact alliances. Similarly in the middle of the nineteenth century several developments interacted to make the unification of Germany possible. While no one would dispute that the role of Otto von Bismarck was of crucial importance in the creation of the German Reich, we should remember that

> men make their own history . . . they do not make it just as they please, but under circumstances directly encountered, given and transmitted from the past.[1]

Bismarck's personality and policies constitute one, but only one, of the determinants of unification which will be analysed in this chapter.

We commence with the power-political contest between Austria and Prussia. Their rivalry in its modern form originated in the mid-eighteenth century when Frederick the Great attacked Silesia in 1740. Only after two long wars did he finally secure it for Prussia in 1763. Thirty years later the French Revolution rocked thrones to their foundations all over Europe, compelling rulers to remember that what they had in common was more important than their power struggles, at least for the time being. Consequently Austria and Prussia joined with the other Great Powers gathered together at the Congress of Vienna after the final defeat of Napoleon to draw up a peace settlement to protect Europe against future French aggression. Barriers were erected to contain the French. In the north the former Austrian Netherlands were joined to Holland; in the south–east the Austrians were given the provinces of Lombardy and Venetia in northern Italy; and in the west the bulk of the Napoleonic creation, the Kingdom of Westphalia, was handed over to Prussia to compensate her for the loss of territory to Russia. This territorial acquisition shifted the centre of gravity of Prussia westwards towards the Rhine and away from the Polish territories which had been her primary interest in the past. During the Vormärz period (the term literally means 'pre–March', i.e. the period in German history before March 1848) it seemed unlikely that Prussia would be called upon to fulfil her obligation to defend the Rhineland. The Restoration governments of Louis XVIII and Charles X were not disposed to cause trouble in central Europe. Nor was the July Monarchy; the war scare of 1840 was no more than a brief aberration. And had it

---

1. Karl Marx, *The Eighteenth Brumaire of Louis Napoleon* (Moscow, 1954), p. 10.

come to war, Prussia could have relied on Austrian help against the common danger despite the failure to resolve the vexed question of control of the federal forces in wartime which Prussia saw as her right, a claim resisted by the Austrians. At the same time, the fact that West-phalia was separated from the core land of Brandenburg-Prussia by 20 kilometres at the narrowest and 200 at the widest points encouraged the Prussians to try and extend their influence over the small interven-ing territories, northwards over the North German plain (the Kingdom of Hannover) and southwards (Electoral Hesse and Nassau) roughly down to the line of the river Main. Given the prevailing philosophy of the day, any large state would have had the same objective. Prussia with her militaristic structure and expansionist history was more likely than most to succeed.

Any change in the balance of power in favour of Prussia would inevitably affect the position of Austria. In the past our image of Aus-trian policy has been deeply coloured by the works of *kleindeutsch* (lite-rally 'little German', i.e. those committed to a Germany which excluded Austria) historians such as von Droysen and von Treitschke who wrote as enthusiastic supporters of Protestant Prussia, the victor of 1866 and 1870. For these historians Austria was an 'unGerman', 'reac-tionary' and Catholic power whose multi-national empire drew her inexorably towards south-eastern Europe and away from Germany, but whose stubborn refusal to recognise the logic of her position retarded unification under the Hohenzollerns. However, seen from the perspec-tive of the Ballhausplatz (the seat of the Austrian foreign ministry in Vienna) Austria also had a 'mission' as legitimate as that of Prussia. For centuries the defender of Catholicism against the Turk, Austria now thought of herself as the pivotal power holding a precarious balance in Europe between Orthodox Russia in the east and 'godless' France in the west. To fulfil this European mission the Austrians believed it es-sential to maintain their presence in the German Confederation (the loose association of states created in 1815) where they exerted much influence over the medium and small states. If the balance of power was upset in Germany, the corollary was an upset in the balance of European power totally unacceptable to Austria. From the days of Metternich to those of Rechberg (Austrian foreign minister from 1855 to 1859) she was willing to recognise a degree of Prussian influence north of the River Main. What she would never do was abandon her position of primacy at Frankfurt where her representative presided over the deliberations of the Federal Diet. However, the maintenance of her position in Germany against Prussia, in northern Italy against France, and in south-eastern Europe against Russia required a consid-

erable military effort which strained her resources to breaking-point on
several occasions. Paradoxically enough the Achilles heel of financial
instability was an added reason why dualism was mandatory for Austria. However much she suspected Prussian intentions, Austria realised
that only by cooperation with the heirs of Frederick the Great could
Prussia be held in check and the strain on Austrian resources corre-
spondingly reduced.

To pursue a dualistic policy proved increasingly difficult after the
1848–9 revolution. Though Frederick William IV had rejected the
crown of a *Kleindeutschland* offered him by the Frankfurt Parliament,
he was enough of a Hohenzollern to want it if the German princes
could be persuaded to offer it to him on a plate. The Erfurt Union
(Prussia's diplomatic version of *Kleindeutschland* in 1849–50) failed because Prince Schwarzenberg, Francis Joseph's new chief minister, took
up the challenge, refusing to be driven out of the Confederation. War
was avoided in 1850 when Prussia backed away and the old political
structures were restored. Suspicion of Prussian policy remained very
much alive in the minds of policy-makers in Vienna while in Berlin
the king and his ministers continued to resent the 'humiliation' of
1850. While this did not preclude superficial cooperation between the
two great German powers to preserve the conservative order of society
against the threat which the forces of liberalism and nationalism were
thought to present to it, nevertheless the episode of the Erfurt Union
served as a warning to the Austrians of what Prussia might well repeat
if the international situation deteriorated.

The tranformation of the international scene after the Crimean War
is a second general factor without which unification would not have
occurred when it did or in the form that it did. The old solidarity of
the conservative powers, linchpin of international order since 1815,
was fatally disrupted by the war in the Crimea. While Britain and
France fought Russia, Austria remained neutral but pursued an intri-
cate policy of armed mediation which alienated Russia from her. To
protect her growing strategic and commercial interests in south-eastern
Europe Austria forced Russia out of the Danubian principalities of
Moldavia and Wallachia and, to add insult to injury, supported Anglo-
French proposals to end the war.

Another destabilising factor weakening Austria's position still further
was the accession to power of Louis Napoleon. Although the new
dictator did not abandon traditional French objectives such as the acquisition of France's 'natural frontiers', his avowed commitment to the
overthrow of the settlement of 1815 introduced an unsettling element
into international affairs. His belief in the principle of nationality

(though not to the point of endangering French interests) posed a general threat to Austria, his uncle's old enemy, and a particular threat in northern Italy where the Austrian presence was a major obstacle to Italian unification under Piedmontese leadership. When war broke out in Italy in 1859 Austria fought alone against France and Piedmont. Russia had no especial interest in western Europe and none in supporting Austria, while Prussia equivocated, attempting to drive a hard bargain over command of the federal forces before she would come to Austria's assistance.

Austrian defeat in Italy and the constitutional changes she was obliged to set in motion in her empire made dualism more necessary than ever for Austrian survival as a European great power. Cooperation with Prussia was, however, more difficult than ever because the changing international scene from the mid-1850s had affected Prussian objectives in Germany. The growing belief in Berlin that Prussia could not rely on the support of most German states or on Austria in the event of a war in the west, coupled with the threat France was now thought to present to the Rhineland, convinced the policy-makers in Berlin that Prussia required a stronger power base to defend herself against France. What the frontiers of the Prussian state should be was indicated by Bismarck, then ambassador in St Petersburg; writing to the Prussian foreign minister in 1859 he urged the latter to seize the opportunity presented by the Italian war:

> the present situation has put the winning card in our hands again provided we allow Austria to become deeply involved in the war with France and then march southwards with our entire army carrying frontier posts in our big packs (*Tornistor*). We can plant them either on the Bodensee or as far south as Protestantism is the dominant faith.[2]

At this time the Prussian government was, as we have seen, torn between self-interest, a sense of loyalty to Austria and distaste for revolutionary politics, and did not heed Bismarck's (unsolicited) advice. Three years later, when Bismarck was in charge of Prussian policy, the likelihood that she would act solely in accordance with her power interests was greatly increased. If she chose to do so, the constellation of forces would be in her favour. Russia would not come automatically to Austria's assistance. And by astute diplomacy it might be possible to neutralise France and thus to isolate Austria. That the object of war was not national unification but the creation of a Great Prussian state is evident from Prussian behaviour in 1866. The legiti-

---

2. Bismarck, *Die gesammelten Werke* (Berlin, 1923–35), 14, no. 724, Bismarck to Gustav von Alvensleben, 23 April–5 May 1859.

mate rights of several rulers north of the river Main were brushed aside by the victorious Prussians; Schleswig-Holstein, the Kingdom of Hannover, Electoral Hesse, Nassau and the city of Frankfurt were annexed outright, creating a solid power base down to the river Main.

The creation of *Kleindeutschland* would not have been possible without the reformed Prussian army. The Erfurt Union failed not only because the romantic conservatism of Frederick William IV held him back at the last minute from war but also because it was recognised in Berlin that Prussia was not strong enough to fight the Austrians. Regent William, who became king in 1861, is often depicted as the compliant associate of his servant Bismarck. In fact the king was one of the makers of *Kleindeutschland* in his own right. A professional soldier by training, he was greatly concerned by the sorry state of affairs revealed during the 1859 crisis when Prussia mobilised several army corps (though with no clear political objective). He determined to reform Prussia's armed forces to enable her to play a role in German affairs commensurate with her military traditions. On his initiative and in the teeth of opposition from the liberal-controlled lower house, the *Landtag*, the army was doubled in size from 50,000 to 110,000 men with greatly augmented reserves. Of course, Prussian liberals were as anxious as conservatives to see Prussia playing an active role in Germany. What they objected to was an increased period of service with the regular army and in particular the demotion of the *Landwehr*, the territorial element in the army introduced by the Prussian reformers in an attempt to break away from the *Kadavergehorsamkeit* (literally the obedience of corpses) of the old Frederician army. But General von Roon, like his royal master, wanted a strongly disciplined fighting force not subject to any civilian influence. This was not only for possible use against other states, but also because conservatives always had an enemy within in mind; an obedient army completely under royal control might be needed to put down uprisings at home which they supposed would result from the spread of liberalism and socialism.

This modernised army under its able chief of staff, Count von Moltke, proved itself at the battle of Königgrätz in June 1866. Not that there was anything inevitable about the Prussian victory. Moltke's controversial encirclement and annihilation strategy did not succeed completely; the bulk of the Austrian army managed to withdraw south of the Danube; and had General Benedek, the Austrian commander, seized his opportunity to attack the first Prussian army, the course of history might have been different. As always, the side making the fewest mistakes won the day. All the same it remains true to say that without the army reforms initiated by Regent William and carried out by war minister Roon and Moltke, Prussia would not have been in a position to risk war with any hope of success.

Before military history staged a welcome come-back in recent years many historians laid heavy emphasis on the economic dimension of the German problem and in particular on the role of the German Customs Union (the *Zollverein*) in bringing about a measure of economic unification; Germany, as John Maynard Keynes suggested, was united 'more by coal and iron than by blood and iron'. Again, one is reminded that the *kleindeutsch* historians depicted the *Zollverein* as a first step on the road to political unification.

Recent research suggests that it was not so simple as that. It is frankly most difficult to assess the extent to which commerce was stimulated by the *Zollverein*. No doubt a larger market did prove beneficial to some enterprises but it has to be remembered that economic growth was influenced by improvements in communications, especially the spread of railways. Furthermore, doubt has been cast on the entire concept of a 'unified' market requiring only a political roof to crown the edifice. Industrialisation, which dated back to the eighteenth century, affected only some German regions where natural resources and skills favoured development. The key to understanding the growth of the *Zollverein* lies not in economics but in finance. The rulers of the medium and small states joined the *Zollverein* to obtain sources of revenue to finance the modernisation many of them undertook in the early nineteenth century, sources which had the additional advantage of being outside the control of local *Landtage*. Hence, despite deep suspicion of Prussia's predatory intentions, Bavaria, Württemberg and Baden renewed the customs treaties in 1852 and again in 1864. Of course, Prussia had an economic whip-hand because of her growing industrial potential in the late 1850s and early 1860s and through control of key communications arteries along the Rhine, Elbe and Oder. But while it is true to say that the *Zollverein* is 'better seen in the context of the individual states' struggle for financial solvency and economic consolidation',[3] Prussian statesmen were well aware of its political significance. Finance minister Friedrich von Motz, under whose energetic leadership the Prussian Customs Union was extended in the late 1820s, admitted that

> the more natural the attachment to a customs and commercial system is . . . the more intimate and deep will be the attachment of those states to some political system.[4]

3. J: Sheehan, *German History 1770–1866* (Oxford, 1990), p. 434.
4. Quoted in H.-W. Hahn, *Geschichte des deutschen Zollvereins* (Göttingen, 1984), p. 56.

And Prussian foreign minister Count Christian Bernstorff remarked after Prussia concluded her first major extra-territorial treaty with Hesse-Darmstadt that, however one-sided the agreement (which made generous concessions to that state), it would 'place Prussia in a position to exert its influence over the [smaller states] in the most equitable manner'.[5] In other words, financial inducements were consciously employed to further the strategic objectives of linking up the western with the eastern territories.

The *Zollverein* did not lead inevitably to the creation of a Prussian-dominated *kleindeutsch* state; as a former US President once remarked: it takes a lot of effort by a lot of people before any development moves into that assured category. Still, one should not go too far in the opposite direction. Recent historical work on the *Zollverein* makes the valid point that, although it did not make unification along *kleindeutsch* lines inevitable, growing economic ties did at least prevent any attempt at a federal solution to the German problem.[6] This was because Austrian and Prussian economic interests were increasingly divergent in the 1860s.

Through an accident of geography Prussia, the most populous state in the Confederation (Austria had a larger total population than Prussia but fewer inhabitants within the part of the state belonging to the Confederation), was well endowed with the raw materials of the first Industrial Revolution: coal, iron and zinc. And as agrarian reform encouraged the movement of poor peasants away from the countryside and the handicraft industry was declining, Prussia possessed an abundant labour reservoir to man her industrial system. In addition the low tariff policy of the *Zollverein* was beneficial to some manufacturers as well as to Prussian landowners (for whose profit the policy was primarily devised).

It would be quite wrong to suppose that the Industrial Revolution did not come to the Habsburg dominions. It is, however, true to say that industrialisation took place at a much slower pace and that it was impeded by Austrian bureaucracy. Prussian officials pursued policies conducive to industrial growth; they actively promoted free-trade ideas; and they helped remove feudal restrictions in the countryside, thereby facilitating the emergence of efficient estates devoted to large-

5. Quoted in L.J. Baack, *Christian Bernstorff and Prussia: Diplomacy and Reform Conservatism 1818–1832* (New Brunswick, NJ, 1980), p. 125.

6. See, for example, Hans Werner Hahn, 'Mitteleuropäische oder Kleindeutsche Wirtschaftsordnung in der Epoche des Deutschen Bundes,' in H. Rumpler (ed.), *Deutscher Bund und deutsche frage 1815–1866* (Vienna and Munich, 1990), pp. 186–214.

scale production. Austrian bureaucrats did much less to free the Habsburg Empire from the grip of feudalism. True, customs barriers between Austria and Hungary were removed in 1850; the next year prohibitive tariffs on foreign imports were abolished and the number of tariffs was cut by almost 50 per cent. A significant expansion of the railway system improved communications; in 1859 trades and professions were freed from all restrictions; and in the countryside the abolition of the *robot* (compulsory labour services) was completed. Though tariff reductions did give an impetus to development, the pace slackened after the depression of 1857 which severely affected Austria. Coal and textile manufacturers were able to veto further tariff reform. The basic problem was caused by high production costs; the inaccessibility of raw materials and transportation problems obliged manufacturers to demand higher protection against foreign competition. So although there was an increase in trade with the rest of Germany in the 1850s, much more trade was carried on inside the Habsburg dominions than with the rest of the world. And, once again, the most serious brake on Austrian progress was chronic insolvency from 1811 onwards. The national debt actually trebled between 1848 and 1866; armed mediation during the Crimean War gravely strained Austria's finances, while the 1859 war brought them virtually to the point of collapse. Only through massive loans (which were then not available for investment) did Austria stagger on. Between 1860 and 1866 she was spending 40 per cent of her state receipts on her army and navy.

Finally, we turn to a consideration of the ideological forces of nationalism and political Catholicism, each of which in its own way contributed to the emergence of a *kleindeutsch* state.

A rough-and-ready definition of nationalism might be the belief that a people bound by a common language or common traditions has a right to set up its own state in which all the citizens – no longer objects to be exploited by tyrannical rulers – participate actively in political life through representative institutions. This definition fits the circumstances of countries such as Britain, Spain and France tolerably well, for in these cases geography has been a major determinant of frontiers. But the ethnic and cultural mixture in central Europe made it extraordinarily difficult until well into the twentieth-century to decide what frontiers a German nation-state should possess.

Three 'national' solutions of the German problem were on offer in the mid-nineteenth century. First there was the *kleindeutsch* state which amounted to Prussian domination of Germany and the complete exclusion of Austria from the German state. Second, there was the *großdeutsch* (greater Germany) idea, the essence of which was the maintenance of the traditional ties with Austria which the vast majority of Germans were reluctant to sever. Third, there was the idea of *Mitteleuropa*, the middle European state, an Austrian scheme whereby the whole of the Habsburg dominions would be included in a huge common market stretching from the Baltic to the Black Sea. Not one of these solutions was national in the modern sense of including only German speakers under one national roof. The *kleindeutsch* state of 1871 included Poles in Posen, Danes in north Schleswig, and French people in Alsace-Lorraine, while it excluded German-speaking Austrians. *Großdeutschland* would have included not only German-speaking Austrians, but also Czechs in Bohemia, Italians in Trieste and Slovenes in Carinthia. *Mitteleuropa* would certainly have included all German speakers but also Czechs, Slovaks, Magyars, Ruthenes, Romanians, Serbs and Croats in one huge racial conglomeration run by the Habsburgs. It should be remembered that political activists at that time applied a quite different yardstick to determine nationality. If the language spoken by the upper classes – the officials, pastors and professors – was German, as it was in large areas of central and eastern Europe, then the area was deemed 'German'. While most Germans had no wish to prevent local populations speaking their Polish, Czech or Danish, nevertheless educated Germans regarded these languages as inferior cultural media.

Clearly the Reich of 1871 which *kleindeutsch* historians lauded as the inevitable outcome of a long historical process was in reality a truncated 'national' state which had ruptured the natural connection with Austria. For that reason among others the German question remained on the agenda long after 1871. After the First World War Poles, Danes and French parted company with imperial Germany. But the Weimar Republic, though a more German state, still excluded the Austrians now reduced to a shadow of their former glory. *Ein Volk, ein Reich, ein Führer* was one of the slogans which helped put the Nazis into power. Hitler's annexation of Austria in 1938 made the Republic a more German state. But the incorporation of Czechoslovakia in 1939 made it a less national state as Hitler's imperialist ambitions rapidly unfolded. After the defeat in the Second World War, because the victorious powers could not decide on the shape and political future of a German state, occupation zones were turned into separate states for the next forty years, dividing the people still further.

If the *kleindeutsches Reich* was not a national state, how did it come to be widely accepted as such in educated circles? The answer lies in part in the more effective propagation of their views by the advocates of *Kleindeutschland*.

Mitteleuropa and *Großdeutschland* had their supporters and their organisations such as the German Reform Society (*Deutsche Reformverein*). But they possessed nothing comparable with the propaganda machine created by the *kleindeutsch* advocates. As industrialisation spread inside the *Zollverein*, a thrusting entrepreneurial and professional class emerged organised through local chambers of commerce and in professional bodies. For economic and national reasons many of them became staunch supporters of unification. Increasingly irritated by restrictions on their economic activities outside Prussia, they persuaded themselves that nothing but benefit would flow from the creation of a German Empire based on the area of the *Zollverein*. In 1858 the Congress of German Economists was founded, attracting to its meetings civil servants, journalists and academics as well as merchants, financiers and industrialists. Their aim was promotion of tariff reform and removal of all restrictive legislation. In 1860 the German Jurists Congress was founded to advance reform of the legal system. In 1861 the German Commercial Association was founded to agitate for a reformed commercial code. Out of the inaugural meeting of the latter came initiatives which led to the creation of the National Society. This body, which took its name from the Italian society which harnessed middle-class opinion behind Cavour, was established to coordinate national liberal political activity. Significantly radicals as well as moderates joined the National Society. Never numbering more than 25,000 members, this society played a crucial role in the creation of a steamhead of opinion principally in northern and central Germany favourable to the establishment of a *kleindeutsch* state. While it enjoyed some lower middle-class support, the upper-class leadership never sought to recruit a mass membership, not only because of fear of popular action likely to erode their own privileged position, but also because they supposed governments would yield to the power of liberal arguments.

National sentiment and economic calculation worked hand in hand. Virulent outbursts of anti-French feeling in 1813 and again in 1840 had not permanently affected relations with their French neighbours, as witness the friendly greetings exchanged in 1848 between the Frankfurt Parliament and the French National Assembly. The year 1859 was, however, a turning-point in Franco-German relations. The French attack on Austria in northern Italy where the first Napoleon had won his spurs aroused excited comment in Germany. While liberals were sympathetic to Italy's struggle for independence, many feared that if France was victorious Napoleon would attempt to seize the so-called 'natural' frontier in the Rhineland. Anti-French feeling quickly manifested itself in the press and at popular festivals, scientific congresses and in *Landtage* all over Germany. The nationalist agitation reached a high point in November with the centenary celebrations of Friedrich Schiller's birth. This time anti-French feeling did not die down. It received a fresh impetus in the spring of 1860 when Napoleon acquired Savoy and Nice from Piedmont as the price of French intervention in northern Italy. All shades of German opinion, liberal and conservative, were united in the belief that an attack in the west was imminent. For the first time demands were heard for the annexation of Alsace and Lorraine to safeguard Germany's frontiers against French aggression.

Anti-French feeling remained a permanent feature of Franco-German relations throughout the 1860s, and strengthened the demand for a strong Reich led by Prussia, the guardian of the Rhineland. Nationalist organisations such as the German Sharpshooters League (*Deutsche Schützenbund*) founded in 1861 and the German Glee Singers League (*Deutsche Sängerbund*) in 1862 institutionalised this intense nationalism. It was kept alive at popular festivals organised by these bodies which attracted thousands of spectators from the broad middle classes. Even wider circles of the population were influenced by popular anti-French literature circulating in the 1860s.

All these organisations, from the Congress of German Economists to the Sharpshooters' League, helped create a climate of opinion favourable to unification. Interlocking directorates and overlapping membership bound the organisers close together. 'The same liberals', remarks one authority, 'who supported the Progressive Party joined the *Nationalverein*, attended the sessions of the Congress of German Economists and addressed the meetings of the gymnasts and sharpshooters'.[7] While it would be quite misleading to imagine that national liberalism altered the thrust of Prussian policy, it is true to say that this steamhead of opinion for a *kleindeutsch Reich* dovetailed neatly into the expansionist designs of that state.

The second ideology, political Catholicism, which emerged as a formidable force at the close of the 1860s, may seem at first sight more likely to retard than advance the creation of a united Germany. That depends to some extent on the feasibility of the *großdeutsch* solution supported (if only nominally) by many Catholics who were opposed to Prussia on religious as well as on political grounds.

In recent years a school of revisionist historians has taken up the

---

7. T. Hamerow, *The Social Foundations of German Unification 1858–1871: Ideas and Institutions* (Princeton, NJ, 1969), p. 358.

cudgels on behalf of the Confederation. Revisionists quote with approval the remarks of a contemporary observer in 1866 who believed that the Confederation was

> the last statesmanlike concept of European diplomacy . . . not only did Germany live at peace with its neighbours; it acted as a brake on any European state which desired to breach the peace of the world. The only error . . . was that it assumed all the members possessed moral stature . . . Prussia had made it clear for a long time that she would not bow to majority decisions. On the day she said that openly the Confederation was smothered to death.[8]

These historians go on to point out, rightly, that far from being the culmination of an inevitable historical development, the Reich of 1871 was the product of a civil war which set German against German, dividing not uniting them. Moreover, where the old Confederation had kept the peace for fifty years, the new Reich plunged Europe into a disastrous war within thirty-four years. Twenty-five years later the same militaristic elements went to war once more, this time to leave Germany more divided than ever before.

It seems unlikely that the Confederation could have been reorganised on federal lines maintaining the Austrian connection and combining maximum freedom for its members with a stronger central authority than the Federal Diet. First, its reputation had sunk so low in the esteem of most liberals – because of its failure to tackle pressing problems and its close association with reactionary measures – that it is difficult to envisage its transformation into a forward looking national state. This was reinforced by the conservative policies pursued by states such as Bavaria and Württemberg, in particular their opposition to a directly elected national parliament. Second, while the Third Germany could preserve its independence by playing Austria and Prussia off against each another (as they had done between 1848 and 1852), as long as Austria preferred dualism the reform schemes of these states (however impracticable) could never be realised. Indeed, as some of them appreciated, a stronger Confederation would not be in Austrian interests because it would inevitably weaken the ties with her non-German possessions. Finally, the rivalries between the states forming the Third Germany militated against close cooperation which might have enabled them to exert some influence. Economically Saxony and Württemberg looked to the *Zollverein* whereas Bavaria was attracted by the markets of the Danubian basin, while politically the attempts of

---

8. Quoted in H.-U. Wehler, *Das deutsche Kaiserreich 1871–1918* (Göttingen, 1980), p. 160.

the latter to become the predominant state in south Germany aroused the suspicions of her neighbours. For all these reasons hopes of a re-formed Confederation maintaining the link with Austria were unrealistic from the start.

On the other hand, the strength of political Catholicism on the eve of the war of 1870 may well have exerted some influence on Prussian policy and thus on the creation of *Kleindeutschland*. That was because the democratic connotations of political Catholicism posed a threat not only to the established order of things in south Germany but also by implication to monarchical power everywhere.

Political Catholicism originated with the reaction of the Catholic Church to the attempts of liberal movements to reduce her monopoly of power in education and over matrimony. As the Church had emerged from the trauma of the French Revolution a more Rome-oriented body, so successive pontiffs adopted an increasingly intransigent attitude towards the modern world. In the old Confederation there were 23 million Catholics and 20 million Protestants. Once Austria's 12 million Catholics were excluded Protestants were in a majority. The Catholic feelings of vulnerability coincided with dislike of Prussian domination of the North German Confederation. The ruthless treatment of defeated states, disregard of dynastic rights and the minimal concessions Bismarck made to liberalism confirmed south Germans in their opposition to eventual union with the north. It was the merger of opposition to Prussia with opposition to liberal attempts to introduce secular education and civil marriage which produced the phenomenon of political Catholicism. In France and Belgium attempts by the state to control the Church led to the emergence of liberal Catholic movements which broke completely the close association of state and Church (throne and altar) characteristic of Catholicism for centuries. In Germany Catholics were much less affected by liberal currents. What the Church authorities borrowed from liberal Catholicism were the techniques of mass political participation to underpin their campaign against liberalism.

After the expulsion of Austria from Germany the four southern states remained in a no-man's land sandwiched between victorious Prussia, defeated Austria and a France determined to prevent further extensions of Prussian power. But despite the conclusion of defensive/offensive treaties with the southern states (entered into because they were conscious of their vulnerability to French attack) it was by no means obvious that the south would gradually be absorbed into the Prussian sphere of influence as Bismarck seems initially to have thought likely. Elections to the new Customs Parliament in 1868 disappointed him. The campaign slogan 'From Customs Parliament to Union Parliament' indicated what national liberals hoped would result from the elections. In fact anti-Prussian and anti-Protestant sentiments carried the day. Forty-nine opponents of union were returned to the Berlin parliament and only thirty-six unionists. The message was clear: while the southern states valued the economic advantages which the *Zollverein* brought to them, deep hostility to Prussian militarism remained the dominant theme.

The important point to bear in mind is that anti-Prussianism was growing stronger, not weaker, by 1870. In Württemberg where the government had not harassed Catholics, nevertheless the Greater German Party for which most Catholics voted cooperated with the People's Party in opposing increased taxation to meet the costs of military reorganisation consequent upon the conclusion of its defensive and offensive treaties with Prussia. In March 1870 the two parties which had a majority in the *Landtag* introduced a motion to cut expenditure and reduce the period of service with the colours – a feature arousing much popular discontent. The government, fearing new elections, postponed a decision until the autumn. Although it attempted to conciliate the opposition in the high summer by offering slight cuts in military expenditure and a reduction in the period of service, it was by no means certain that this would have resolved the crisis. The government was determined to make no new concessions while the opposition was assured of support from grass-roots organisations pledged to a taxation boycott.

In Baden and Bavaria where governments had attempted to curtail Church activities, parties hostile to Prussia had been founded. The Catholic People's Party founded in Heidelberg in 1869 demanded freedom for the Church to manage her own affairs, unification on a federal basis with the inclusion of Austria in a German Reich, and the introduction of universal suffrage. The last demand was significant; it had dawned on Catholic politicians that a broad franchise would, with the help of the rural clergy, enable them to mobilise the masses and swamp the urban basis of political liberalism. But it was in Bavaria that political Catholicism became a major force in response to government attempts to reduce Church control over schools. In the winter of 1868–9 the Bavarian People's Party or Patriotic Party was founded. It won an overall majority in the chamber in May 1869, and despite intense government pressure maintained its hold after elections in October. In February 1870 the crisis deepened when both houses of the *Landtag* carried a no-confidence motion which eventually forced the Hohenloe ministry, which was favourable to union with the north, to resign. Subsequently the lower house proposed cuts in the military budget and a reduction in the period of service with the colours. In July the new minister-president and the finance minister declared these proposals totally unacceptable, making a head-on collision between government and opposition inevitable.

The outbreak of the Franco-Prussian War and the outburst of patriotic feeling which swept through the south has obscured the fact that the two largest states in the area were gripped by a political crisis much more serious than the one facing Prussia in the first half of the 1860s. Opinion had been mobilised and polarised in both states. On one side crown, military and civil service were defending privileged positions against determined opponents with grass-roots support such as the Prussian liberals had never sought in their struggle with the Prussian crown.

It would be going much too far to suggest that Bismarck plunged the North German Confederation into war in 1870 merely to divert attention from a serious internal threat to the stability of the conservative order of things. However, we know that he was concerned about the deteriorating situation. The British ambassador reported in February 1870 that Bismarck had said that in the event of serious complications in Bavaria the Prussian army would march into that state at once. And in March after the fall of Hohenloe it was rumoured in Berlin that three army corps had been designated for use in Bavaria and Württemberg.

At the same time Bismarck was worried about the situation facing him in Prussia. National Liberals were becoming increasingly restive as evidence mounted of deepening southern opposition to final unification. In February Eduard Lasker, the liberal leader, attempted to force the pace with a motion asking the *Reichstag* to recognise the national aspirations of Baden (which had a pro-Prussian government) and help it join the north. Behind this lay the hope that the other southern states would follow suit, making the creation of *Kleindeutschland* an accomplished fact. If France chose to fight over this issue, well and good. Patriotic feeling would then drive the south into the northern camp. Bismarck opposed the motion, having no desire to allow the National Liberals to dictate the course of events. Yet he needed their political support more than ever before. For without it the government could not secure favourable majorities in the forthcoming *Landtag* and *Reichstag* elections, it was extremely doubtful whether the Iron Budget would be renewed, i.e. the arrangement entered into in 1867 whereby military expenditure was outside *Reichstag* control for the next four years. Furthermore, the price of agreement might well be some movement towards responsible government, for frustrated National Liberals were turning more and more to constitutional issues, encouraged to some extent by the establishment of the liberal Empire in France in January 1870. But Bismarck was adamantly opposed to further political concessions. That he was on the look-out for some way out of the impasse by reviving the flagging national issue is suggested by his determined attempt in the spring of 1870 to obtain an imperial title for King William – with no success, for neither Württemberg nor Bavaria were eager to confer such an honour on a Hohenzollern. Therefore it seems not unreasonable to suppose that National Liberal reactions to deadlock over final unification combined with serious political unrest in south Germany – for which the growth of political Catholicism was largely responsible – may well have played a part in the decision to go to war in 1870.

These reflections lead naturally to a consideration of the Bismarck factor. The qualities and objectives of this extraordinarily talented statesman have been aptly summarised by a recent writer:

> The Minister-Presidency of Prussia was not his objective but only a means to a higher goal. The issue for him was the territorial expansion and consolidation of Prussia in a revolutionary Europe, a path he was convinced could only be traversed by establishing Prussian hegemony in Europe at the expense of Austria but in conformity with the interests of the other European powers. The means were revolutionary, the goal conservative . . . Add to this his tendency to extremes, his eagerness at moments of tension to go to the limits, his towering ability to juggle with several balls at once, to oversee a situation in all its complexity, to separate tactical means from strategic goals but nevertheless to keep both in view, finally the tendency – which bordered on self-destruction – to go *va banque* when a situation reached crisis point – in all this lay his superiority over his opponents at home and abroad.[9]

Hagen Schulze quite rightly emphasises the particularist character of Bismarck's policy. Significantly his hero was Frederick the Great and his yardstick for measuring the worth of a Hohenzollern was simply whether the ruler had acquired territory for his kingdom. All his life Bismarck remained a servant of his king (provided he got his way); and all his life his objective remained the creation of a Great Prussian state stretching from the Rhine to the Oder and from the Baltic Sea

---

9. H. Schulze, *Der Weg zum Nationalstaat: Die deutsche Nationalbewegung vom 18. Jahrhundert bis zur Reichsgründung* (Munich, 1985), pp. 113–14. The book by Schulze referred to here has now appeared in an English translation. The details are as follows: H. Schulze, *The Course of German Nationalism: from Frederick The Great to Bismarck, 1763–1867* (Cambridge, 1991).

to Lake Constance. That this would involve war with Austria was a near certainty in his view:

> The only parade ground for our policy is Germany [he wrote in 1853] . . . and it is precisely this that Austria believes she needs as a matter of urgency; there is no room for both [of us] . . . we take the breath away from each other's mouths; one of us must yield or be forced to do so by the other.[10]

While Bismarck was never a nationalist in the liberal sense which implied popular participation in the affairs of state, nevertheless the authoritarian Prussian state was perfectly compatible with the conservative philosophy of nationalism. This postulated the existence of several German states, each a manifestation of the *Volksgeist* (spirit of the people) and each with the right to an independent political existence. Prussian expansionism at the expense of smaller states could, therefore, be clothed in nationalist garb of a sort. This was what Bismarck meant when he declared in 1858 that there was 'nothing more German than Prussian particularism properly understood'.[11] Furthermore, the coincidence of the power drive of the Prussian state with the liberal demand for a *kleindeutsch* state was a bonus mark for Bismarck, prompting the frank remark years later after the Reich of 1871 had come into being that

> whether one considered the main issue from the Borussian angle to be the leading role of Prussia or from the national angle to be the unification of Germany, both objectives coincide.[12]

Much has been written about Bismarck's extraordinary diplomatic expertise exemplified above all in his handling of the Schleswig-Holstein crisis. One of the keys to this, as to all his skilful diplomatic operations, lay in an acute awareness of the intimate and ever-changing relationship between domestic policy and international affairs. But whereas conservatives believed that the stability of the established order at home depended on stability abroad, and National Liberals that disorder abroad would bring about political change at home, Bismarck saw another possibility: stability of the monarchical order at home combined with disturbance of the balance of power abroad. 'Great crises', as he commented years before, 'represent the weather that is conducive to Prussia's growth if we use them without fear and perhaps

10. Bismarck, *Die gesammelten Werke*, 14, no. 1,480, Bismarck to Leopold von Gerlach, 19–20 December 1853.
11. Ibid., vol. 2, no. 343, 'Einige Bemerkungen über Preußens Stellung im Bunde' (March, 1858), p. 317.
12. Ibid., vol. 15, p. 198.

very ruthlessly'.[13] In exploiting favourable situations he displayed an acute sense of timing, an understanding of the relationship between means and ends, and an ability to keep several options open to the last possible minute.

When the male line of the Danish royal house died out in November 1863 the German liberals demanded immediate occupation of the duchies and the recognition of Duke Friedrich as ruler of an independent Schleswig-Holstein, this in defiance of the Treaty of London in which the Great Powers recognised Prince Christian as lawful successor to the Danish throne and to the duchies. Bismarck had two objections to this: first, the creation of another small state in north Germany controlling the mouth of the Elbe was not in Prussian strategic interests; and second, it would give an enormous impetus to liberalism certain to weaken the power of monarchy everywhere – or so conservatives thought for they grossly over-estimated the revolutionary potential of liberalism. While resolutely refusing to be stampeded by German liberals into precipitate action against Denmark, Bismarck was able to some extent to deflect their wrath yet not antagonise the Great Powers: Prussia, with Austrian support, occupied Schleswig to compel the Danes to abide by promises made to the German powers in 1851–2 but broken by the virtual annexation of Schleswig in March 1863. Securing the cooperation of Austria was less of a diplomatic masterstroke than is often supposed: Austria dared not assume the leadership of a national crusade; she could only hope that by working with Prussia she could contain that restless power and keep it on a conservative keel. Bismarck was careful to reassure the great powers that Austria and Prussia recognised King Christian and were concerned only to make him keep the Danish promises. But, of course, Bismarck calculated that Denmark had no time to comply with the ultimatum. And once in possession of the duchies he calculated that the situation could then be moulded in Prussian interests. By the end of 1863 he favoured the annexation of the duchies to round off Prussian territory in north Germany.

The flexibility of his diplomacy was evident at the London Conference in the summer of 1864 when the Great Powers attempted to revolve the dispute in the spirit of the old Concert of Europe. Bismarck did not rely on Prussian military strength alone to rule out any restoration of the status quo – he was able to point to the explosive state of German public opinion (which now expected the creation of an independent Schleswig-Holstein in the very near future) to demon-

13. Ibid., vol. 1, no. 473, Bismarck to Baron von Manteuffel, 15 February 1854.

strate how impossible that would be. The dangerous option of an independent state − which he reluctantly supported − was scotched because the Danes would not abandon their compatriots in North Schleswig. Partition − which Bismarck would have accepted to be rid of the North Schleswig Danes − was unacceptable to Denmark. Thus the Conference collapsed, the war continued and Austria and Prussia ended up in possession of the duchies. Denmark's mistaken policy, Austria's willingness to work with Prussia, the wish of Britain, France and Russia to avoid conflict and the military power of Prussia, all contributed to a favourable situation which Bismarck could not have created but which a less able practitioner of the diplomatic arts might not have been able to exploit so successfully.

The 'revolutionary means' in Bismarckian diplomacy to which Schulze refers is exemplified in his handling of France. In the conservative circles in which Bismarck grew up it was axiomatic to suppose that the forces of revolution could be held at bay only if the three great conservative powers stood shoulder to shoulder as they did in the days of Metternich. The rise to power of Napoleon III aroused in conservatives the sort of alarm and foreboding which Hitler's appointment as Chancellor did in the 1930s. Only by keeping Napoleon in diplomatic purdah could a *bouleversement* of the international status quo be prevented. Bismarck, second to none in his defence of the class interests of the Junkers, showed a deeper appreciation of the nature of the Napoleonic regime than most of his conservative contemporaries. Ideologies come and go, so that a country's 'interests' or what the rulers think these 'interests' are, are a better guide to policy. Napoleon was unlikely to launch a revolutionary 'war of liberation' but was more likely to exploit situations to advance French interests. That thought transformed an ideological pariah into a possible ally for Prussia. And, as relations with Austria rapidly deteriorated after 1864, the cornerstone of Bismarck's diplomacy was the attempt to neutralise France during what he was convinced would be an inevitable conflict with Austria for mastery in Germany.

It was essential to keep the floating mine away from the Prussian ship by reassuring Napoleon − as Bismarck did at the Biarritz meeting in October 1864 − that any agreement Prussia made with Austria such as the Gastein Convention (which divided the duchies between the two German powers) was of a purely temporary nature. For any suggestion that Prussia would help Austria retain Venetia would alarm Napoleon (one of whose objectives was to acquire the province for Italy) and would encourage him to negotiate with Austria, offering her assistance against Prussia in return for Venetia.

At Biarritz Bismarck dropped vague hints of compensation for France should Prussia become master of Germany. Arguably Napoleon proved too slippery a character even for Bismarck. In the spring of 1866 with a German war a certainty, Bismarck's attempts to obtain specific promises of neutrality from France failed. Napoleon was determined to keep a free hand to intervene at a crucial moment in what contemporaries thought would be a long war. Consequently the war of 1866 was a high-risk operation for Prussia against whom the vast majority of states were ranged. No one foresaw the dramatic victory at Königgrätz which decided the outcome in a few weeks. Bismarck was well aware of the *va banque* nature of the decision to fight. Talking to the British ambassador hours before the ultimatum to the neighbouring states expired he remarked that:

> If we are beaten, I shall not return here. I shall fall in the last charge. One can but die once; and if we are beaten it is better to die.[14]

Bismarck was, in fact, much more the inveterate gambler running great risks than the accomplished crystal-gazer of popular legend who planned wars with foresight and deliberation and with absolute confidence that Prussia would win.

Though very much a man of the eighteenth century in his whole-hearted commitment to the aggrandisement of the state he served, Bismarck was very much a man of the new century in his quick appreciation of the growing importance of public opinion. True, he was scathing in his comments on 'German public opinion': 'our growth in power', he remarked to an erring diplomat, 'cannot issue forth from legislative chambers or from the press but from Great Power politics carried on by force of arms'.[15] Nevertheless, he made considerable efforts to try to manipulate *kleindeutsch* opinion in Prussian interests. He founded a new press organ, intervened frequently to correct articles and tried through his contact men to influence the foreign press. His efforts were largely wasted because of his blatant illiberalism. To push the army reforms through the *Landtag* in the teeth of liberal opposition he persecuted his opponents, censored the press and even removed the immunity of deputies in a determined attempt to smash them politically. No rapprochement with liberalism was possible as long as the constitutional crisis continued in Prussia.

When schemes for the reform of the Confederation were circulating in the early 1860s Bismarck's 'revolutionary' proposal for a directly

14. Lord Augustus Loftus, *Diplomatic Reminiscences* (London, 1984), vol. 1, p. 60.
15. Bismarck, *Die gesammelten Werke*, vol. 14/2, no. 999, Bismarck to Robert von Goltz, 24 December 1863.

elected German parliament was dismissed on all sides. Conservatives were horrified that one of their number could flirt with the revolution and liberals rejected it as a desperate ploy by an old reactionary for whom time was running out. Both were wrong. Bismarck realised from his observation of Napoleonic France that universal male suffrage could benefit the conservative interest in the countryside; the rural vote mobilised by landowners could, in the absence of a secret ballot, swamp urban liberals whose mistrust of the masses robbed them of a long-term political future. But that lay in the future – on the eve of war opinion was solidly against Bismarck.

If liberals, especially in Prussia, were better disposed towards Bismarck after 1866 that was not because the minimal concessions made to liberal opinion in the constitution of the North German Confederation satisfied them, but simply that the completion of the *kleindeutsch* state seemed imminent. And it was widely supposed that when the four southern states joined in Bismarck would not be able to resist pressure for fully responsible government. To further concessions he was, however, adamantly opposed, both as a champion of monarchical prerogative and also because of the need to reassure the south German governments that entry into the Confederation at some future date would not threaten their conservative regimes. It has been suggested earlier that concern about the domestic situation in Prussia, coupled with the rising tide of radicalism in the south, may have been significant factors influencing the decision to go to war in 1870.

That war was not fought primarily to complete the unification of Germany on *kleindeutsch* lines. Although Bismarck was very ready to orchestrate national resentment against French demands for territorial compensation during the Luxemburg crisis, he had not the slightest intention of waging a national war in 1867 to unify Germany; while National Liberals would have supported war with enthusiasm, the southern governments might well have refused to come to Prussia's aid under the terms of the defensive and offensive treaties. When war did come in 1870 Bismarck ensured that the threat from France – real or supposed – lay at the centre of the dispute over the Hohenzollern candidacy. He calculated quite correctly that fear of 'French aggression' would spark off a wave of anti-French feeling sweeping the southern governments into war.

That war would be the likely outcome of the candidacy Bismarck must have known from the spring of 1870 onwards. How the situation would unfold he cannot possibly have known. But just as the Danes played into his hands by their (understandable) intransigence in the winter of 1863–4, so did France in 1870. After the withdrawal of the candidacy − a victory for France and a severe blow to Bismarck − they demanded a promise from the King of Prussia that the candidacy would never be renewed. The king's firm (but courteous) refusal was depicted by Bismarck in the celebrated Ems telegram and in the circular to German embassies abroad as an indignant rebuff to an insufferably rude ambassador who persisted with his impertinent demand. The intention was to arouse German national feeling on a point of honour and to provoke the sensitive French − deeply worried about their loss of influence over German affairs − into a declaration of war. Thus Bismarck succeeded in locating the causes of the war in unreasonable French demands, not in German pressure to complete the *kleindeutsch* state. These circumstances ensured that when the southern governments did negotiate entry into the new German Reich Bismarck − not the National Liberals − was in control of the situation. Nor did he neglect the international perspective. By shifting responsibility for the war on to French shoulders Bismarck effectively tied the hands of the great powers. Only later in the century did the alteration in the balance of power consequent upon the creation of the Reich in 1871 become a matter of concern to them.

SUGGESTIONS FOR FURTHER READING

W. Carr, *The Wars of German Unification* (London, 1991).

L. Gall, *Bismarck: The White Revolutionary*, 2 vols (London, 1986).

M. Hughes, *Nationalism and Society: Germany 1800–1945* (London, 1988).

H. Schulze, *The Course of German Nationalism: From Frederick the Great to Bismarck, 1763–1867* (Cambridge, 1991).

O. Pflanze, *Bismarck and the Development of Germany: The Period of Unification 1815–1871* (Princeton, 1990) 2nd edn .

J. Sheehan, *German History 1770–1866* (Oxford, 1990).

CHAPTER SIX

Bismarck's heir: Chancellor Bernhard von Bülow and the national idea 1890–1918

Katharine A. Lerman

On 30 March 1909 Bernhard von Bülow, the fourth Reich Chancellor of imperial Germany, stood up to defend his record in the German *Reichstag*. Chancellor speeches were major events in public life before the First World War and Bülow was renowned for the brilliancy of his verbal swordsmanship. He gave a bravura performance in which he stressed his lifelong commitment to the national idea and his role as custodian of the national interest. 'In nearly forty years of service', he declared,

> in often difficult, often very difficult circumstances, I have proved my loyalty to King and Fatherland, Kaiser and Reich. In foreign as in domestic policy I have never known any guiding star save the good [*Wohl*] of the monarchy, the good of the country, reasons of state [*Staatsraison*], the national idea and the Kaiser idea, which for me are indissolubly linked.[1]

Bülow's words, however, had a hollow ring to them in March 1909 for it was common knowledge that he had lost the confidence of Kaiser Wilhelm II as a result of his handling of the *Daily Telegraph* affair the previous November. In addition, as early as August 1908, Bülow had recognised that the government might be 'heading for a fiasco' with its Reich financial reform and that while its failure 'would give me *une très belle sortie* . . . for our country, its domestic well-being and its external prestige, it would be a blow from which it would be difficult to recover.'[2] In March 1909 one of his closest advisers told

---

1. Bülow's parliamentary speeches can be found in the *Stenographische Berichte* of the *Reichstag* and Prussian *Landtag* (Berlin, 1897–1909), and also in J. Penzler (ed.) *Furst Bülows Reden*, vol. 1 (1897–1903), vol. 2 (1903–6) and H. Hötzsch (ed.) vol. 3 (1907–9) (Berlin, 1907–9).

2. Zentrales Staatsarchiv (ZSA) Potsdam, Hammann Papers, 14, Bülow to Hammann, 3 August 1908 and 14 August 1908.

him that the fundamental problem with the reform was the lack of clarity over the government's aims. Without the will to resolve the issue, Bülow faced certain parliamentary defeat. By May Bülow was already preparing his next and final speech for the *Reichstag* which he knew would be his 'swan-song' and which he delivered on 16 June. Concerned not to appear irritated, annoyed, piqued, depressed or sorry for himself, he told his chancellery chief, 'At this of all times I must appear superior, distinguished and self-assured, as a *statesman*'.[3] Eight days after his speech the *Reichstag* rejected the inheritance tax and Bülow left Berlin for Kiel to secure the Kaiser's agreement to his resignation.

Throughout his career Bülow repeatedly maintained that he was motivated solely by the national interest. He believed he was emulating imperial Germany's first Chancellor, Otto von Bismarck, when he subscribed to the view that patriotism was the highest morality in politics and that everything else should be subordinate to the *salus publicae*. Historians' verdicts on Bülow's nine-year chancellorship, however, have generally been harsh, and the fourth Chancellor has traditionally been seen as a man who squandered Bismarck's legacy and irreparably damaged the public interest. While several historians have discerned some reformist potential in German domestic politics during his chancellorship, especially during the period of the so-called Bülow Bloc parliamentary coalition of 1907–9, it is rare to come across the view that Bülow was 'far more weighty and courageous a statesman than his historical reputation would allow'.[4] The marked deterioration in Germany's diplomatic position and the bitter antagonisms which were evident in German domestic politics by 1909 appear to speak for themselves. As Johannes Haller, who wrote one of the first historical assessments of the Bülow years, concluded:

> In the Bülow era glossing things over and hushing things up, cover-ups and cooking the books were elevated into a system. If we suffered a set-back, it was made into a success, and even if the failure was all too evident, in the given circumstances it had still to be a welcome result. The Chancellor, unsurpassed in the art of just about 'arranging' things yet again and sorting out even the most muddled situation, really accustomed the nation to locking the stable door only after yet another horse had bolted. Thus arose that atmosphere of comfortable optimism and sweet self-deception in which vigorous political thinking was lulled to sleep

3. Bundesarchiv (BA) Koblenz, Loebell Papers, 6, Bülow to Loebell, Whit Monday 1909.

4. T. Cole, 'Kaiser versus Chancellor: the crisis of Bülow's chancellorship 1905–6', in R.J. Evans (ed.) *Society and Politics in Wilhelmine Germany* (London, 1978), p. 41.

[*einschlief*], the feeling of responsibility became numb, the ability to [make] a free, personal decision was suffocated by shallow smooth-talking, until the great mass of the nation, half-dreaming, ultimately stumbled towards its fate, a host of blindmen with a blind leader at their head, [staggering] towards the abyss.[5]

How was it that a man who was so conscious of his role in history as Bismarck's heir, and so insistent about his commitment and devotion to the new German nation-state, could attract such condemnation? This chapter will explore Bülow's conception of the national idea, his contribution to German foreign and domestic policy between 1897 (when he became state secretary of the Foreign Office) and 1909, and how his emphasis on the national idea came to hinder rather than facilitate the emergence of a patriotic consensus in Germany before the First World War.

BÜLOW'S CONCEPTION OF THE NATIONAL IDEA

Bernhard von Bülow liked to be compared with Otto von Bismarck. The wars of unification were the most formative experience in his adolescence and he never spoke of what Bismarck had achieved without reverence and awe. Moreover, throughout his life he insisted on his personal and political loyalty to his predecessor, whom he had met for the first time as a young boy. His father, Bernhard Ernst von Bülow, was state secretary of the Foreign Office under Bismarck in the 1870s, and Bülow himself spent seventeen years in the German Diplomatic Service under Bismarck's watchful eye. Herbert von Bismarck, the Chancellor's son, complimented him in 1885 on being 'really the only one of all our diplomats who lets himself be impregnated with the political ideas of my father.'[6] When Bülow became Chancellor in 1900, he was widely regarded as a worthy successor to Bismarck and one of the most intelligent and talented men in the German ruling elite. Selected by Kaiser Wilhelm II as early as 1895 to be 'his Bismarck',[7] Bülow deliberately fostered an image of himself as

5. J. Haller, *Die Aera Bülow: Eine historisch-politische Studie* (Stuttgart and Berlin, 1922), pp. 148–9.

6. W. Bussmann (ed.) *Graf Herbert von Bismarck: Aus seiner politischen Privatkorrespondenz* (Göttingen, 1964), Bülow to Herbert Bismarck, 31 October 1885, p. 331.

7. See J.C.G. Röhl, *Germany Without Bismarck: The Crisis of Government in the Second Reich, 1890–1900* (London, 1967), p. 158.

the legitimate and deserving heir of the first Chancellor. His parliamentary speeches and public pronouncements, his private letters and memoranda, his book, *Deutsche Politik* (Berlin 1916), and the four volumes of his posthumously published memoirs, all contain appeals to Bismarck's memory, attempts to place and justify his own political actions within the Bismarckian tradition, and evidence of a self-conscious desire to go down in history as a man who consolidated and built upon Bismarck's legacy.

Bülow's relationship to Bismarck was a paradoxical one and there is abundant evidence that he did not fully understand Bismarck. But it is impossible to discuss his political ideas without reference to Bismarck for, in the late 1880s and early 1890s, Bülow developed a concept of 'the national idea' which reflected both his recognition of Bismarck's achievement in unifying Germany around Prussia and his perception of the weaknesses inherent in the Bismarckian Empire, particularly as manifested after Bismarck's dismissal in 1890. In addition Bülow inherited a 'method' from Bismarck, for he saw the first Chancellor as a statesman and *Realpolitiker* who had no fixed principles or beliefs in politics but, rather, swam with the current and achieved what he could for the nation. Finally, he came to appreciate the function Bismarck fulfilled as a symbol of German unity and power. This not only encouraged Bülow as Chancellor to promote 'the Bismarck myth' and his own role (unlike his two predecessors) as Bismarck's real epigonus, but also it led to a lifelong confusion in Bülow's mind of appearances with reality. As a diplomat observing events in Germany from St Petersburg in the 1880s, he believed that Russia's fear of Germany was significantly increased after the Reich Chancellor made a 'colossal speech'; and he wrote that the 'unqualified machinations' against Bismarck after the death of Kaiser Wilhelm I in 1888 'shattered . . . respect and confidence in Germany, that is, the foundations of our power position and of world peace.'[8] In his memoirs Bülow stated revealingly that the Germans were disliked, even before Bismarck made German power an object of envy, because 'we underestimated the value of forms, of appearances and, as the Greek philosopher demonstrated long ago, mankind judges by appearances and not by the reality of things.'[9] As Chancellor, Bülow consciously attached supreme importance to the politics of prestige. How his policies were seen became more important than what they achieved.

---

8. Bussmann, *Bismarck*, Bülow to Herbert Bismarck, 12 February 1888, p. 508 and 13 April 1888, p. 513.
9. B. von Bülow, *Denkwürdigkeiten*, 4 vols. (Berlin, 1930–1), vol 1, p. 27.

Bülow borrowed his concept of the national idea from the German historian, Heinrich von Treitschke, and in his memoirs he claimed that Treitschke's *German History* and Bismarck's speeches constituted the basis of his political thought and feelings. Nevertheless Treitschke's influence on Bülow should not be exaggerated. Bülow admitted when he first read Treitschke that he found some passages offensive, and as Chancellor he did not hesitate to criticise Treitschke's views. In urging the benefits of a heightened national consciousness, Bülow drew on his experience of the summer of 1866 and his participation as a volunteer in the Franco-Prussian War. He was completely out of sympathy with those Prussian conservatives who complained about the 'dilution' of Prussia in 1866 and with constitutional liberals who rejected the authoritarian structure of the new Reich. Rather he revelled in the nationalist euphoria. As he wrote later in *Deutsche Politik*, Bismarck had achieved in one decade what had been mismanaged and neglected for centuries.

It was after Bismarck's dismissal that Bülow began to refer to the national idea in his correspondence, and it was clearly in part a device to enable him to come to terms with the departure of the great man. As Bülow emancipated himself personally and politically from the influence of the Bismarck family in the 1890s, he sought to separate Bismarck from his achievement and transferred his loyalty to the new Kaiser. 'The Bismarckian epoch belongs now to history', he wrote to his friend Karl von Lindenau three weeks after Bismarck's resignation.

> Its fruits must be ripened and in my opinion that is only possible by working together, united and devoted, under the Kaiser and for the Kaiser, in whom I have confidence because I believe that there is much of significance in him.[10]

A year later he told another close friend, Philipp zu Eulenburg-Hertefeld, that he would have preferred it if Bismarck had remained in office but they now had to demonstrate that the Reich could be ruled without him. Even the greatest individuals were transitory phenomena. 'The idea, the national idea, is above all change and has to be helped to victory *à tout prix et quoiqu'il arrive* [at any price and whatever happens]. There is no salvation except through this formula.'[11] Bülow's successful elevation of the national idea above all other considerations was indicated in 1897, shortly before his appointment as state secretary of the Foreign Office, when he wrote in a personal memorandum that

---

10. BA Koblenz, Bülow Papers, 99, Bülow to Lindenau, 9 April 1890.

11. J.C.G. Röhl (ed.) *Philipp Eulenburgs politische Korrespondenz*, 3 vols (Boppard am Rhein, 1976–83), vol. 1, Bülow to Eulenburg, 28 May 1891, p. 685.

he wished Bismarck would die soon as he only made the task of governing more difficult.

Given the political instability which ensued after Bismarck's dismissal, the urgency of a solution to the Empire's domestic problems and Bülow's own role in the intrigues to restore stability by increasing the power and prestige of the monarchy and (not least) securing his own appointment as Wilhelm II's Chancellor, it is perhaps not surprising that Bülow's private correspondence in the 1890s was preoccupied with the internal weaknesses of the Empire – the problems of confessional disunity, particularism and class conflict, the constitutional clash between monarchical authority and the pretensions of a democratically elected *Reichstag*, and the potential dangers, as well as strengths, inherent in Kaiser Wilhelm II's personality. Moreover, Bülow drew on his knowledge and understanding of German history, and he attributed German disunity in the past more to internal divisions between Germans than to the hostility or manipulations of foreign powers. Again and again the national idea was offered by Bülow as the panacea for these problems. Concerned about the *Reichsverdrossenheit* (weariness with the Reich) in the south German states, Bülow pointed out to Philipp Eulenburg that the population in the south had been particularist, ultramontane, *großdeutsch*, and even in favour of the Napoleonic Confederation of the Rhine, but had never supported the Hohenzollerns. Germany's entire internal and external future, he wrote in 1895, depended on the progressive strengthening of the ties between the south German states and the Reich, the nurturing of the national idea. Without the national idea, the Prussian monarchy, too, would be like 'a mill-wheel without water'. Prussia's fortunes were now inseparably linked to those of the Reich and any weakening of the Reich idea would be a step on the road to disaster. And of all Bismarck's policies as Chancellor Bülow was most critical of the *Kulturkampf* which had undermined national unity by setting Protestants against Catholics, Germans against Germans. The Catholic Centre Party, Bülow maintained in 1892, represented the old Germany which had fought in the Thirty Years' War under the imperial Habsburg flag and which had to be merged with the Hohenzollern Reich if the latter's unity and future were to be secure. Bülow's emphasis on the national idea was his response to the deep pessimism about the political situation which pervaded all levels of the German ruling elite by the middle of the 1890s. He believed that the monarchy could be popularised by strengthening the bonds between the imperial crown and the nation and rallying all nationally minded elements behind it. This in turn could be achieved by banging the national drum and creating a closed phalanx of conservative, liberal and Catholic support in opposition to the unpatriotic socialists.

Bülow's prolific correspondence before 1897 reveals an acute awareness of the divisions between Germans, the new and unfinished nature of the Bismarckian Empire, and the overriding need for consolidation which could come only through 'constantly striving forwards' and creating national feeling. Indeed, Bülow's political ideas and observations, as well as the importance he attached to the national idea, are ultimately intelligible only within the context of the continuing struggle for national unification. Even before Bismarck's resignation Bülow wrote:

> The German, who is still in many ways lacking the excitable national pride and the schooled sense of political advantage of other peoples, abandons himself all too easily to self-opinionated defiance and naive doctrinairism when the sky appears to him [to be] completely cloudless. Despite the best prospects of peace, our domestic and foreign policy should be geared to [the possibility] that the end of the century could easily bring us the decisive struggle for the monarchical nation-state.[12]

While Bülow repeatedly urged that the conduct of policy had to be calm, cautious and consistent, he always returned to the benefits of a heightened national consciousness and the integrative potential of German nationalism. In 1890 he insisted that everything, including domestic policies, had to be subordinated to Germany's unity and position as a European power. But the 'social imperialist' hue to much of what Bülow wrote in the 1890s – the idea that an ambitious foreign policy would divert attention away from problems at home – is unmistakable, as is the sense in which the promotion of national feeling became an end in itself. 'I am putting the main emphasis on foreign policy', Bülow wrote after moving into the Wilhelmstrasse in 1897. 'Only a successful foreign policy can help to reconcile, pacify, rally, unite.'[13]

BÜLOW'S ROLE IN GERMAN FOREIGN POLICY

At first glance Bülow's stress on his Bismarckian credentials and his custodianship of Bismarck's inheritance appear particularly incongruous

12. Ibid., Bülow to Eulenburg, 2 March 1890, p. 471.
13. Röhl, *Germany Without Bismarck*, p. 252. For a now classic social imperialist interpretation of German policy before 1914, see H.-U. Wehler, *The German Empire 1871–1918* (Leamington Spa, 1985).

in the light of his contribution to German foreign policy between 1897 and 1909. For, with the exception of Kaiser Wilhelm II, no other individual came to symbolise more the overweening arrogance, aggressive insecurity and deluded optimism which characterised German *Weltpolitik* before the First World War. His appointment as state secretary of the Foreign Office in 1897 coincided with Germany's embarkation on an ambitious programme of naval expansion and popular imperialism which promised to break through the confines of Bismarckian diplomacy and underline the claims of a new nation-state to world power status. It was Bülow who told a rapturous *Reichstag* in December 1897 that the times when the German people had left the earth and sea to their neighbours were over and that Germany, too, demanded her 'place in the sun'. Well before his resignation in 1909, his mere continuance in office was construed as a major obstacle to any improvement in Anglo-German relations. 'The road which Germany took in 1897 led to diplomatic isolation, war, military defeat and the collapse of the monarchy' was John Röhl's judgement of the significance of the ministerial changes of 1897.[14] Far from consolidating Bismarck's legacy, Bülow's conduct of German foreign policy precipitated the destruction of the Bismarckian Empire and the demise of the Prussian monarchy which that Empire had been designed to safeguard.

What is equally curious, however, especially when he knew he was destined for high political office several years before 1897, is the complete absence of any discussion of *Weltpolitik*, the need to acquire colonies or Germany's 'world historical' task in Bülow's correspondence before 1897. Bülow wrote extensively about Germany's historical and political development, but it is clear that he saw Germany's international position in traditional, conservative and continental European terms. In the 1890s his reflections on German foreign policy hinged upon such issues as the reliability of Germany's alliance partners, the security of the Empire within the European state system and the danger of a hostile coalition directed against Germany. Commenting on Germany's problems from abroad, Bülow appeared to take little cognizance of the economic shift that was taking place in Germany in the 1890s and how Germany's rapidly growing population, burgeoning industry and expanding commerce and trade were creating new imperialist pressures. Indeed, in 1890 he still assessed the internal strength of the Empire exclusively in military and moral terms. Finally, although he was in favour of annexations during the First World War and convinced once war broke out that France had to be destroyed

14. Röhl, *Germany Without Bismarck*, p. 277.

economically, there is no mention in his correspondence before 1897 of the need for territorial adjustments in Germany's favour or any specific foreign policy aims. Nor is there any evidence before his meeting with the Kaiser and Tirpitz in June 1897 that he believed that Germany needed a huge battlefleet.

What emerges from Bülow's correspondence before 1897 is, rather, a commitment to the political boundaries of the Bismarckian nation-state within Europe and a sometimes naive optimism and faith in its future. Unlike the Pan-German nationalists whose wild ambitions and expansionist ideals he later attacked in the *Reichstag*, he had a political, not an ethnic concept of the nation. Far from dreaming of the inclusion of Austrian Germans in a future Greater German Reich, he was concerned with the internal balance and cohesion of the Empire, as well as the ascendancy of Prussia, and he clearly viewed the prospect of a greater number of Catholics or new national minorities with alarm. As with Bismarck, Bülow saw language and culture as legitimising a political entity which had primarily served to secure the position of Prussia. He thus found it perfectly acceptable that the new German nation-state excluded Germans but included the formerly French provinces of Alsace and Lorraine, as well as substantial numbers of Poles and Danes. While Germany's relationship with Austria was complicated by considerations of language, culture and religious confession, Bülow regarded the Dual Monarchy essentially as a foreign power to be mistrusted. He was convinced that there could be no return to the situation before 1866 when Austria and Prussia had struggled for control over German affairs; nor could there be a return, after the incorporation of the south German states into the Empire in 1871, to a Prussia or north Germany confined to the frontiers of the Rhine and Main. Prussia's future was inseparably linked to the Reich, and Bülow appeared wedded to the territorial status quo.

Of course these observations are in no sense intended to conceal that there was a broadly aggressive thrust in Bülow's political outlook before 1897. 'I believe in the rising star of the German nation', he wrote to Philipp Eulenburg in 1887,[15] and on several occasions he maintained that, provided Germany kept up her defences, she could await 'elemental events' or 'the decisive struggles of the future' with equanimity. Bülow had a simplistic, Social Darwinist view of international relations according to which youthful and vigorous nations emerged victorious from their struggles against the sick and dying. International diplomacy was analogous to a battlefield or a chessboard on

15. Röhl, *Eulenburg*, vol. 1, Bülow to Eulenburg, 25 December 1887, p. 258.

which one made one's moves and played to win. There was also a certain rigidity in his thought. Like Friedrich von Holstein (the influential counsellor in the Foreign Office) and others in the 1890s, he over-estimated the conflict of interest between Russia and Britain, and believed that if Germany kept free from trouble and made no precipitate moves or commitments, she could reap the whirlwind that would eventually come. He did not share Bismarck's interest in the ascendancy of Germany within a stable Europe but, rather, believed Germany would profit from the conflicts of others. 'The sharper the antagonism between Russia and England, the better for us', he wrote in 1895.[16] But the key point here is that he believed time was on Germany's side and he had certainly not formulated any clear foreign policy goals. Convinced of the cultural superiority of the German nation and confident in Germany's strength, his ideas certainly did not exclude the possibility of an eventual war against Britain, but he generally inclined towards the more complacent outlook of *tout arrive à qui sait attendre* (everything comes to him who waits).

It is frequently assumed that Bülow was in full control of German foreign policy from his installation as foreign secretary in 1897 and that *Weltpolitik* was his policy. Unlike his predecessor, Adolf Marschall von Bieberstein, Bülow was a professional diplomat who was seen as having expertise in this area; his first speech in the *Reichstag* in December 1897 heralded what appeared to be a fundamental reorientation in German foreign policy; moreover, it was clear that the official responsibility of the Reich Chancellor, Chlodwig zu Hohenlohe-Schillingsfürst, for the conduct of foreign policy became purely nominal between 1897 and 1900 and that Bülow was 'the real Minister of Foreign Affairs'.[17] When Bülow became Chancellor in October 1900 the basic continuity of German foreign policy was unaffected. Oswald von Richthofen, who was under state secretary in the Foreign Office between 1897 and 1900, became Bülow's successor as foreign secretary, but there was no question that he remained Bülow's deputy.

Nevertheless, attempts by historians to show that Bülow not only managed the day-to-day conduct of German foreign policy but also had a 'grand design' or 'world power concept' which he pursued consistently from 1897 have generally been difficult to substantiate and ultimately unconvincing. There is no evidence of a grandiose foreign policy concept in Bülow's thought before 1897 and, even allowing for the rather lame argument that he could not reveal the full scope of his

---

16. Ibid., vol. 2, Bülow to Eulenburg, 28 September 1895, p. 1552.

17. Haus-, Hof- und Staatsarchiv Wien, PA III, 151, Szögyényi to Goluchowski, 9 April 1898.

intentions for understandable diplomatic reasons, the official documentation for such a thesis remains poor after 1897. As Peter Winzen has acknowledged, if one leaves aside the issue of *Weltpolitik* and colonial acquisitions, Bülow's approach to foreign policy issues was remarkably consistent. From the middle of the 1890s Bülow (and Holstein) advocated a policy of cautious reserve in international relations, believing that Germany should not lean too heavily towards either the Franco-Russian combination or Britain and that she would thereby profit from the conflict of interest between them. This 'free hand' policy was entirely compatible with the building of the navy from 1898. Finally, if Bülow did have a grand design or *Weltmachtkonzept* when he took over the conduct of German foreign policy in 1897, its underlying assumptions (for example, the expectation that Britain would remain isolated and on relatively good terms with Germany) were questionable by 1902 at the latest, but Bülow continued to be responsible for German foreign policy until his resignation in 1909.

All the available evidence suggests that, far from developing his own grand design or world power concept, Bülow 'inherited' his foreign policy in 1897. Once he was initiated in June 1897 into plans hatched by the Kaiser and Alfred von Tirpitz to embark on an ambitious naval armaments programme, he did not make a 'decisive breakthrough from a continental to a world political concept'[18] but, rather, agreed to conduct German foreign policy in accordance with the needs of the navy. Bülow freely admitted that he was assigned his foreign policy task in 1897. In 1912 he wrote:

> The task I was set when the conduct of foreign affairs was assigned to me on 26 June 1897 on the *Hohenzollern* was to make possible our transition to *Weltpolitik* (trade, shipping, overseas interests, the consequences of the huge development of our industry, our increasing prosperity, the increase in our population) and above all the building of the German navy, without clashing with England, for whom we were in no way a match at sea, but preserving German dignity and our position on the continent.[19]

He did not himself integrate the naval programme into a comprehensive strategy aimed at world power. He agreed to subordinate considerations of diplomacy to the requirements of naval armaments. Bülow already knew well that 'the value of a person for H.M. depends on his willingness or usefulness to cooperate directly or indirectly in

18. Winzen, 'Prince Bülow's *Weltmachtpolitik*', in *Australian Journal of Politics and History*, 22 (1976), p. 232.

19. ZSA Potsdam, Rath Papers, 9, Bülow to Rath, 12 February 1912. Bülow gives the same version of events in his memoirs and in *Deutsche Politik*.

increasing our supply of ships'.[20] Moreover, he believed in swimming with the current: not only was *Weltpolitik* already a fashionable word by 1897 but also the Kaiser made his famous *Weltreich* speech in January 1896. In his correspondence with the Kaiser after 1897 Bülow always referred to the fact that he was implementing Wilhelm's great plans and pursuing his aims. There is no conclusive evidence that behind the well-worn formula of *Weltpolitik* Bülow had any grandiose *Weltmachtkonzept* of his own which he sought to put into effect.

Bülow was prepared to play a specific and subordinate role in a military monarchy. He unfailingly supported Tirpitz, the state secretary of the Reich Navy Office, and never questioned naval or military demands. In 1906, when Tirpitz's resignation appeared a real possibility, he wanted to avoid everything which looked as if he might be withdrawing his support from the state secretary, 'especially as he is now finally beginning to have the confidence in me to which I indeed have a claim after supporting him constantly for seven years and which is also in H.M.'s interest.'[21] He wanted Tirpitz to have no doubts about how sincerely and seriously he wanted him to remain in office. Bülow never interfered in naval matters; he had only a very superficial grasp of the technical details of the naval legislation, and he never questioned the wisdom of the naval programme until his position was irreparably weakened in 1908. At the same time the coordination between the Foreign Office and those responsible for naval and military matters was clearly inadequate during his chancellorship, although this also reflected structural deficiencies in the Bismarckian constitution. During the Russo-Japanese War vital information about the condition of the Russian fleet never reached the Foreign Office and never entered into the calculations of Bülow and his subordinates. Similarly, the Chancellor and Foreign Office were informed only very belatedly in February 1905 about an operations plan, already approved by the Kaiser in December 1904, to invade Denmark and seize vital Danish waterways as a preliminary to a war against Britain. Bülow expressed no objections to the plan (and nor did he raise diplomatic objections to the notorious Schlieffen Plan) but was merely concerned that it should be kept secret. The 'incalculable catastrophes' if the information became known clearly weighed more heavily on the Chancellor than the consequences of such an invasion.[22] The whole areas of naval ar-

20. N. Rich and M.H. Fisher (eds) *The Holstein Papers*, 4 vols (Cambridge, 1955–63), vol. 4, Holstein to Bülow, 17 February 1897.

21. PA Bonn, IA Deutschland, 122, no. 9, Bd. III, Bülow to Hammann, 7 July 1906.

22. See J. Steinberg, 'Germany and the Russo-German War', *American Historical Review*, 75 (1970), esp. pp. 1,970 and 1,978–9.

maments and military and naval planning were effectively 'off-limits' for the Chancellor. Bülow believed it was consistent with his patriotism and his loyalty to the monarchy not to make any objections to the demands of the generals and admirals.

With such crucial areas of decision-making beyond his control, the Chancellor's 'responsibility for the conduct of His Majesty's foreign policy' must necessarily be qualified and questioned. In addition Bülow's style of foreign policy management throws into doubt whether he was capable of pursuing a consistent strategy or *Weltmachtkonzept*. As soon as he became Chancellor in 1900 he informed the Foreign Office that, since he was intending to devote his attention to domestic policy and his relations with the Kaiser, beyond continuing to sign important political instructions and telegrams, he wanted to be shown only matters 'of real personal significance for me'.[23] Bülow delegated major aspects of German foreign policy to his subordinates, especially Holstein, Richthofen and later Alfred von Kiderlen-Wächter, who all complained they were overburdened with work. His sudden interventions, which, as during the First Moroccan Crisis, were often prompted by his concern to maintain the Kaiser's confidence, contributed to the notorious 'zig-zag course' of German foreign policy between 1900 and 1909 which baffled even German ambassadors. In addition, after Richthofen's death and Holstein's resignation in 1906, Bülow found that he could trust neither the new state secretary, Heinrich von Tschirschky und Bögendorff, nor the latter's successor in 1907, Wilhelm von Schön, both of whom were personally chosen by the Kaiser. Tschirschky criticised the Chancellor's lack of activity and wrote to a friend in 1907 that even Otto Hammann, Bülow's Press Chief and one of his closest advisers, 'asked me recently whether I really knew what B[ülow] did all day.'[24] While the novelty of Bülow's ostensibly relaxed style of leadership was appreciated in the Foreign Office when he took over in 1897, the virtually anarchic conditions which prevailed by 1908 could barely be concealed. It was Bülow's negligent behaviour, in passing on the text of the Kaiser's interview to the Foreign Office without reading it himself and without giving his subordinates adequate instructions, which precipitated the *Daily Telegraph* affair of November 1908, though he chose to blame the Foreign

---

23. PA Bonn, IA Deutschland, 122, no. 13, Bd. I, Bülow to Foreign Office, 19 October 1900.

24. A. Monts, *Erinnerungen und Gedanken des Botschafters Anton Graf Monts*, ed. K. Nowak and F. Thimme (Berlin, 1932), Tschirschky to Monts, 23 May 1907 (P.S. of 25 May), p. 451.

Office. Kiderlen-Wächter, who was summoned to the Foreign Office to take charge of the Bosnian Crisis and to deputise for the distraught state secretary, was appalled at the conditions he found there, complained that Bülow did not bother at all about foreign policy, and resigned himself to having to do everything on his own. Bülow, he acknowledged privately, was a greater *Schweinehund* than he had ever imagined. He was lazy and superficial, and acted only when his position with the Kaiser was at stake.[25]

Bülow never abandoned his conviction that the best foreign policy was a pragmatic one and that there was no room for any kind of formulae in diplomacy. He believed that he could rely on his own diplomatic instincts and proven experience to manage affairs successfully and that he would reach the right decision almost intuitively. His interventions in foreign policy frequently bear the hallmarks of hasty improvisation and indecision (as evidenced, for example, in the negotiations for a Russian alliance in 1904–5 and his inability to decide whether the Björkö Treaty corresponded to Germany's real interests) and historians have searched futilely among the Foreign Office records for evidence of mature consideration on Bülow's part. While he may have believed that he was being 'frightfully clever and Bismarckian' (Jonathan Steinberg) in pursuing a cautious and pragmatic policy which involved no firm commitments, he also of course really had no option after the passage of the navy laws of 1898 and 1900 but to approach foreign policy like 'the caterpillar before it has grown butterfly wings'.[26]

The confusion which surrounds 'Bülow's foreign policy' between 1897 and 1909 arises primarily from the gulf which separated his rhetoric from reality. For while Tirpitz, Holstein and possibly even the Kaiser may have had a clear sense of what they hoped to achieve, Bülow was willing to be the front-man for the policies (or, in the case of the Kaiser, the emotional needs) of others. Bülow was prepared to pursue an empty prestige imperialism which sacrificed genuine German interests to the desire for a propaganda victory at home. His parliamentary speeches and press propaganda in 1901–2 confirm the impression that he preferred to antagonise Britain than alienate an Anglophobic German public. In early 1906 Bülow accepted that Ger-

---

25. See E. Jäckh (ed.) *Kiderlen-Wächter der Staatsmann und Mensch: Briefwechsel und Nachlass*, 2 vols (Berlin and Leipzig, 1924), vol. 2, esp. pp. 12–18 and 100; F. Thimme (ed.) *Front Wider Bülow* (Munich, 1931), p. 56.

26. BA Koblenz, Richthofen Papers, 5, Bülow to Richthofen, 26 July 1899. See also P. Kennedy, *The Rise of the Anglo-German Antagonism 1860–1914* (London, 1980), p. 239.

many's Moroccan initiative had led to isolation and defeat at the international conference in Algeciras, and he was concerned only that this was not how the conference was perceived at home. 'After agreement has been reached', he told Hammann in March 1906, 'the impression must be aroused that from the beginning I had in mind a definite goal – and indeed achieved exactly that – which, however, could not be revealed immediately.'[27] Bülow's presentation of the results of the Moroccan Crisis as a success for Germany was later described by Friedrich Wilhelm von Loebell, the Head of Reich Chancellery, as his 'greatest rhetorical achievement'.[28] Nevertheless Bülow's concern to depict all foreign policy initiatives in this way reflects a deep insecurity about the extent of national consciousness in Germany. It also suggests a fundamental insecurity and self-consciousness in his own identity as Reich Chancellor of a new and dynamic European power. As he told Loebell in October 1908, when requesting him to draft a short speech on the Bosnian Crisis:

> I believe it will have a good effect! It demonstrates that the Reich Chancellor is on the alert. It corresponds to what the Ministers in England, France [and] Italy have done. The longer I am Reich Chancellor, the more I see it is above all a question of the Chancellor holding his ground [*sich behauptet*], standing in the foreground and not letting himself be effaced.[29]

BÜLOW'S APPROACH TO DOMESTIC POLITICS

The relationship between foreign and domestic policy during Bülow's Chancellorship is a complex one which cannot be reduced to any simple formula. Bülow himself believed that the energies of the nation should be harnessed to serve the maintenance of its position in the world. But he also saw a nation's position in the world as dependent on the degree of national feeling and solidarity among its people. In 1905 he told the German ambassador in Washington that 'for the power position of a state neither the population figure nor the unity of

27. ZSA Potsdam, Hammann Papers, 11, Bülow to Hammann, 18 March 1906.
28. BA Koblenz, Loebell Papers, 27, unpublished memoirs, p. 77.
29. ZSA Potsdam, Reichskanzlei, 798/2, Bülow to Loebell, 10 October 1908.

language is decisive, but the agreement or divergence of national aspirations and goals.'[30] Bülow had a keen appreciation of the functional uses of nationalism, and, as we have seen, he hoped to exploit foreign policy successes to overcome divisions and promote social cohesion at home. He also consciously used foreign policy issues to distract attention from domestic problems, and he deliberately accentuated his role as the leader of German foreign policy when he needed to bolster his personal position and prestige. An unambiguously aggressive foreign policy between 1897 and 1909 was incompatible with the Tirpitz Plan which required a period of international stability and calm while the navy was being built. *Weltpolitik*, as officially propounded by Bülow, was deliberately vague, and frequently appeared to mean no more than the peaceful cultivation of Germany's overseas interests without endangering the security or future of the nation. Bülow variously sought to arouse national feeling, safeguard the fleet, reassure Germany's neighbours and satisfy domestic opinion. Finally, there was less homogeneity of outlook within the German ruling elite than is often assumed, and Woodruff D. Smith has recently indicated that German *Weltpolitik* (in a broadly imperialist sense) was not only tailored to the requirements of mass consumption, but also resulted from efforts to create consensus within the ruling elite itself.[31] When Bülow became Chancellor in 1900 and assumed responsibility for German domestic policy, he was determined to counteract the divisions and centrifugal tendencies within the executive and present the government as united around national issues. Since German foreign policy was an important element in this, Bülow's ultimate inability to impose unity on the conduct of foreign policy and the failures in German foreign policy from 1905–6, not only undermined the Chancellor's wider popularity and prestige, but also had a highly detrimental effect on his position within the executive.

The essence of Bülow's approach to domestic politics from 1900 was his desire to rally a broad range of support for the government and the monarchy. This not only entailed bringing together all nationally minded elements in the *Reichstag*, including the Catholic Centre Party, but also encouraged him to begin his chancellorship by touring the south German states and reassuring their governments of his commitment to the Bismarckian federal constitution. Bülow hoped to rally support for the government by pursuing a calm, consistent domestic

30. T. Schieder, *Das Deutsche Kaiserreich als Nationalstaat* (Cologne and Opladen, 1961), p. 92.

31. W. D. Smith, *The Ideological Origins of Nazi Imperialism* (Oxford, 1986), p. 6.

policy which gave priority to national issues and sought to avoid any kind of domestic confrontation or crisis. He told the Prussian Ministry of State in October 1900 that the best way to avert domestic conflict was to reduce the quantity of legislation to the absolute minimum. The less the political parties had to do, the less they would have to fight over.

This highly conservative approach to domestic politics was not very realistic or practical at a time when enormous strains were being placed upon traditional social and political structures as a result of rapid economic change and an intensive naval armaments programme. In addition, Bülow inherited a number of thorny domestic issues in 1900, notably the conflict in the Prussian *Landtag* over government plans to extend the canal system and the need to revise Germany's tariff and commercial policy, which could not long be deferred. But, after witnessing the divisive course of German domestic politics in the 1890s, Bülow's instinct was always to withdraw or postpone contentious issues if at all possible. He preferred to close the Prussian *Landtag* in May 1901 rather than suffer a defeat over the Canal Bill and be pushed into a dissolution. In 1902 he also wanted to postpone a resolution of the tariff issue since he feared a government defeat. Later in his chancellorship he deferred the reorganisation of the Reich's finances until it was a matter of the utmost urgency.

When domestic issues could not be avoided Bülow sought to turn them into 'life and death questions' for the Reich. The tariff, the reorganization of the colonial administration and the Reich financial reform were whipped up by the Foreign Office Press Bureau into vital national issues which had to be resolved in accordance with the government's wishes if the security and future of the nation were not to be endangered. If the Social Democratic Party's (SPD) obstruction of the tariff succeeded, Bülow told his Press Chief in 1902, this would signify 'the greatest danger for peace, order, economic prosperity [and] constitutional institutions'.[32] He acknowledged that the longstanding dispute over the succession to the small principality of Lippe-Detmold was originally of little significance; but in 1904, when the death of the Regent renewed the crisis and Bülow wanted to enhance his personal role in achieving a settlement, he was prepared to argue that it threatened 'the foundations of the Reich'.[33] The Reich's financial preparedness was as important as its military preparedness, he insisted in the

32. ZSA Potsdam, Hammann Papers, 7, Bülow to Hammann, (17 October 1902).
33. PA Bonn, IA Deutschland, 122, no. 1a secr., Bd. 2, Bülow to Foreign Office (Posadowsky), 14 October 1904.

Reichstag on 19 November 1908, and failure to bring the financial reform to a successful conclusion would irreparably damage Germany's prestige abroad and strength at home.

Bülow's parliamentary speeches before 1909 consistently called for the nation's representatives to transcend their party differences and focus exclusively on what was good for the nation as a whole. While this salutation sometimes paid off, it reflected a fundamental naivety about the sources of political and ideological conflict. In *Deutsche Politik* Bülow wrote dismissively of the political parties which could not unite to resolve 'essentially unimportant questions of legislation' and which fought out 'slight differences of opinion on details of financial, social or industrial policy, with such acrimony as if the weal and woe of the Empire depended on them.' The varied life of a nation could not be 'stretched or squeezed to fit a programme or a political principle'.[34] But, even when the political parties were convinced of the national importance of a Bill (as they were with respect to the financial reform in 1908–9), this did not necessarily help them to agree on the substantial questions of detail. Patriotism could not bridge the divisions between the 'bourgeois' parties when they were intent on defending their sectional interests. For all his pragmatism and concern to find 'the middle way', Bülow further confounded the problem of building such a consensus because he clearly did not have a personal position on many issues of domestic policy, frequently had only limited contact with the relevant state secretaries, and was inclined to tack with the wind in consultations with parliamentary deputies. Throughout his chancellorship he was primarily concerned about the level and range of support for an initiative in the parliaments and whether it had the backing of the Kaiser. During the first eighteen months of the Bülow Bloc, the nature of the conservative–liberal coalition was allowed to determine what legislation was introduced into the *Reichstag*.

The one major initiative in domestic policy to which Bülow committed himself wholeheartedly as Chancellor was the Germanisation of Prussia's Polish provinces. This policy, which culminated in the Expropriation Law of 1908, had the support of the Kaiser, and Bülow believed he was continuing along the path which Bismarck had set. Bülow professed sympathy for the tragic course of Polish history and he recognised that there was little danger by 1900 that the Prussian Poles would receive any foreign backing for their aspirations to na-

34. B. von Bülow, *Deutsche Politik* (Berlin, 1916) pp. 184–5. Earlier version translated into English as *Imperial Germany* (London, 1914). See p. 117.

tional independence. The issue for Bülow was whether the Eastern Marches would be German or Polish. If the German Empire wanted to retain Posen and West Prussia, it was imperative that Germans settled in these areas, that the 'right compound' was applied to 'the national cell tissue' in good time. German colonisation of the Polish provinces was a 'national duty' and Bülow maintained his policy confirmed the nation's belief in the power of its national culture.

Bülow's concern about social and political divisions and his overriding desire to avoid domestic crises reflected his conviction that the national idea, the degree of national consciousness and purpose, was paramount in internal affairs. The intensity of national feeling was the most important quality in a political party, and it was the internationalism of the SPD, not least its apparent willingness to see Alsace and Lorraine returned to France, which Bülow saw as the major gulf separating it from the other parties. But Bülow's fear of domestic conflict also stemmed from his anxiety that a domestic crisis might lead to the internal disintegration of the Reich. In a political system which gave enormous power to the Kaiser and permitted the *Reichstag* no effective control over the executive, there was no satisfactory mechanism for the resolution of class tensions.

In the 1890s Bülow had been concerned to avoid civil conflict arising from a clash between the Kaiser and the *Reichstag* or from conservative pressure to launch a preventive strike against the socialists. Although the Kaiser expressed his hope in 1895 that Bülow as Chancellor would help him to 'clean up this rubbish heap of parliamentarism and the party system at home',[35] Bülow himself warned against a *Staatsstreich*, the violent overthrow of the Bismarckian constitution and the disenfranchisement of the working class. Rejecting Bismarckian methods of repression and exceptional laws as inappropriate after 1890, he argued that it was better to rely on the healing powers of time and nature than to resort to medicine or drastic operations on the body politic. Bülow remained convinced that the German people were too law-abiding to approve of a *Staatsstreich*, and that the disunity of the bourgeois parties had contributed significantly to the growth of the SPD. If the socialists were isolated by rallying the liberal middle classes and the Catholics behind the government, wooing the working class with material benefits and banging the national drum, they could then be left to die a slow death. He was later to see the patriotic attitude of the SPD in 1914 as vindicating his views.

Whenever the pressure increased for more drastic action against the

35. Röhl, *Germany Without Bismarck*, p. 158.

socialists, as after the SPD's electoral gains in 1903, Bülow worried about the 'incalculable consequences' of a domestic conflict. In December 1906 he was prepared to dissolve the *Reichstag* over a national issue and launch a nationalist election campaign against the SPD and Catholic Centre only because he knew that he would otherwise be ousted from office. The campaign itself was a highly risky undertaking and, since the Centre actually gained seats in the elections of 1907, it was only a qualified success. Moreover, in excluding the Centre from the bourgeois coalition against the socialists, Bülow embarked on a course which contradicted the domestic strategy he had urged since the 1890s. He was merely fortunate that the elections signified a defeat for the SPD and thus alleviated conservative pressure for more extreme, unconstitutional action in the last years of his chancellorship.

The government's apparent victory in the elections of 1907 and the inclusion of left liberals in the Bülow Bloc did not, however, open the way to progressive reform. From the 1890s Bülow and his friend, Philipp Eulenburg, had been determined to find a 'third way' between the twin perils of reaction and revolution, and Bülow's conception of 'personal rule in the good sense', with the Kaiser exercising his power constitutionally through loyal advisers, was seen as the best way of maintaining the delicate constitutional balance in imperial Germany while satisfying the Kaiser's pretensions to autocratic rule. In 1897 when he moved to Berlin, Bülow described the cultivation of his relationship with the Kaiser as his 'main task' and he wrote that if he did not keep in close contact with the monarch constantly 'the *status quo*, which was welded together with difficulty, will fall apart at the seams'.[36] This seemed the best way to obviate the need for extreme solutions to the political problems of the Empire, but it also ruled out the possibility of reform. The most flattering interpretation of Bülow's commitment to maintain the constitutional status quo is that he hoped to 'help Germany over' the difficult reign of Kaiser Wilhelm II, but this seriously underestimates his personal ambition.

In his memoirs, written after the collapse of the monarchy, Bülow claimed that Bismarck had given too much power to the Kaiser and that after 1890 Germany should have evolved in the direction of parliamentary government. He also claimed that he himself had tried to give Germany greater parliamentary freedom through his Bülow Bloc experiment between 1907 and 1909. But this was a myth which he himself debunked in *Deutsche Politik*.

The statement uttered from time to time that my idea was to change the

36. BA Koblenz, Bülow Papers, 99, Bülow to Lindenau, 20 November 1897.

distribution of power between the Crown and the Parliament in favour of the latter, that is, to introduce parliamentary government in the West European sense of the words, belongs to the thickly populated realm of fables. In my eyes the dividing line between the rights of the Crown and of Parliament were immutably fixed.[37]

Quite apart from his professions of royalism, Bülow consistently rejected parliamentarism as unsuited to the German character. The slow-witted Germans would not tolerate all the chopping and changing; a serious and cautious people, they would find the unavoidable fluctuations frivolous or become immersed in doctrinaire disputes. But above all Bülow believed that the introduction of a parliamentary system would destroy the unity of the nation. In 1894 he maintained that if Kaiser Friedrich III had lived long enough to inaugurate parliamentary government in Prussia, 'Prussia would today be a kind of Belgium or Baden if it still existed at all.'[38] On another occasion he declared that if the German nation-state adopted parliamentarism, it would suffer the same fate as the Polish Commonwealth, dissolve internally and end up being partitioned. In Bülow's opinion the Prussian monarchy, the army and the civil service were all more representative of the true interests of the German people than the *Reichstag*.

Bülow's record between 1900 and 1905 (when his position was strongest), his attitude to Prussian suffrage reform (which he wanted tied to a reform of the *Reichstag* suffrage) and his handling of the *Daily Telegraph* affair (when he failed to secure constitutional guarantees from the Kaiser) all indicate further that he was in no sense a reformer. While he toyed with ideas of constitutional reform, such as the introduction of Reich Ministries, as a method of bolstering his position in 1906, he rejected the options once it became clear that his own freedom of manoeuvre would be curtailed. Bülow's concept of the national idea essentially committed him to the political and constitutional status quo. As he wrote to Loebell in 1912, he had 'tried to maintain the existing order of things north of the Rhine and east of the Elbe' not merely because he was a Prussian conservative through and through but above all because he was convinced that 'Prussian values [*Preußentum*], Army and agriculture are the firmest foundations of Germany's power position, our unity and our future.'[39]

The wide gulf which separated Bülow's public rhetoric from the reality of his position and role became as evident in his management of domestic policy as it was with respect to German foreign policy.

37. Bülow, *Deutsche Politik*, p. 340 (English edn, p. 277).
38. Röhl, *Eulenburg*, vol. 2, Bülow to Eulenburg, 15 December 1894, p. 1431.
39. BA Koblenz, Loebell Papers, 7, Bülow to Loebell, 10 February 1911.

While the Chancellor talked and wrote about politicising the nation, reviving the bureaucracy, adapting to the modern world and recognising the forces of change, his conception of how this might be done was essentially circumscribed and narrow. Even in the 1890s Bülow not only equated the national interest with the interests of the Kaiser and government but also identified the interests of the monarchy with his own political career. During his chancellorship he increasingly equated the national interest with his own political survival and reputation. His press directives reveal how, while publicly urging the nation to focus on the big national tasks, he himself became preoccupied with the minutiae of selling his public image. Bülow wanted to be perceived as King Karl in Ludwig Uhland's poem who steered the ship of state into safe harbour. By 1909 his overriding concern was to draw attention to his own services in preserving the security, dignity and interests of the nation.

Yet by 1909 Bülow's harping on the national interest had helped to destroy any semblance of patriotic consensus in Germany. The government was thoroughly demoralised and there was evidence of a creeping fatalism and pessimism in both political and military circles in Berlin. The federal states resented the humiliating role they had been assigned in the resolution of such vital 'national' issues as the tariff and financial reform. There was widespread public disgust at the system of rule and the image of the regime was tarnished after a series of diplomatic failures, political crises and homosexuality scandals. Bülow's willingness to swim with the current and his apparent reluctance to defend the Kaiser during the *Daily Telegraph* affair of November 1908 had helped to alienate the government's traditional supporters on the right, many of whom were already chafing over their pairing with the liberals in the *Reichstag*. Moreover, the Chancellor's repeated exhortations to be guided solely by the national interest, while at the same time apparently espousing a policy of 'drift' in domestic affairs and leading Germany into diplomatic isolation, had contributed to the fragmentation and radicalisation of the political right. Bülow, who had sought to stifle the embryonic 'national opposition' from 1900 by heaping scorn on the 'beer-hall politics' of the Pan-German League and publicly staking his claim to be the sole custodian and interpreter of the Bismarck myth, was confronted by a nationalist offensive which directly

40. See especially R. Chickering, *We Men Who Feel Most German: A Cultural Study of the Pan-German League, 1886–1914* (Boston, Mass, 1984), pp. 63–9, 213–23, 253–62; G. Eley, 'Some thoughts on the nationalist pressure groups in imperial Germany', in P. Kennedy and A. Nicholls (eds) *Nationalist and Racialist Movements in Britain and Germany before 1914* (London, 1981), pp. 40–67.

attacked his conception of the national idea.[40] Bülow's chancellorship ensured that the competence of Germany's rulers could be credibly challenged in the name of patriotism. Far from promoting social cohesion and what Bülow called a healthy national egoism, *Weltpolitik* and domestic stagnation exacerbated the divisions within German society. The failure to spread the financial burden of the naval armaments programme more equitably demonstrated conclusively that his conception of the national idea was no substitute for domestic political consensus.

Although Bülow's political views must be located within the broad tradition of German conservatism, his personal background and political mentality cannot be seen as very typical or representative of the German ruling elite before 1914. While he came from a privileged and aristocratic north German family with a long tradition of service to the state, he was born a Dane, married an Italian Catholic and chose to live abroad during his long retirement, as he had done for much of his life before 1897. While extolling the national idea and the superiority of German culture, he clearly took pride in his cosmopolitanism and cultivated a suave, urbane manner which was attractive not least to Kaiser Wilhelm II because it contrasted with the traditionally rather dull and dour exterior of the Prussian bureaucrat. His insistence on his loyalty to the Prussian monarchy and the traditional pillars of the Prussian state was couched in unfamiliar, modern and progressive language which easily made him suspect to many conservatives in Berlin. While he acknowledged that German unification had been achieved by men of conservative political persuasion, he also recognised that the national idea had been born in liberal circles.

Bülow, like many of his generation, was in a sense a victim of the struggle for national unification. Intoxicated by Prussian successes in the 1860s but highly conscious of the imperfections, the unfinished nature of the Bismarckian Reich, he believed that the only way to hold it together was through the manufacture of national feeling. Convinced of Germany's peculiar path to nationhood and that Bismarck was 'only conceivable on German soil, only completely comprehensible to the German', Bülow compared Bismarck to a mirror in which the nation could see itself reflected.[41] The dominance of this single image came to prevent him from appreciating the multifarious layers of German identity.

Yet ultimately even his professed love for all things German can appear spurious and insincere. Again and again, Bülow chastised the

41. Penzler, *Reden*, vol. 1, Bülow's speech of 16 June 1901 at unveiling of Begas's memorial statue in Berlin, pp. 225.

Germans in the *Reichstag* for being dogmatic, self-opinionated, doctrinaire, unpolitical, unpatriotic, slow-witted and plodding. In 1902 he complained about 'a lack of patriotism and political stupidity such as can only be found unfortunately in our country'.[42] In his memoirs his description of the Kaiserin as 'typically German' is almost insulting as he compares her irreproachable and dutiful nature to the soulfulness, zest, toughness, coquetry, passion and charm of foreign women.[43] Somehow one has the impression that, for Bülow as for Hitler after him, the German people could not quite live up to his expectations.

The journalist Theodor Wolff later wrote of Bülow that 'his feeling for a few persons closely related to him was the only warm feeling in him, the only one that did not merely flicker on the surface and evaporate in fine phrases'.[44] When Bülow left office in July 1909 there were few to express regret about his departure. A vain, superficial and ultimately rather lonely figure, he sought refuge in Italy but never gave up his hope of being recalled to office until the last year of the war. Devastated by Germany's defeat and scathing about Weimar democracy, Bülow took some comfort from Hindenburg's election as President in 1925 and Stresemann's conduct of foreign policy. He died at the age of 80 in October 1929, convinced that better days would come for the German people when they were once again infused with national feeling.

SUGGESTIONS FOR FURTHER READING

B. von Bülow, *Memoirs*, 4 vols (London, 1931–2).

B. von Bülow, *Imperial Germany* (London, 1914).

R. Chickering, *We Men Who Feel Most German: A Cultural Study of the Pan-German League, 1886–1914* (Boston, Mass, 1984).

G. Eley, *Reshaping the Right: Radical Nationalism and Political Change after Bismarck* (London and New Haven, Conn, 1980).

R. J. Evans (ed.) *Society and Politics in Wilhelmine Germany* (London, 1978).

42. ZSA Potsdam, Hammann Papers, 7, Bülow to Hammann, 19 July 1902.
43. Bülow, *Denkwurdigkeiten*, vol. 1, p. 263.
44. T. Wolff, *Through Two Decades* (London, 1936), p. 10.

I. Geiss, *German Foreign Policy 1871–1914* (London, 1976).

P. Kennedy, *The Rise of the Anglo-German Antagonism 1860–1914* (London, 1980).

P. Kennedy, and A. Nicholls (eds) *Nationalist and Racialist Movements in Britain and Germany before 1914* (London, 1981).

K. A. Lerman, *The Chancellor as Courtier: Bernhard von Bülow and the Governance of Germany, 1900–1909* (Cambridge, 1990).

N. Rich, *Friedrich von Holstein: Politics and Diplomacy in the Era of Bismarck and Wilhelm II*, 2 vols (Cambridge, 1965).

J. C. G. Röhl, *Germany Without Bismarck: The Crisis of Government in the Second Reich, 1890–1900* (London, 1967).

J. C. G. Röhl and N. Sombart (eds) *Kaiser Wilhelm II: New Interpretations* (Cambridge, 1982).

W. D. Smith, *The Ideological Origins of Nazi Imperialism* (Oxford, 1986).

B. Vogel, *Deutsche Rußlandpolitik: Das Scheitern der deutschen Weltpolitik unter Bülow 1900–1906* (Düsseldorf, 1973).

H.-U. Wehler, *The German Empire 1871–1918* (Leamington Spa, 1985).

P. Winzen, *Bülows Weltmachtkonzept: Untersuchungen zur Frühphase seiner Außenpolitik 1897–1901* (Boppardamam Rhein, 1977)

P. Winzen, 'Prince Bülow's *Weltmachtpolitik*', *Australian Journal of Politics and History*, 22 (1976).

CHAPTER SEVEN

Scholarship, state and nation, 1918–45

Michael Burleigh

In Germany, separate academic studies of Russia and Eastern Europe at the nation's universities commenced in the decade before the First World War.[1] Government needed expertise especially on Russia, and the demand was met by the exiled Baltic German publicist Schiemann, and his talented protégé, the historian Otto Hoetzsch, who became the first incumbents of chairs in multi-disciplinary Russian and East European studies.[2] During the First World War, military and industrial interests assisted in the foundation at Breslau and Königsberg of institutes devoted to East European studies, and the more thorough economic exploitation of that region. The radically altered circumstances of the Weimar Republic saw a fresh wave of institutional expansion, with new centres of expertise in Berlin, Danzig, Leipzig and Munich. Here, however, the emphasis was upon the provision of a scientific basis for revisionist territorial claims against the post-Versailles successor states to the east of Germany.[3]

Following a temporary lull in public activity due to the exigencies of the Hitler–Pilsudski Pact, *Ostforschung* – or research on the East – as this congeries of disciplines had come to be known, thenceforth enjoyed boom conditions. A new series of institutes was established in

1. For the early history of the discipline see H. Giertz, 'Das Berliner Seminar für osteuropaische Geschichte und Landeskunde', *Jahrbuch für die Geschichte der USSR und der volksdemokratischen Länder Europas* (1967), 10, pp. 184–5; M. Hellman, 'Zur Lage der historischen Erforschung des ostlichen Europa in der Bundesrepublik Deutschland', in F. Wagner (ed.) *Jahrbuch der historischen Forschung* (Stuttgart, 1980), pp. 14–16, and G. Camphausen, *Die wissenschaftliche historische Russlandforschung im Dritten Reich 1933–1945* (Frankfurt am Main, 1990).

2. Biographies include K. Meyer, *Theodor Schiemann als politische Publizist* (Frankfurt am Main, 1956), G. Voigt, *Otto Hoetzsch, 1876–1946* (East Berlin, 1978), and U. Liszkowski, *Osteuropaforschung und Politik: Ein Beitrag zum historischpolitischen Denken und Wirken von Otto Hoetzsch*, 2 vols (Berlin, 1988).

3. M. Burleigh, *Germany Turns Eastwards: A Study of Ostforschung in the Third Reich* (Cambridge, 1990, 2nd edn.) pp. 22ff.

Cracow, Poznan and Prague, while individual *Ostforscher* entered the service of the most notorious agencies of a barbaric regime.[4] After 1945, the staff in lightly sanitised versions of these institutes lent their collective expertise to the refashioned animosities of the Cold War. The immediacy of the Communist threat in the Soviet-occupied Zone, and the tragedy experienced by millions of ethnic German refugees, also offset the need to confront the part played by an entire academic discipline under the Nazi regime. Finally, to close the vicious circle, the claims made by these West German institutes, not to speak of the integrationary requirements of the SED and other Eastern European Communist regimes, resulted in the creation there of departments and institutes, whose purpose was to monitor 'imperialist *Ostforschung*' as the scientific face of West German or NATO 'revanchism'.[5]

This barest of outlines of the institutional history of *Ostforschung* already suggests a high level of political responsiveness on the part of the people who persistently subscribed to the usual canons of scholarly objectivity. The prodigious archival and published legacy enables us to ask and answer a number of questions about the relationship between professional experts and the state; about the degree of permeability evinced by mainstream conservative nationalism under the impact of *völkisch* and scientific racism; and finally, concerning the continuities and discontinuities of nationalist thought and practice between Weimar, the Third Reich and the Federal Republic.

The overwhelming majority of the scholars discussed in what follows operated with a mind set on 'the East' which was heavily influenced by centuries of Prussian-German contacts with Poland and Russia, as well as by the state of contemporary relations. Broadly speaking the received picture consisted of a mix of negative and positive elements. The Germans were 'bearers of culture' to the Slavs. The latter had arrived in the region posterior to the former. Their backwardness was epitomised by the mismanaged political economy of Poland and the tottering political structures of Tsarist Russia. Metaphorically, this backwardness was often expressed through the notion of a 'cultural gradient' declining from the 'civilised' West towards the

---

4. The most recent studies of these institutes in occupied Poland are C. Klessman, *Die Selbstbehauptung eine Nation* (Düsseldorf, 1971), S. Gaweda, *Die Jagiellonische Universität in der Zeit der faschistischen Okkupation 1939–1945* (Jena, 1981), and B. Piotrowski, *W sluzbie rasizmu i bezprawia: 'Uniwersytet Rzeszy' w Poznaniu (1941–1945)* (Poznan, 1984).

5. Burleigh, *Germany Turns Eastwards,* pp. 300ff. See also H. Elsner, 'Abteilung für Geschichte der imperialistischen Ostforschung', in M. Hellman (ed.) *Osteuropa in der historischen Forschung der DDR* (Düsseldorf, 1972), vol. 1, pp. 123–31.

The State of Germany

'uncivilised' East. The German mission to bring civilisation and order to the Slavs was gradually given a biological accent in the form of the slogan '*Drang nach Osten*', whereby the Germans were somehow compelled to venture eastwards. Since by the late nineteenth century this notion was wildly at variance with a general demographic drift westwards, the perception grew that the Germans were holding back an uncontrollable Slavic flood or wave. The East as a literary and historical construct was thus simultaneously a land of opportunity and demographic menace, notions which have endured to the present time.[6]

If for much of the late nineteenth century these ideas lent a crude legitimacy to Prussian-German rule in partitioned Poland, during the Weimar Republic they were employed to justify German claims to lost territories. Archaeologists, historians, philologists and geographers provided the scientific armaments for their government's claims to parts of Poland and Czechoslovakia, while government rewarded them by licensing and financing institutional expansion. This relationship became both closer and released from any ethical or professional constraints.

From the 1920s academic studies were used to substantiate revisionist territorial claims in the East. Much of this work reflected racist modes of thought, although the provenance of the racism was usually cultural-historical rather than seriological. The facts of post-war political frontiers, which of course were not the single handiwork of the victors at Versailles, were systematically undermined through *parti pris* interpretations of history, or by the application of dubious geographical concepts. Scholars, such as Wilhelm Volz, working under the aegis of the Leipzig *Stiftung für Volks- und Kulturbodenforschung* maintained that in addition to the territories more or less densely settled by Germans there was a further area, in which, regardless of mere numbers, their cultural influence was allegedly paramount.[7] The layout of villages, the contours of fields, the style of brickwork, and the contrast between 'order' and 'chaos' would be the criteria for where political frontiers ought to run. However, it is important to stress the differences between this cultural chauvinism, and more specifically National Socialist modes of thinking. What would the latter have made of Volz's assertion that 'Race does not decide ethnicity . . . rather will and consciousness of nationality'?[8] The historians devoted a great deal of sterile

6. On these concepts, see W. Wippermann, *Der 'Deutsche Drang nach Osten': Ideologie und Wirklichkeit eines politischen Schlagwortes* (Darmstadt, 1989).

7. See A. Penck, 'Deutscher Volks- und Kulturboden', in K.C. von Loesch (ed.) *Volk unter Völkern* (Breslau, 1926), pp. 62–73.

8. W. Volz (ed.) *Der ostdeutschen Volksboden: Aufsätze zu den Fragen des Ostens* (Breslau, 1926), pp. 5–6.

assiduity to questions such as: who settled the contested regions first, or who had made the greatest contribution to their culture? They trawled deep in time to establish a continuous German presence before and after the Slav migrations; and recent history to stress the artificiality and transience of the Polish nation-state in contrast to the dynamic, state-forming, capacities of the Germans and their rulers. This last concern also involved giving generous attention to a series of submerged nationalities, such as the Kashubians and Pomeranians, as a means of further subverting the legitimacy of the Polish nation-state.[9]

All of these tendencies were well represented in a collective volume edited by Karl Brandi and Albert Brackmann, entitled *Deutschland und Polen*, which appeared in August 1933. Brackmann's own contribution can be said to exemplify the culturally argued chauvinism which permeates the book:

> While the Slav peoples of Europe, including the Russians, still lay in a deep intellectual slumber, the monk Widukind wrote his Saxon history in the monastery of Corvey on the Weser, the nun Hroswitha in the abbey of Gandersheim her song to Otto the Great and her classical dramas, and in Magdeburg Bruno of Querfurt his life of St Adalbert and bishop Thietmar his chronicle . . . Where then could one find in Poland cultural centres like Corvey or Gandersheim or Magdeburg – not to speak of the centres of ancient civilisation on the Rhine? Gnesen and Posen were settlements of the most primitive type.[10]

Some of the contributions also reveal a casual reliance upon biology as a causal agency, with 'Nordic blood' accounting for resistance which the Saxons met from other Slavs, or the wholly anachronistic use of contemporary geopolitical concepts, not to speak of the language of late-nineteenth-century nationalism. Thus Max Hein could write:

> As in the year 1000 it was again the Germans . . . who sought to realise the christianisation and germanisation of the Prussians and their addition to the German Lebensraum and to the German, and at the same time West European, sphere of civilisation. The Prussian venture of the Teutonic Order is, on the one hand, the fulfilment of a great German cultural mission in the East, and on the other, the expansion of the all too narrow Lebensraum in the old Reich.[11]

Deutschland und Polen was one of the earliest products of the increasingly close relationship between certain scholars and government agen-

9. Burleigh, *Germany Turns Eastwards*, pp. 30–1; 60–1; 117–31.

10. A. Brackmann, 'Die politische Entwicklung Osteuropas vom 10–15 Jahrhundert', in Brackmann (ed.) *Deutschland und Polen. Beiträge zu ihren geschichtlichen Beziehungen* (Munich 1933), p. 30.

11. M. Hein, 'Ostpreussen', *Deutschland und Polen*, p. 126.

cies. The book was heavily subsidised by the latter and, via Brackmann the editor, the contributions were cut to suit the dictates of the current political line.[12] This process had begun as early as 1931, when interested government departments expressly decided to license Brackmann's personal institutional ambitions on the grounds that this 'had the advantage that the work can be carried out under a certain political control'.[13] The line between scholarship and government was drawn a year later by the Social Democratic minister-president of Prussia, Otto Braun: 'scholarship can supply the politicians with the material from which they can draw their conclusions'.[14]

The end product of this collaboration was a Berlin-based research institute, the *Publikationstelle* or 'PuSte', and half a dozen multi-disciplinary regional research associations to which every prominent scholar in the field was attached. Collectively, these bodies had the following functions: the coordination of scholarship in the Reich dealing with the East; subsidising of scholarship conducted by ethnic Germans in Eastern Europe, and the maintenance of contacts between them and their colleagues in the Reich; the monitoring and translation of hostile scholarship; the political vetting of applications to use German archives; and finally, the censorship and control of German scholars studying ethnic minorities in the Reich, lest they inadvertently cast doubt on the ethnic homogeneity of Germany.

The principal beneficiaries of the governmental largesse channelled through these organisations were ethnic German scholars living and working in Eastern Europe. In the case of the North East German Research Association (NODFG), two eager young scholars, Walter Kuhn and Kurt Lück, were kept afloat through the good offices of Brackmann and government money.[15] Both were obsessively interested in the history and current circumstances of German ethnic minorities in Poland and the western Ukraine, with Lück shoring up one such community through the foundation of a rural credit agency.[16] While Kuhn was primarily involved in the application of biological concepts to explain the expansion and contraction of these settlements,

12. For the details see Burleigh, *Germany Turns Eastwards,* especially pp. 61–8.

13. BA (Koblenz), R421/1812, 'Vermerk über die kommissarische Beratung am 11 Dezember 1931 betreffend wissenschaftliche Ostmarkenforschung', Reich Ministry of the Interior to State Secretary in the Reichskanzlei.

14. BA (Koblenz), R431/1812, 'Protokoll über die Besprechung im grossen Sitzungssaal des Preussischen Staatsministeriums in Sachen der Ostmarkenforschung am 24.2.32', p. 215.

15. For the financial arrangements see for example, BA (Koblenz) R153/1309, 'Vorschläge über Beihilfen', pp. 5–6.

16. See H. von Rosen, *Wolhynienfahrt 1926* (Siefgen, 1982), p. 64 for Lück's work on behalf of the ethnic German peasants.

Lück graduated from mindlessly cataloguing the contribution of German civilisation to the Poles,[17] to 'modernistic' ventures into the analysis of ethnic stereotypes. Vast quantities of literary, oral and visual evidence from 'below' were deployed in the interests of proving the permanency of Polish–German nationality conflicts, and hence, as a way of depicting German aggression as essentially reactive and self-defensive.[18] Other scholarship to benefit from this academic version of *'Osthilfe'*, included Peter Heinz Seraphim's studies of the 'economic danger that lies in the existence of . . . Jewish population groups for these people and states', investigations designed to establish 'which possibilities exist for the solution of the eastern Jewish problem'.[19] In the late 1930s Seraphim converted these studies into a racist version of developmental economics, with the Jews as the obstacle to rural Eastern Europe's route to 'modernity'.[20]

The corollary of promoting studies of ethnic Germandom, or on the allegedly deleterious influence of Jews on the economies of Eastern Europe, was tight control over studies of Slavic ethnic minorities within Germany. This control ranged from withholding research funds from younger scholars working on ostensibly innocuous aspects of the history and culture of Lusatian Sorbs,[21] to interference with the publications of distinguished professors of Slavic philology, notwithstanding assurances that they 'not only served the truth but . . . also worked throughout as a German Slavist'.[22] Government-inspired interference further encompassed such semantic issues as the substitution of the word 'resettlement' for 'colonisation' in descriptions of the German presence in the East.[23] Such

17. K. Lück, *Deutsche Aufbaukräfte in der Entwicklung Polens* (Plauen, 1934).

18. K. Lück, *Der Mythos vom Deutschen in der polnischen Volksüberlieferung und Literatur* (Leipzig, 1943, 2nd edn). This insidious line of argument has been present in some of the work which sparked off the West German 'Historikerstreit'. See R.J. Evans, *In Hitler's Shadow* (London, 1989), especially p. 56.

19. BA (Koblenz), R153/98 P. H. Seraphim, 'Bericht über den Entwurf einer Arbeit Das Judentum im osteuropaischen Raum', 9 January 1936.

20. P.H. Seraphim, 'Das ostjüdische Ghetto', *Jomsburg, 1 (1937)*, pp. 439–65; Seraphim, 'Die Judenfrage im General-gouvernement als Bevölkerungsproblem' *Die Burg* 1 (1940), pp. 57–62. On Seraphim see G.F. Volkmer, 'Die deutsche Forschung zu Osteuropa und zum osteuropäischen Judentum in den Jahren 1933 bis 1945', H.J. Torke (ed.) *Forschungen zur osteuropäischen Geschichte*, vol. 42 (Berlin, 1989) pp. 148ff.

21. See for example BA (Koblenz), R153/1263 Wolfgang Kohte to the Deutsche Forschungsgemeinschaft 21 August 1937 concerning a grant application by Dr Paul Wirth.

22. BA (Koblenz), R153/1258 Professor Reinhold Trautmann to Albert Brackmann, 13 April 1939.

23. Geheimes Staatsarchiv (West Berlin) Rep. 92, *Nachlass* Brackmann, no. 82, Brackmann to Klante 21 June 1937 and Brackmann to Aubin 21 June 1937, relaying the information that the Ministry of the Interior wanted the word 'colonisation' avoided at all costs.

interventions seriously annoyed committed Nazi historians like Hans Mortensen, who indignantly complained 'I, for my part, would never publish or make known anything that would damage Germany or the German people, even if it was the scholarly truth'.[24] Censorship ventured into the absurd when, for example, Emil Meynen's *Deutschland und Deutsches Reich* was banned in 1936 because his claim that Germany encompassed German-speaking areas such as Alsace-Lorraine or Switzerland was regarded as diplomatically inopportune at that moment in time. The question inevitably arose, not least in Meynen's mind, 'how can we sing the national anthem: '*Von der Etsch bis an den Belt*'?[25]

Since individual words were subjected to the quickly changing exigencies of high politics, how did political change affect such fundamental conceptual components of historical writing as the state, and how responsive were these scholars to the rise of that Nazi universal form of scientific explanation, namely biological racism? Historians of academic life in Nazi Germany writing immediately after the war, for example Max Weinreich, would have regarded the contention that Nazism had had a 'progressive' impact on the historical and social sciences, as the triumph of a small academic truth over the large fact of German academia's dismal descent into illiberalism.[26] This post-war consensus is no longer universal. One minor by-product of the search for Nazism's intended or inadvertent 'modernising' effects on German society, has been the argument that certain allegedly 'progressive' developments in modern German social history owed as much to the mould-breaking of the indigenous Right, as to the influences of American and French sociology. Who needs Braudel or Bloch when one already has Otto Brunner?[27] In the case of Ostforschung, it is claimed that the multi-disciplinary, regional rather than national, and socially extensive nature of the subject, anticipated many of the prac-

24. BA (Koblenz), R153/627 Mortensen to Brackmann 15 January 1938.

25. For the details of this anecdote see M. Rössler, '*Wissenschaft und Lebensraum*': *Geographische Ostforschung im Nationalsozialismus* (Berlin, 1990), pp. 67–9.

26. M. Weinreich, *Hitler's Professors: The Part of Scholarship in Germany's Crimes against the Jewish People* (New York, 1946).

27. This question was first formulated by C. Klessmann in his 'Osteuropaforschung und Lebensraumpolitik im Dritten Reich', P. Lundgreen (ed.) *Wissenschaft im Dritten Reich* (Frankfurt am Main, 1985), p. 353. Since then the question has exercised the minds of a number of North American and German academics. See J. van Horn Melton 'From folk history to structural history: Otto Brunner and the radical conservative roots of German social history' (unpublished manuscript, 1989), and W. Schulze, *Deutsche Geschichtswissenschaft nach 1945* (Munich, 1989) for examples. For a critique of the 'modernisation' thesis in general see M. Burleigh and W. Wippermann, *The Racial State: Germany 1933–1945* (Cambridge, 1991).

tices of a modern social history, whose intellectual ancestry has conventionally been traced from either external influences, or the subterranean stream of the German historical Left. This is certainly how some of the *Ostforscher* regarded matters at the time. Thus, in 1937 the Breslau historian Hermann Aubin argued that the territorial losses after the First World War had forced historians to abandon the limitations imposed by 'dynastic-territorial historiography'. The 'tearing asunder' of 'German *Lebensraum*' after 1918 led historians to abandon history based on the nation-state in favour of ethnological and cultural-geographic concepts which in turn made the present political frontiers seem epiphenomenal and hence revocable.[28] This brand of regionally focused 'total' history would in turn serve to mobilise popular consciousness of the *Volk*'s potential horizons. This conceptual shift was made explicit by Erich Keyser in an article published in 1933:

> Historians in the nineteenth century forgot that a substantial part of the *Volk* were not comprised within the borders of Germany, but like the Austrian or Baltic Germans were foreigners in their own states . . . The *Volk* is more than the nation; it comprises the totality of those who shaped by blood, soil, and culture, are the real subjects of history. The nation, on the other hand, is purely a political entity . . . In this regard nineteenth-century historical writing, quite apart from its liberalism, differed from ethnic history in that it was predicated solely on the state rather than on the *Volk* . . . The national idea is directed towards the state, while the idea of the *Volk* transcends the state and its borders.[29]

Although it is, of course, debatable whether in the *longue durée*, a concern with ordinary people, or indeed, inter-disciplinary or regional studies actually represent an advance over other more traditional forms of historical inquiry – a point often made by the Left as well as by the self-appointed guardians of academic orthodoxy on the Right – none of these historiographical issues should obscure the fact that in Germany, the 'progressive' methods were accompanied by a reliance upon race as a causal agent, and served political ends which moved smoothly from revisionism to murderous racial imperialism. By 1942, for example, Erich Keyser was crediting *Ostforschung* with a role in proving that 'the German East, from the Elbe to the Gulf of Finland, from

28. H. Aubin, 'Zur Erforschung der deutschen Ostbewegung', F. Petri (ed.) *Grundlagen und Perspektiven geschichtlicher Kulturraumforschung und Kulturmorphologie* (Bonn, 1965), pp. 108–9; Klessman, 'Osteuropaforschung und Lebensraumpolitik', pp. 372–3; Burleigh, *Germany Turns Eastwards*, pp. 304ff.

29. E. Keyser, 'Die völkische Geschichtsschreibung', *Preussische Jahrbücher* 234 (1933), pp. 5–6.

the Inn to the Black Sea, deserves to be the unitary *Lebensraum* of the German people'.[30]

If it is essential to counter attempts to restore the work of Aubin, Brunner and the rest to its 'rightful' place within a 'modernist' story of historiography, through the omission of any reference to their use of *völkisch* racism, so one should be equally careful, in the interests of both accuracy and fairness, to establish the thin line separating them from full-blown scientific racists. In the case of some of the *Ostforscher* mentioned above this can be done by examining their relationship with the Leipzig-based anthropologist Otto Reche, the driving force behind the Society for Blood Group Research, the North East German Research Association's expert on racial questions, and an adviser to the Hereditary Health courts.[31]

Although already elderly by the outbreak of the Second World War, Reche spotted a role for himself as a scientific adviser to government agencies concerned with the occupied eastern territories. In late September 1939 he began bombarding Brackmann with unsolicited schemes for the ethnic rearranging of the conquered areas, schemes which Brackmann then relayed to both the Ministry of the Interior and then the SS.[32] Working on the principle that 'we need Raum but no Polish lice in our fur', Reche made the following stark suggestions:

> The newly acquired land must be made empty of all foreign ethnic elements; all foreign races, foreign peoples are to be resettled . . . The present inhabitants of the newly ceded areas are racially, and therefore in character, talents and capabilities too, for the most part totally useless. Above all the *c.* two million Jews and Jewish hybrids must be pushed out as soon as possible. . . . The emigrant Poles can take their moveable goods – in so far as this does not prejudice the interests of the German state – with them; one may proceed less charitably with the Jews.[33]

Having drawn a blank with the Ministry of the Interior, which was preoccupied with economic questions, Brackmann helped Reche find the right address, namely the Race and Resettlement Office of the SS. Reche's memoranda went to SS-*Gruppenführer* Günther Pancke, and

30. E. Keyser, 'Die Erforschung der Bevölkerungsgeschichte des deutschen Ostens', in H. Aubin, O. Brunner, W. Kohte and J. Papritz (eds) *Deutsche Ostforschung. Ergebnisse und Aufgaben seit dem erstern Weltkrieg* (Liepzig, 1942), p. 91.

31. Burleigh, *Germany Turns Eastwards*, p. 127.

32. BA (Koblenz), R153/288 Brackmann to Essen (RMdI) 28 September 1939; Brackmann to Reche 1 November 1939.

33. BA (Koblenz), R153/288, O. Reche, 'Leitsätze zur bevölkerungspolitischen Sicherung des deutschen Ostens', 24 September 1939, pp. 1–6.

via him to the *Reichsführer-SS*.[34] Having established the connection, Reche proceeded to volunteer his thoughts on the racial quality of prospective German settlers in the East; on the need for the creation of a 'warrior nobility' consisting of SS veterans; and on the practicalities of fingerprinting 'Jews and other scoundrels'.[35]

Reche in turn figured as one of the contributors selected by Aubin, Otto Brunner and Wolfgang Kohte for the massive Brackmann *Festschrift*. Although Aubin personally solicited Reche's chapter, he began to have serious reservations once the finished typescript appeared on his desk. By the third page, Aubin was reduced to scribbling 'again pure fantasy' in the margins.[36] The final version, which Aubin saw fit to publish, had two related agendas. An historical part, designed to demonstrate that residual barbarian Germans had 'enslaved' the incoming Slavs, but had then interbred with them in the way of Germans in East Africa with the Hottentots(!), and a contemporary investigation of the questions 'what have we before us of racial value?' and how was one to establish the necessary 'biological boundaries against elements that are racially far apart from us?'[37] Brackmann's response to this extraordinary venture into biological ahistoricity was that it would be 'an extraordinarily important foundation for all other works in the field of German ethnic research'.[38]

Although Aubin and Brackmann were aware of the dangers for conventional scholarship latent in the studies of men like Reche, they were also tantalised by political power, regardless of who happened to exercise it, and desirous of the ultimate validation their society could confer, namely recognition of their work's relevance. Confronted by a regime which awarded no prizes for intellectual inquiry *per se*, they desperately stressed the applied nature of what they were doing, and its relevance to policy measures of the present. It is important to stress that the scholars themselves took this particular initiative, for example with Aubin announcing in September 1939: 'We must make use of our experience, which we have developed over many long years of effort. Scholarship cannot simply wait until it is called upon, but must make itself heard'.[39]

34. Berlin Document Center (Reche file), Pancke to Reche 8 November 1939, etc.

35. BDC (Reche file) Reche to Pancke 14 November 1939 and 18 November 1939 enclosing 'Entwurf für einen bevölkerungsstatistischen Fragebogen'.

36. BA (Koblenz), R153/1049, Aubin to Papritz, 12 November 1941 with notes on Reche's contribution.

37. O. Reche, 'Stärke und Herkunft des Anteils nordischer Rasse bei den Westslawen', Aubin *et al.* (ed.) *Deutsche Ostforschung*, vol. 1 p. 88.

38. BA (Koblenz), R153/1050 Brackmann to Otto Reche 10 July 1942.

39. BA (Koblenz), R153/291 Aubin to Brackmann 18 September 1939.

Many members of this branch of the academic profession slid into progressively collusive relationships with the operative agencies of the Nazi regime. There is no evidence whatsoever that they had any scruples in dealing with policemen, thugs and murderers. Aubin, Brackmann and their staff quickly made their talents known to Governor-General Hans Frank in occupied Cracow, with a view to exerting a decisive influence upon the construction of a German system of higher education and research in place of a once thriving Polish academic culture which Frank and his associates had destroyed.[40] Aubin lectured before Frank in a university whose professors were in concentration camps, and Brackmann tried to secure an influence over Frank's pet project, the *Institut für deutsche Ostarbeit* in Cracow. Although his influence was short-circuited by more skilled operators on the ground, he and his colleagues elsewhere continued to have scholarly contacts with an institution which represented the apogee of scholarship fully instrumentalised in the service of political power. As experts on ethnic questions, and as firm believers in the policy of separating different ethnic groups, the *Ostforscher* were also involved in the creation of new boundaries, and its corollary, the physical relocation of whole populations. For many of them, this was – and in some cases remains – a matter of firm conviction.[41] As early as September 1939, groups of *Ostforscher* in Breslau and Berlin were working on ways of consolidating the German populations in areas mainly inhabited by Poles, which included the expropriation of the property of the alleged political activists and the deportation of post-First World War migrants.[42] From the winter of 1940, Walter Kuhn and Kurt Lück, by now an SS-*Haupsturmführer*, were active in repatriating Volhynian Germans, who themselves were racially 'screened', to villages from which the indigenous Polish inhabitants had been forcibly deported to the *Generalgouvernement*.[43] Lück was also heavily involved in the deliberate falsification of atrocity stories concerning Polish attacks on ethnic Germans in the wake of the September 1939 invasion, stories which were intended to legitimise systematic and massive brutalities carried out by the Germans against Poles and Jews in the name of racial purity.[44] Finally, Brackmann's staff were responsible for sup-

40. Burleigh, *Germany Turns Eastwards*, pp. 257ff.

41. Ibid. pp. 157–8. Interview with Dr J. Papritz in Marburg on 11 August 1986.

42. BA (Koblenz) R153/291 Wolfgang Kohte to the President of the Reich Statistical Office 3 October 1939, see also the paper 'Bevölkerungsfragen im Polen', 1 November 1939.

43. See BA R57/1836 Prof. W. Kuhn to the Chef der Sicherheitspolizei und des SD-Einwandererzentrale Nord-Ost 'Lodsch' 22 January 1940 and BDC file Kurt Lück.

44. K. Lück, *Marsch der Deutschen in Polen. Deutsche Volksgenossen im ehemaligen Polen berichten über Erlebnisse in den Septembertagen 1939* (Berlin, 1940).

plying the Gestapo and SS agencies with cartographical and statistical data on the 'Jewish Question', materials which were intended to give racial policy greater efficacy and precision.[45]

This spiral of collusion continued following the German invasion of the USSR; the *Publikationsstelle* continued to channel detailed economic and ethnological information to a host of government agencies, while assisting in the systematic plundering of Russian academic institutions. Beyond making off with entire libraries and archives, some of the *Publikationsstelle* staff were seconded to SS departments, where plans were being laid for the racial, economic and political refashioning of the entire eastern region. Specifically, one of Brackmann's cartographers worked for Professor Konrad Meyer's SS planning bureau, the agency responsible for the infamous *'Generalplan Ost'*.[46] Under the terms of this plan millions of Germans would be gradually settled in a network of towns and defensive villages; the indigenous population having been literally decimated or deported. Even the landscape itself was to have been altered, with hills, trees and prefabricated villages, so that the 'German man can feel at home'.[47] These connections suggest that the *Ostforscher* had moved very far from the idea of the classical nation-state: in theory and in practice.

After 1945, most of the surviving *Ostforscher* passed smoothly back into West, and sometimes, East German academic life. In a political climate which did not ask many questions, they were successful in weaving their specific concerns into the refashioned animosities of the developing Cold War. It seems likely that this was done with the blessing of various Western intelligence agencies who began tapping the wisdom of the *Ostforscher* shortly after the war. Copies of the old institutes and new journals were accompanied by a number of familiar academic reappointments.[48] However, during the 1970s, and probably under the impact of détente, their influence slipped from having one of their number in Adanauer's cabinet, to being the scientific flank of an expellee lobby to which politicians nodded, but increasingly did not bow. Territorial claims based on the presence of substantial ethnic

45. BA (Koblenz R153/286 RSHA to the PuSte on 2 November 1939 acknowledging 'Anteil der jüdischen Bevölkerung an der Gesamtbevölkerung der polnischen Haupt-und Kreisstädte und sonstigen Städten über 10,000 Einwohner innerhalb des deutschen Interessengebietes'.

46. Burleigh, *Germany Turns Eastwards*, pp. 163–4. See also M. Burleigh, 'Die Stunde der Experten', in M. Rössler and S. Schleiermacher (eds) *Der 'Generalplan Ost': Aspekte der nationalsozialistischen Planungs- und Vernichtungspolitik* (Nordlingen, 1991), pp. 93ff.

47. Rössler, *'Wissenschaft und Lebensraum'*, pp. 181–2.

48. Burleigh, *Germany Turns Eastwards*, pp. 300ff.

minorities have been marginalised by the realities of late-twentieth-century diplomacy, by the migration of ethnic Germans to the Federal Republic, and by the resurgence of a nation-state whose vocation is economic prosperity and the absorption of the economically prostrate former GDR rather than the achievement of a greater territorial extent. Although the post-war continuities are considerably fainter than those linking the conservative nationalism of the Weimar period with the racial imperialism of the Third Reich, on a psychological level some would maintain that there are still outstanding problems. While a united German state will probably remain inward looking for the immediate future, there are vestiges of an older sense of a German civilising mission, bringing 'order' to the 'chaos' of Eastern Europe, in the words and actions of some of the entrepreneurial and bureaucratic *Macher* heading eastwards to Leipzig or Dresden. There does not seem to be much talk of what the people there can contribute to the emergent state in the way of recompense.

SUGGESTIONS FOR FURTHER READING

M. Burleigh, *Germany Turns Eastwards: A Study of 'Ostforschung' in the Third Reich* (Cambridge University Press, 1988; 2nd edn. 1990); M. Burleigh and W. Wippermann, *The Racial State: Germany 1933–1945* (Cambridge University Press, 1991); G. Camphausen, *Die wissenschaftliche historische Russlandforschung in Dritten Reich 1933–1945* (Frankfurt am Main, 1990); G. F. Volkmer 'Die deutsche Forschung zum osteuropäischen Judentum 1933–1945', in H.-J. Torke (ed.) *Forschungen zur osteuropäischen Geschichte* (Berlin, 1989) vol. 42.

CHAPTER EIGHT

The collapse of nationalism in Nazi Germany

William Sheridan Allen

The career of Adolf Hitler abounds in ironies. He rode to power on a promise to unite all Germans, to make them respected and powerful, and to build a permanent bulwark against international Communism. After a dozen years of rule he left Germany divided and weak, a people morally discredited and the object of near universal suspicion and contempt, and he brought the Soviets into Berlin for the next two generations. But the greatest irony is that Hitler achieved supreme leadership by appealing to nationalism; he was widely viewed as 'Germany's greatest nationalist'; yet his Third Reich permanently damaged the German popular faith in nationalism. How and why that happened is the topic of this chapter.

My analysis will require at least some theoretical assertions, inevitably controversial in view of the expanding debate over the nature and role of modern nationalism.[1] I will argue that there are different types of nationalism, that Hitler and his most fanatical followers used a vocabulary of nationalism common to most types but with a content not shared by most of his supporters, that major aspects of the nationalist programme became malfunctional when Hitler carried them out, and that during the Third Reich the different types of nationalism that had helped bring Hitler to power were re-evaluated after he turned them into policy. Because Germans who had applauded the verbiage of nationalism found its actualisation threatening, they rejected nationalism. What was once seen as a unitary phenomenon splintered completely. Above all I will argue that nationalism in Germany became discredited because its effects no longer served its supposed purposes. Instead of enhancing security and well-being, nationalism as practised by Hitler

---

1. For an analysis of general theories see J. Breuilly, *Nationalism and the State* (New York, 1982), pp. 18–36, 365–73. My approach to nationalist functions is much narrower than his, though I certainly second his argument that for Germany nationalism produced a 'pseudo-solution' (pp. 349f). Further evaluations of theory are in M. Hughes, *Nationalism and Society: Germany 1800–1945* (London, 1988), pp. 1–23.

became a threat to personal security and so it lost its appeal to most Germans. What survived the Third Reich was a public attitude quite different from the sentiments represented by Nazi extremists.

I

Prior to the Third Reich, in the Kaiser's time and even more so in the years of the Weimar Republic, nationalistic sentiments became increasingly pervasive throughout Germany. By the eve of the First World War, German nationalism in one or another form had become almost universally prevalent, especially within the middle classes and the political Right. Then it deepened: as happened in virtually all combattant countries, the First World War intensified nationalist fervour in Germany. What had once seemed to many as just a trick of the 'establishment' was now perceived, through the passions of total war, as a pre-requisite for surviving a life-and-death struggle. The sufferings of the First World War certainly left most Germans opposed to any renewed armed conflict, a view that was to continue throughout the Third Reich. Yet the wartime commitment to the nation persisted after the fighting stopped and remained almost as intense during the 1920s as it had been during the actual war years.

Germany's defeat and its extended post-war national humiliation were widely assumed, in the Weimar era, to be both an instance of foreigners exploiting Germany and the reasons for the many social and economic ills that beset the Weimar Republic. This causal linkage even applied to events that were, at the most, only lightly connected with the Armistice of 1918 or the Treaty of Versailles: hyperinflation, the structural unemployment of the 'rationalisation era', the agricultural crisis, the political and sexual turmoil of the 'flapper years', the Great Depression. Yet all were blamed, by right-wing orators, on Germany's international weakness. With Germany effectively disarmed, manifestly defenceless against foreign incursions, saddled with emotional burdens of war guilt, and supposedly crushed by reparations debts, national solidarity seemed wholly defensive in nature. Even the Left expressed this attitude. It was the Social Democratic leader Philip Scheidemann who said: 'Any hand must wither that puts itself and us in these chains' (by signing the Treaty of Versailles).[2] Socialists excori-

2. D. Lehnert, 'The SPD in German politics and society', in R. Fletcher (ed.) *Bernstein to Brandt: A Short History of German Social Democracy* (London, 1987), p. 115.

ated the Right for 'hurrah patriotism', i.e. for insincere patriotism, rather than for nationalism *per se*.[3] Even the Communists used the vocabulary of nationalism, arguing that only a Soviet Germany could adequately defend the country. As for the many parties of the moderate and extreme Right, nationalism became more than ever the standard language of their political appeals, even if various leaders and constituents understood the common vocabulary differently.

This was at least partly because, as had been true even in the nineteenth century, nationalism served different functions for different groups. It also had differing qualities. For almost all Germans there was a real sense of pride in the achievements of their united nation and its culture. Germany had blossomed in science, technology, social welfare, urban administration, music, education, trade and manufacture. Consequently there was much to be proud of. National pride also enhanced personal self-esteem for those who needed that; at the very least it provided everyone with a sense of identity. Few Germans, even if they disliked some aspects of their country, wanted to feel shame over their identification with Germany, or at least with German culture.[4] Providing identity and pride was perhaps the most modest function of nationalism and also the most widespread.

For others, however, nationalism had more specifically goal-directed and less lofty uses. Ever since Bismarck discovered how politically beneficial an appeal to nationalistic sentiments could be, German conservatives used nationalism as a ploy to disarm their foes and to win broad electoral support. In time some conservatives came to believe their own rhetoric, but there also remained an element of the cynicism and insincerity that Bismarck had displayed. Certainly there were very few conservatives who were willing to sacrifice their own self-interest for the good of the nation (in fact most of them thought that the two things were one and the same). By the 1920s the tradition was well established in Germany that nationalism was, among other things, a potent weapon against the Left. It is worth remembering that in Kaiser Wilhelm's time the Socialists were excoriated as *vaterlandslose Gesellen* ('the unpatriotic guys').

Nationalism also had a social function. For the middle classes of Germany, aspiring to escape a status that left them permanently ranked below the aristocracy regardless of their achievements, but also at risk

---

3. W. S. Allen, *The Nazi Seizure of Power: The Experience of a Single German Town 1922–1945* (New York, 1984, rev. edn), p. 43.

4. As a Marxist, then a Zionist, Hannah Arendt criticised almost everything in the country of her birth, but still identified with the German language: E. Young-Bruehl, *Hannah Arendt: For Love of the World* (New Haven, Conn, 1982), p. 199.

of sliding into the proletariat, nationalism meant a claim to social up-grading and social security. From the time of the French Revolution of 1789, nationalism has carried revolutionary implications by elevating group allegiance over individual self-interest. Customarily the nation has been portrayed as a sort of family: *la patrie, das Vaterland*. Conse-quently nationalism has a potential for social equalisation, all members of the family having theoretically the same claims to its protection and the same status. Social distinctions based on birth or wealth may thus be challenged on the grounds that common nationality should over-ride them. Status, say many nationalists, should be based on the value of an individual's contributions to the nation's needs.

Down to Hitler's time Germany showed extraordinary status–con-sciousness: foreigners found few things more absurd than the German quest for and insistent use of titles as appendages to their names. One of the handiest things about the social levelling functions of national-ism was that it could change the status of members of the middle class without also demanding any equalisation of income or property. Un-like socialism, nationalism did not threaten to obliterate objective class differences. It was also morally gratifying because it appealed to the very edifying concept of *noblesse oblige*. The middle and upper classes should respect workers out of a sense of duty. Whatever other func-tions nationalism performed for the German middle classes, it certainly supplied them with an attractive social ideology.

Apart from its political and class functions, nationalism could also provide psychological protection against the threat of change. It is an ideology that insists that the inherited qualities of the nation are unique and precious and therefore must be preserved against internal as well as external threats. By exalting the value of individual identifica-tion with the nation and by demanding national cohesion, it concen-trates collective hostility against anyone who might deny the supreme importance of the nation as a group. Therefore it can be used to justify intolerance, the repression of dissidents, the persecution of mi-norities, and the enforcement of conformity. In times of upheaval, such as the first third of the twentieth century clearly were for Ger-many, large numbers of people – regardless of their social or political adherence – may focus their anxieties upon others who are different. The 'other' may seem a threat because of his otherness. It is conveni-ent to claim that people who are different threaten the cohesion of the national community. While such scapegoating will not cure the basic problem of existential insecurity, it has the psychological advantage of providing a clear target for otherwise shapeless anxieties. Further, if persecuting minorities is done in the name of the national collectivity, that not only provides the anxious individual with potential allies but also lends some respectability to what would otherwise be considered unjustifiable attitudes.[5]

This list of functions performed by nationalism in Germany before the advent of the Third Reich is brief and incomplete, yet even so it is enough to indicate that German nationalism had many different qualities and attracted people for quite divergent reasons.[6] As has been found in other countries too, there are many kinds of nationalists – some good, some bad, some indifferent.[7]

Note also that the above set of functions performed by nationalism consists of items really related to domestic needs. None of them links directly to what was to be Hitler's actual programme: war, imperialism and genocide. At the moment of his triumphant accession to the leadership of Germany in 1933, Hitler began the process of dissolving the apparent common bond of the disparate nationalists (by carrying out *his*, not *their* programme) so that their actual differences about nationalism could become apparent to them.

In the period when Nazism was gaining enough mass backing to put Hitler into office as Reich Chancellor, Hitler appealed to Germans by focusing on all the functions of nationalism described above. He promised to unify the Germans and thereby strengthen the country so that it would no longer be exploited by foreigners. He evoked pride in Germany's achievements and called the Germans a *Herrenvolk*. He was adamantly opposed to 'Marxists' and proposed to stamp out the SPD and KPD and to convert the workers to nationalism. (This, incidentally, was probably what won him the most votes.) He offered a new national community, the attractive *Volksgemeinschaft* that would elevate all patriotic Germans into a common status as 'racial comrades'. And he threatened to crack down on all forms of deviation: sexual, artistic, ideological.

These promises, delivered with enough vagueness so that each group could believe that Nazism was chiefly pursuing that group's own goals, were directly attuned to the functions nationalism was presumed to provide. That, plus the disintegration of Weimar democracy and the vast pool of 'protest votes' available, won the NDSAP about two-fifths of the electorate in free elections.[8] It made the cre-

5. I owe much of this analysis to my colleague at SUNY/Buffalo, Dr. Norman Solkoff, Distinguished Professor of Psychology.

6. Hughes, op.cit., pp. 3–5, 15–17, 122, 194f.

7. This point is more fully developed by N. Davies, *God's Playground: A History of Poland*, vol. 2: *1795 to the Present* (New York, 1984), pp. 9–13.

8. I have analysed this more extensively in 'The Nazi rise to power: a comprehensible catastrophe', in C.S. Maier *et al* (eds) *The Rise of the Nazi Regime: Historical Reassessments* (Boulder, Col, 1986), pp. 9–18.

ation of the Third Reich possible. But it was also to provide a perversion of what Germans really wanted.

II

From the start of his rule, Hitler tried to make nationalism perform its expected function, as he had promised. The results, however, were not what Germans had expected. During the period of the Nazi 'seizure of power' (the first six months of the Third Reich, conveniently marked off by the law of 14 July, 1933, that made the NDSAP Germany's only legal party) and the consolidation of the regime (conveniently marked by Hitler's purge of the Stormtroopers and his assumption of Hindenburg's powers, both in the summer of 1934), Hitler most definitely carried out one of his campaign promises. He destroyed the trade unions plus the Social Democratic and Communist organisations.

Ian Kershaw has argued that this above all was a widely applauded policy,[9] though it was obviously unpopular among that third of the country who were adherents of these working-class organisations. In any case, for those to whom nationalism was primarily a weapon against the Left, Hitler's attack on 'Marxism' fulfilled long-held desires. Yet many were also appalled by the Stormtrooper thuggery that accompanied the destruction of the Left. Such concerns were both allayed and heightened by the lawless violence used against the *SA* in June 1934. The 'execution' without trial of Ernst Roehm and hundreds of others meant than any German could be subjected to the same fate. Thus the price paid for the entire policy was the elimination of the *Rechtsstaat*: official lawlessness and state terrorism became evident to all.[10]

Since the rule of law had been one of the great achievements of the German nation, dating back to the reign of Frederick the Great, even ardent nationalists were very uneasy over this aspect of the Nazi dicta-

9. See I. Kershaw, *Popular Opinion and Political Dissent in the Third Reich: Bavaria 1933–1945* (Oxford, 1983) and *The Hitler Myth: Image and Reality in the Third Reich* (Oxford, 1987).

10. That non-politically motivated denunciations and Gestapo actions based on them became customary is shown in R. Gellately, *The Gestapo and German Society: Enforcing Racial Policy 1933–1945* (Oxford, 1990), Ch. 5 and *passim*.

torship. Worse still: by carrying out the anti–Marxist desires of conservative Germans, Hitler showed that a curse can be attached to the fulfillment of wishes. Beyond that, once the Left had been smashed, did one really continue to need the Nazis? The question was both pertinent and irrelevant since the dictatorship was, by 1934, unchallengeable.

Before Hitler's shattering of the organised working-class movements, many Germans had perceived them as a threat to their security. After it their lives were insecure in different and more immediate ways. This same pattern was to be followed in most of the other features of the Third Reich. In other words, originally appealing expectations of nationalism were shown to be malfunctional.

A second example consists of the problematical assumption of the post-First World War years that a united Germany could successfully overcome the consequences of Germany's defeat in 1918. Of course many of the punitive provisions of the Treaty of Versailles had already been negotiated away by the Weimar Republic. Reparations payments ended with the 'Hoover Moratorium' of 1931. Hitler promised to reverse the defeat of 1918 and from 1933–39 he did that and more. That was, on one level, undoubtedly gratifying to Germans who had been upset by losing the First World War. On the other hand, very few Germans wanted to go to war again, the memory of what war had cost being far too fresh. Therefore Hitler's aggressive foreign policy frightened his countrymen. By the summer of 1934 both the Gestapo's 'morale reports' and the reports of the Social Democratic underground used the same term to describe the noticeably evident fear of war among the population: *Kriegspsychose* ('war psychosis'). From then on each of Hitler's serial coups produced an ever-growing public anxiety.[11] That he succeeded repeatedly in getting his way without war until September 1939 did not cause popular exultation over national triumphs so much as bewildered relief that disaster had once again been avoided.

During such moments as the confrontation with Czechoslovakia and the Western democracies over the Sudetenland in September 1938, the public was not gripped by war fever but by numb fear. Eyewitness accounts from Berlin on the occasion of a military parade at the height of the Sudetenland crisis describe Germans watching it in stony silence, 'the most striking demonstration against war I've ever seen' (William Shirer).[12] When the Second World War actually broke

11. M.G. Steinert, *Hitler's War and the Germans: Public Mood and Attitude during the Second World War* (Athens, Ohio, 1977), pp. 7f and *passim*.
12. W.L. Shirer, *Berlin Diary: The Journal of a Foreign Correspondent 1934–1941* (New York, 1979), pp. 142f "Sept. 28, 1938".

out in 1939, foreign newsmen reported Germans to be stunned and gloomy, but jubilant when a false rumour of peace was circulated a month later.[13] Not even the *Wehrmacht's* stunning victories over the French and British in 1940 proved reassuring, let alone an occasion for celebration. When the news of the German army's capture of Paris hit Berlin, its citizens responded with indifference.[14]

As Hitler's war turned catastrophic, with defeat, retreat, massive casualties, and constant bombing of the Reich, Germans learned the lesson of how dangerous aggressive nationalism could be. What national solidarity there was in the face of catastrophe was forced on Germans by circumstances: the beleaguered country had become, in contemporary language, a 'community of fate'. But that is a far cry from eagerness to fight or to risk all on behalf of the nation's gain.

In sum: during the 1920s many Germans believed that their lives would be bettered if Germany became strong enough to prevent foreign domination. As Hitler achieved and exceeded that goal, most Germans became fearful of his recklessness, which could endanger their lives. When war did come, they experienced directly how destructive and dangerous radical nationalism could be. This was not what they had hoped for when they had applauded diatribes against 'the fetters of Versailles'. The vocabulary of defensive nationalism remained a staple of Nazi propaganda. The reality of agressive nationalism undercut the original function of protecting the people.

Even the most popular of Nazi concepts, the socially homogenising 'folk community', fell prey to a similar cleavage between expectation and actualisation. Hitler and many Nazis sincerely tried to introduce new standards of status, not least because they felt contempt for the old order and saw it as a threat to any war effort. At the beginning of the Third Reich there was widespread enthusiasm among middle-class Germans for the 'idealism' of patriotic solidarity. Workers, however, never bought it. They viewed the entire programme as a corrupt sham and their non-cooperation was a big problem for the regime.[15] The material side of this 'social revolution' was rapidly undermined by Germany's rearmament, while specific groups, such as farmers, became bitter over the inadequacy of Nazi policies.[16]

13. Ibid., pp. 191, 201, also 205, 207f. See also J.W. Grigg's recollections, UPI dispatch, 2 September 1979.

14. Shirer, op.cit., pp. 395, 403f.

15. Analysed and documented in T.W. Mason, *Arbeiterklasse und Volksgemeinschaft: Dokument und Materialien zur deutschen Arbeiterpolitik 1936–1939* (Opladen, 1975). An English translation is supposed to be published in the near future.

16. D. Schoenbaum, *Hitler's Social Revolution: Class and Status in Nazi Germany 1933–1939* (New York, 1968).

Even the erstwhile enthusiasts became appalled by the incredible corruption perpetrated by Nazis who were supposed to implement 'folk community' programmes, like Labour Front leader Robert Ley.[17] One constantly repeated Nazi slogan was *Gemeinnutz vor Eigennutz* (the 'collective benefit precedes the individual's'). But it was common knowledge that Nazi leaders were determined to gain and defend their own power, at the expense of each other, even to the detriment of their common cause. What Germans concluded, obviously, was that their leaders were hypocrites. Furthermore, Germans grew to resent the regimentation imposed upon them by local party leaders – the 'little Führers' – trying to implement 'folk community' policies.[18] Ultimately the 'folk community' meant little more than the Nazi Block Warden exacting contributions from each household for 'Winter Aid', which funds, most Germans believed, were corruptly appropriated by Nazi bigwigs for their self-enrichment. What most ordinary Germans got out from the 'folk community' was a lot of propaganda.

Also the persecution of dissidents and minorities failed to end psychological insecurity, as had been expected, because it became too widespread and violent. Conservative Germans applauded the Gestapo's putting 'Marxists', homosexuals and Jehovah's Witnesses into concentration camps, but began to grow nervous over the violence against Germany's Jews.[19] The single most widespread cause of public disaffection from Nazi actions came on the occasion of the *Kristallnacht* pogrom in November 1938.[20] Shame and concern over this disgraceful incident carried over into the war years, where many Germans believed that their cities were targeted for Allied bombing according to whether or not a synagogue had been burned in their town on *Kristallnacht*. As the news of the Holocaust gradually became whispered about at home, usually because of reports by soldiers on leave from the Eastern Front, Germans were increasingly ashamed. For example, most of those in the 20 July 1944 plot felt driven to resist Hitler primarily because of his crimes against the Jews.[21] The same was true of the student dissidents in the 'White Rose' organisation.[22]

17. R. Smelser, *Robert Ley: Hitler's Labour Front Leader* (Oxford, 1988).

18. The resentments are discussed in Kershaw, *Hitler Myth*.

19. The extent of public complaint is detailed in K.A. Schleunes, *The Twisted Road to Auschwitz: Nazi Policy towards German Jews 1933–1939* (Urbana, Ill, 1990, expanded edn).

20. I analysed this in 'The German popular response to *Kristallnacht*: value hierarchies vs. propaganda', in L.H. Letgers (ed.) *Western Society after the Holocaust* (Boulder, Col, 1983), pp. 69–82 and 98–108.

21. P. Hoffmann, *The History of the German Resistance 1933–1945* (Cambridge, Mass, 1977) and *German Resistance to Hitler* (Cambridge, Mass, 1988).

22. I. Jens (ed.) *At the Heart of the White Rose: Letters and Diaries of Hans and Sophie Scholl* (New York, 1987).

Ultimately everyone was potentially threatened by Nazi assaults against anyone who was 'different'. By the end of the Third Reich the SS was seriously considering the mass extermination of all 'ugly' people.[23] Hardly any Germans knew about that, but most came to know about the Nazi attempt to murder all mentally retarded or congenitally ill Germans. By September 1939 one could also be beheaded for listening to the wrong radio station. The persecution of 'others' had come to exemplify the French proverb: 'In eating, the appetite increases.'

Since all the above malfunctions of nationalism were heavily promoted by Nazi propaganda which was so incessant and pervasive in the Third Reich, why was it not successful? It was, to the extent that it reinforced the Nazi leaders in their convictions, confused and isolated individuals, and convinced even those who did not believe it that everyone else was believing it. But Nazi propaganda could not reverse previously held convictions. No propaganda can. Beyond that, Germans had become highly sensitised to and quite sceptical of any propaganda as a result of the feverish politics of the Weimar era.[24] That they came to disbelieve their own government is evidenced by the fact that almost all Germans listened to the BBC during the Second World War. They literally risked their necks for accurate information.

But the primary reason for the failure of Nazi propaganda was that when it conflicted with reality, as discovered through experience, reality won. A major instance of this was that despite a constant propaganda campaign by Goebbels from 1942 to the end of the war, to persuade all Germans that they would win the war if they never surrendered, almost all Germans did surrender when their home towns were approached by Allied armies.[25] Of those who did not, the usual reason was that they were forced to continue fighting, not that they had been convinced to do so by the propaganda.

Finally, one should note that the very structure of the Nazi dictatorship undercut nationalism. As a form of self-identification, nationalism cannot be imposed. It has to be felt and believed by an individual. But the Third Reich discouraged voluntary commitment in all regards because it was determined to regiment its own people. The incessant controls, the herding of people into compelled demonstrations of en-

---

23. R. Hilberg, *The Destruction of the European Jew* (New York, 1979), p. 642ff.

24. W. S. Allen (ed. and trans.) *The Infancy of Nazism: The Memoirs of Ex-Gauleiter Albert Krebs 1923–1933* (New York, 1976), p. 81.

25. J. Stephenson, '"Resistance" to "No Surrender": Popular Disobedience in Württemurg in 1945', in F.R. Nicosia and L.D. Stokes (eds) *Germans against Nazism: Nonconformity, Opposition and Resistance in the Third Reich* (Oxford, 1990), pp. 351–67.

thusiasm, the coerced conformity, all had the effect of treating the people as objects: the *Herrenvolk* as serfs. In response, even once willing enthusiasts became passive, bored, resentful, apathetic, withdrawn.[26] Ultimately very few Germans volunteered for any aspect of their nation's needs because almost all Germans had come to expect their rulers to tell them what they had to do. Under the stress of the Second World War, Germans became chiefly concerned with their own and their family's survival. This privatisation was the antithesis of nationalism. Or to put it another way, Hitler had finally created the conditions wherein nationalism no longer made any sense.

III

The death and destruction of the Second World War ended almost all nationalistic sentiments in Germany, especially the most radical ones. But some survived even Hitler. He had taken nationalism to the extreme limits and had thereby discredited it, disillusioning his one-time followers. It was not simply that nationalism had been shown to be life-threatening rather than life-enhancing. On top of that direct experience came the post-war evidence of the crimes committed in Germany's name. It was overwhelming and undeniable and Germans realised that they had partaken of a moral, rather than just a physical, catastrophe. Some argued that Hitler was an aberration and that Germans could retrieve their self-esteem by returning to the good parts of their national heritage.[27] West German political leaders have consistently and freely voted for reparations to the victims of Nazism and to the state of Israel, in the clear conviction that atonement can pave the way for renewed pride in Germany. Officially and privately Germans have extolled their martyred countrymen who resisted Hitler, especially those who, like the 20 July 1944 conspirators, had explicitly claimed to be risking their lives in order to restore Germany's national honour.

So the nationalism of pride and self-identification survived Nazism, though that pride was often for aspects of Germany that Hitler hated. Though nothing done by the Treaty of Versailles matched the break-up of the Reich into two separate and antagonistic states, such as pre-

---

26. Allen, *Seizure*, pp. 282–92: 'Life in the Third Reich'.
27. F. Meinecke, *The German Catastrophe* (New York, 1947).

vailed from 1949 to 1989, there was nothing during those years comparable to the nationalistic outrage of the 1920s. Since 1945 calls for the reunification of the fatherland were generally ritualistic. A substantial number of West Germans grew comfortable with Willy Brandt's formula: 'One nation; two states'. During and since the reunification of the two Germanies, the predominant emotion in West Germany was not nationalistic exaltation, but pragmatic concern about how much this new unity was going to cost. Some leading intellectuals, such as Günter Grass and Hans-Ulrich Wehler, publicly opposed the whole idea of a united Germany.[28]

One post-Hitlerian surprise was the adoption of some nationalistic attitudes by the SPD, beginning already in 1945. But that stance stemmed at least partly from deliberate calculation: the Social Democrats wanted to avoid being outflanked by nationalists ever again. None of their leaders ever indulged in radical rhetoric. They simply insisted that foreign exploitation was as repugnant as the domestic variety and that democracy required self-determination. And by the 1960s the Social Democratic nationalism was as muted as their erstwhile 'Marxism' had become. That was at least partly because even mild nationalistic appeals did not win them many votes. Germans were too cool towards the whole notion of the nation.[29]

Almost all this change in the nature and extent of German national sentiments is largely a legacy of the Third Reich. The most nationalistic government the world has known left its people very doubtful about anything other than an understandable and rational acceptance of the indisputable fact that they were Germans: a self-identification that, like the heritage of most nations, involves both pride and shame.

SUGGESTIONS FOR FURTHER READING

W. S. Allen, *The Nazi Seizure of Power: the Experience of a Single German Town, 1922–1945* (rev. ed., London, 1989).

R. Bessel (ed.) *Life in the Third Reich* (Oxford, 1987).

B. Engelmann, *In Hitler's Germany: Everyday Life in the Third Reich* (New York, 1986).

28. G. Grass, *Two States – One Nation?* (New York, 1990).
29. Hughes, *Nationalism and Society*, p. 226 and *passim*.

R. Gellately, *The Gestapo and Germany Society: Enforcing Racial Policy, 1933–1945* (Oxford, 1990).

S. A. Gordon, *Hitler, Germans, and the 'Jewish Question'* (Princeton, New Jersey, 1983).

R. Grunberger, *The 12-year Reich: A Social History of Nazi Germany, 1933–1945* (New York, 1971).

P. Hoffmann, *German Resistance to Hitler* (Cambridge, Mass., 1988).

M. Hughes, *Nationalism and Society: Germany 1800–1945* (London, 1988).

I. Kershaw, *The 'Hitler Myth': Image and Reality in the Third Reich* (Oxford, 1987).

I. Kershaw, *Popular Opinion and Political Dissent in the Third Reich: Bavaria 1933–1945* (Oxford, 1983).

D. Peukert & J. Reulecke (eds) *Die Reihen fast geschlossen: Beiträge zur Geschichte des Alltags unterm Nationalsozialismus* (Wuppertal, 1981).

D. Schoenbaum, *Hitler's Social Revolution: Class and Status in Nazi Germany, 1933–1939* (New York, 1966).

M. Steinert, *Hitler's War and the Germans: Public Mood and Attitude during the Second World War* (Athens, Ohio, 1977).

CHAPTER NINE

Nationalism and German politics after 1945

Peter Alter

April 1945 was the cruellest month. Hitler's Third Reich, the scourge of Europe for twelve long years, was at last finished, politically and militarily as well as morally. Most German cities lay in ruins, devastated by bombs, shelling and fire. Millions of refugees and 'displaced persons' were on the move. As the Allied forces liberated German-occupied Europe and directed their offensive towards the centre of the Reich the concentration camps revealed horrors which were beyond human imagination and comprehension. The collapse of the National Socialist dictatorship was accompanied by the dissolution of the German state. After Germany's unconditional surrender on 8 May 1945 the country was occupied by the four victorious powers. The traditional territorial organisation of the Germans had come to an end. Total war was followed by total defeat – and the defeat of 1945 was incomparably more far-reaching and final than that of 1918, affecting people's lives more directly. In 1918 the horrors of war had remained largely on battlefields abroad; in 1945 they were brought to German soil proper. It seemed to be *finis Germaniae*.

The unconditional surrender of May 1945 brought an era of German history to a close. It was a turning-point of the most fundamental kind. The enormity of what had happened and the task of rebuilding Germany led contemporaries to speak of a *Stunde Null* (hour zero) – appropriately at the time, although years later it became apparent that no comprehensive new start had actually taken place in Germany in 1945. But most Germans felt that after the end of the Nazi dictatorship a break with basic traditions of their history was necessary, and the will to make this break was there. These traditions included thinking in militarist and nationalist categories, which was now held responsible for developments that had led to the establishment of the Nazi regime in Germany in 1933, and to the unleashing of the Second World War in 1939. German policy, the deluded activities of the Nazis, who were responsible for the war and the Holocaust, had perverted the national idea. Thus it was only natural that in 1945 nationalism was often linked with National Socialism as a criminal ideology, and that the Germans had grave doubts about the nation and the national state. As principles of state organisation, it seemed, they had run their course.

The momentous change in the thinking of the Germans which will be outlined here was rooted in the experience of National Socialism and the Second World War. The direct confrontation with a ruthless dictatorship, with crime and destruction had an impact on the German mentality which is still visible today. In the West German state on the territory of the former Reich, the Federal Republic of Germany, the national state and a national consciousness were no longer the highest values; freedom, peace and tolerance now ranked above them. The conviction that national egoism and rivalry between states did not provide an adequate basis for the coexistence of the European peoples had gained ground. In the mid-1960s the philosopher Karl Jaspers published a political polemic, *What is becoming of the Federal Republic?*, in which he expressed dismay about the political consciousness of the West Germans:

> It has been said that there is a *vacuum* in our political consciousness. It is true that we do not yet have our hearts in a political objective, nor do we have a feeling of standing on ground that we have created ourselves. . . The vacuum will not be filled by a national consciousness. That is either missing, or it is an artificial one.[1]

Even when the unification of the two states which were successors to the eclipsed German Third Reich was on the international agenda in 1989–90 the West German people were reluctant to accept the rhetoric of nation, and many in fact distrusted and rejected it. In the summer of 1990 the Munich historian Thomas Nipperdey observed that rejecting the nation was 'something specifically German'. He warned his readers against the 'fatal inclination'

> to impose our non-national-consciousness on other oh-so-backward peoples. It seems that the world is once again to be saved by the most progressive, a better, post-national entity, and one feels the arrogance of the seemingly so noble rejection of the national. We should not feel superior.[2]

1. K. Jaspers, *Wohin treibt die Bundesrepublik? Tatsachen, Gefahren, Chancen* (Munich, 1966, repr. 1988), pp. 177–8. For their generous advice and help I am very grateful to my colleagues Angela Davies, Eva A. Mayring and Lothar Kettenacker.

2. T. Nipperdey, 'Die Deutschen wollen und dürfen eine Nation sein', *Frankfurter Allgemeine*, 13 July 1990, p. 10. Almost a year after unification the Berlin writer Peter Schneider wrote: 'Faced with unification, West German society turns out to be morally and intellectually unprepared for the challenge. The problem is precisely *not* the new German nationalism some people fear but the almost total lack of it. In the ruins of the National Socialist megalomania, West Germans fell back on a very convenient credo: I only believe what I see (in the till)' (*Time*, 1 July 1991, p. 40).

I

The rejection of the nation and its elevation into an absolute value after the *Wertzusammenbruch* (collapse of all values) at the end of the war, the turning away from the idea of the national state as the value central to all politics, grew out of the experience of the 'German catastrophe'.[3] In defeated and occupied Germany, therefore, the process of settling accounts with the past from the start also concentrated on nationalism and its consequences for German history. 'Nationalism', now frequently equated with National Socialism, acquired unequivocally negative connotations. As a polemical term and a term of political demarcation, it has retained these to the present day in Germany. Nationalism was seen as the opposite of devoted patriotism, which does not necessarily relate to the nation, and permits competing loyalties to exist. Nationalism was considered the antithesis of free democracy and a 'healthy' national consciousness, whatever these terms might mean. The public debate after 1945, however, took place within a very small circle. The participants were leading intellectuals, who had either opposed the Nazi regime or had survived the dictatorship abroad in forced or voluntary emigration. The debate did not widen and enter party politics until the 1950s, when political and economic conditions in West Germany had settled.

In 1945 and immediately thereafter, the mass of the German population was, of course, preoccupied almost exclusively with simply surviving. Its attitude towards political issues therefore tended to be one of apathy and indifference.[4] Many people believed that in the foreseeable future the occupying powers would take over politics, operating over the heads of the Germans. It is, unfortunately, not possible to make more precise statements about the level of awareness among the German people, their political attitudes and their political thinking in the early post-war period due to lack of information. However, there is much to suggest that the idea that the German population harboured a powerful but unexpressed potential for resentment and nationalist feeling in 1945 and thereafter is incorrect. Even the millions of refugees, brutally expelled from eastern Germany and other parts of central, eastern and south–eastern Europe, seem not to have provided a

---

3. F. Meinecke, *The German Catastrophe: Reflections and Recollections* (Cambridge, Mass., 1950). The German edition was published in 1946.
4. B. Marshall, 'German reactions to military defeat, 1945–1947: the British view', in V.R. Berghahn and M. Kitchen (eds) *Germany in the Age of Total War* (London, 1981), pp. 218–39.

breeding ground for surviving or new nationalisms, as some contemporaries predicted. Militant political revisionism and right-wing nationalism were never to play more than a marginal and, apart from occasional flowerings, rapidly diminishing role in the politics of the Federal Republic after its founding in 1949.

There is evidence to suggest that nationalism was already being firmly condemned a few weeks before Germany's surrender to the Allies. When the Thuringian concentration camp, Buchenwald, near Weimar, was liberated by American troops in April 1945, a number of former inmates, all supporters of democratic socialism, drew up a list of demands and ideas which were to guide Germany's new politics. Some of these ideas found their way into Allied occupation policy, and also into the programmes of the newly established German parties. The Buchenwald Manifesto of 13 April 1945, 'For Peace, Freedom, Socialism', was an ambitious and pioneering attempt 'to rescue Germany from this historically unprecedented collapse and to secure for it again the respect and trust of the council of nations', by opening up a perspective for the future. It contains statements about Germany's future domestic and foreign policy. In foreign policy, the manifesto calls for all forms of nationalism to be abandoned. The authors advocate the creation of a 'European-wide awareness'. They continue: 'To achieve this we need a new spirit. It is to be embodied by a new type of German – that of the German European. Nobody can re-educate us, if we do not do it ourselves in freedom.' As the first concrete steps on this long path the Manifesto recommended that Germany should come to an understanding with its direct neighbours in the east and west, Poland and France, and cooperate with them. It also suggested that 'Germany should enter the Anglo-Saxon cultural area'. The authors of the Manifesto combined this suggestion with the wish that their country be accepted into 'the international organisation for peace and security as soon as possible'. In other words, they wanted Germany to become a member of the United Nations, which was then in the process of being set up.[5]

The language of the Buchenwald Manifesto was rather vague and general, but its authors made sufficiently clear the direction in which they wanted Germany to go. The dissolving of a traditional national consciousness in a European consciousness which the Manifesto demanded was also put forward at the same time by the liberal economist, Wilhelm Röpke, as the objective of all German policy in the

5. The Buchenwald Manifesto is printed in M. Overesch, *Deutschland 1945–1949: Vorgeschichte und Gründung der Bundesrepublik. Ein Leitfaden in Darstellung und Dokumenten* (Königstein, 1979), pp. 171–6.

new Germany. A German by birth, Professor Röpke had emigrated in 1933 and had been teaching in Geneva since 1937. His book, *The German Question,* was published in Switzerland in the spring of 1945. Two years later, a third edition had to be printed. The book was translated into English, French and Italian. Its arguments and demands captured the contemporary imagination.

The influence of Röpke's work on the German public and on German politicians in the post-war period cannot be overemphasised. According to the historian Hans-Peter Schwarz, it was 'the most consistent and well-founded blueprint for German politics' in the German language in existence at the end of the war.[6] In it, Röpke diagnosed the Germans, and at the same time prescribed a therapy for all their ills and troubles. He believed that the Germans were now ripe for a moral revolution. In his opinion, the fact that it had not happened in 1918 was a disaster. At the end of the First World War,

> the poison of nationalism was not got rid of, but under the influence of defeat, collapse, and economic and social upheavals, was only propagated further. The very serious readiness for a searching self-examination that existed after November, 1918, was quickly dissipated and reduced to impotence in face of the opposite determination to return all the more defiantly to the old spirit.[7]

The Germans had paid the penalty in 1933 and 1945. In 1933, 'with the Third Reich, the German Reich founded by Bismarck came to its end'.[8] Twelve years later, the Germans suffered

> the complete bankruptcy of a spirit, a policy, a type of patriotism and of collective morality, which the Nazis had utilized in order to carry matters to the uttermost extreme. In blind obstinacy the wrong path was pursued to the end, until the leaders themselves saw no way out except through taking their own lives. The people, as such, will not commit suicide, but will turn back provided that they are shown a way back.[9]

Röpke recommended a threefold revolution for the Germans: political (decentralisation), economic (liberalism) and moral. 'The solution of the German question', Röpke went on,

> contained in this threefold revolution is the only one that holds out the promise of real permanence. It permits the fulfilment of all just and reasonable claims from the victors for the future security of Europe in face of Germany [*sic*]; and at the same time it is the solution which every

6. H.-P. Schwarz, *Die Ära Adenauer* (Stuttgart, 1981), p. 393.
7. W. Röpke, *The German Question* (London, 1946), p. 180.
8. Ibid., p. 188.
9. Ibid., p. 184.

German patriot with clear vision and goodwill must desire for his homeland, once he has himself recognized the nature of the German question. Germany had become a danger to her neighbours because she had become infected with a grave malady. It is therefore the common interest of victors and vanquished that she should at last be thoroughly cured.[10]

Röpke drew the general conclusion that

only if the Germans are cured of regimentation and proletarianization will they really turn away for good from the narcotics of nationalism and totalitarianism, and recoil in disgust from every sort of political mass-hysteria.[11]

Another great liberal of the post-war period agreed with Röpke's assessment and his prediction about the difficulty of Germany's path back into the community of nations. Theodor Heuss, who had been a member of the *Reichstag* in Berlin until 1933 and was elected the first President of the Federal Republic in 1949, condemned the nationalist excesses of Germany's most recent past no less firmly. Like Röpke, he recommended a fundamental purification. 'For twelve years we were in the hell of history', Heuss said in March 1946 in a lecture he gave in destroyed Berlin.

For a long time we will be in the purgatory of purification. And then Paradise? No, Paradise exists only in utopian novels…We shall be happy without Paradise if only we get back to the firm ground of a free life. We should receive this in the name of democracy…When it comes to democracy, the Germans have to go right back to the beginning and learn to spell the word, even if they call themselves democrats today. They are in the ghastly position of having no word that denotes what the English call 'fairness'.[12]

At the same time Alexander Abusch, a Communist journalist and later Minister for Culture in the GDR, who had left the country during the Nazi period, made a similar complaint: 'Many Germans discovered patriotism, belatedly and incorrectly, as an extreme form of supernationalism.'[13] And, like Röpke and Heuss, he believed that a 'moral renewal of the German people' was inevitable:

Under the curious conditions of long-term occupation by the armies of

10. Ibid., p. 194.
11. Ibid., p. 193.
12. T. Heuss, 'Um Deutschlands Zukunft', in Heuss, *Aufzeichnungen 1945–1947* (Tübingen, 1966), pp. 206–7.
13. A. Abusch, *Der Irrweg einer Nation: Ein Beitrag zum Verständnis deutscher Geschichte* (Berlin, 1946), p. 184.

the United Nations,[14] the German nation must renew itself, its leaders as well as the rank-and-file. This means that it must translate the most urgent lessons of its history into new action, and at last complete the democratic revolution of 1848 and 1918 in one step.[15]

Historians also had their say in this debate about German nationalism, German faults and guilt. Friedrich Meinecke, the doyen of German historians and 84 years old at the time, concluded his famous book of 1946 on *The German Catastrophe* with a chapter on 'roads to survival'. Meinecke, who saw nationalism that was becoming amoral as the 'immediate prelude to Hitlerism',[16] accepted that 'the work of Bismarck's era has been destroyed through our own fault'.[17] Nevertheless, he claimed, 'even a partitioned Germany robbed of her national political existence, which is our lot today, ought to remember with sorrowful mourning the unity and strength that she previously enjoyed.'[18] In terms of foreign relations Meinecke could conceive of Germany 'only as a member of a future federation, voluntarily concluded, of the central and west European states'.[19] He suggested that in order to be prepared for this the Germans needed to 'work under the auspices of humanity for the purification and intensification of our moral existence'.[20] Even a scholar as wise and perceptive as Meinecke, however, could suggest only in extremely vague terms what this purification and intensification actually involved. 'The areas in which we must spiritually establish ourselves again are marked out for us. These areas are the religion and the culture of the German people.'[21] Meinecke made a special plea for contemplation of the 'sacred heritage of the Goethe period'.[22] He wanted to see every German town and larger village possess 'in the future a community of like-minded friends of culture', for which he suggested the name *Goethegemeinden* (Goethe Communities).[23]

The 'roads to survival' which Meinecke pointed out reveal his idealism, but also show that he was out of touch with real life. They testify to his helplessness in the face of what had happened, the de-

14. United Nations was the term for the wartime coalition from January 1942.
15. Abusch, *Der Irrweg*, p. 268.
16. Meinecke, *The German Catastrophe*, p. 24.
17. Ibid., p. 115.
18. Ibid., pp. 108–9.
19. Ibid., p. 110.
20. Ibid., p. 112.
21. Ibid.
22. Ibid., p. 9.
23. Ibid., p. 120.

pressing present, and the overwhelming tasks of the immediate future. More pragmatic men such as Meinecke's colleague at the University of Freiburg, Gerhard Ritter, and the journalist Ernst Friedlaender, both of whom tended towards the liberal conservative camp, also spoke of the spiritual renewal of Germany. But when it came to condemning thinking in national categories, they were more restrained. During the war Ritter had been close to the resistance around Carl Goerdeler, the Lord Mayor of Leipzig, and he became a leading historian in the early years of the Federal Republic. As early as 1946 he expressed the opinion that a people 'which on principle dispenses with "national consciousness" loses itself. This makes it morally worse, not better.'[24] Retaining national values, however, for him was not the same thing as giving up the idea of 'educating German young people and Germans in general to strive for world peace and greater, democratic freedom'.[25]

Ernst Friedlaender, who had spent many years abroad, had worked as a leader-writer for the new weekly, *Die Zeit,* since 1946. Early in 1947 he called for a thorough debate on national thinking, which he wanted to distinguish from *nationalist* thinking. 'We have every reason', he wrote in *Die Zeit*

> to come to some decision concerning the terms 'nationalism' and 'nationalist'. Since Germany's surrender the public meaning of these words has become exclusively and solely derogatory. Before the surrender, for twelve years the same words had had an unquestionably positive meaning in official propaganda. This is part of the absolutely necessary process of reassessing values that is in progress in Germany. But what is at issue here is less the words than the values.[26]

His quarrel was not with the liberal nationalism of the early nineteenth century, but with 'imperialist nationalism' of a later age. This variant of nationalism, according to Friedlaender, was

> unscrupulous national egoism that, as the example of Nazism has shown, can lead to unprecedented crimes, can precipitate a world war. This nationalism has lost the moderation which grants all peoples an *equal* right to existence, to freedom and dignity.

In Friedlaender's opinion, 'justified anti-nationalism' must not be allowed to

---

24. Gerhard Ritter to Erwin Eckert, 8 July 1946, in K. Schwabe and R. Reichardt (eds) *Gerhard Ritter: Ein politischer Historiker in seinen Briefen* (Boppard, 1984), p. 414.
25. Gerhard Ritter to Hellmuth Ritter, 23 June 1947, in ibid., p. 430.
26. E. Friedlaender, 'Nationalismus, 6 February 1947', in N. Frei and F. Friedlaender (eds) *Ernst Friedlaender: Klärung für Deutschland: Leitartikel in der ZEIT 1946–1950* (Munich and Vienna, 1982), p. 35.

become an anti-nationalism that attacks the nation and the people instead of nationalism. And that is why it is absolutely necessary to draw a clear, universally comprehensible dividing line between the 'national' and the nationalistic, which allows us to say yes to the one, and no to the other. Without it, we are groping in the dark, not only with respect to our thinking and values, but also in our practical politics.[27]

Friedlaender's conclusion was a plea for the 'national', or, as it was often put later, for a 'healthy' national consciousness:

> Today, in any case, when the subject of debate is nationalism as it relates to the politics of power, which can clearly be distinguished from the 'national' without any risk to the spiritual health of the people, there is no cause to throw the national overboard. We have no reason to agree with a minority among us which, tormented by national fear of itself and national self-hatred, would prefer to let Germany disappear, which would agree to Germany being divided up for the benefit of all its neighbours…After all, it is neither good nor healthy if in our present state of emergency organisation we are to be 'undernourished' in terms not only of physiological, but also of national calories. For this, too, produces symptoms of deficiency. These can give rise to mental cramps, which are the opposite of the re-education we are working for.[28]

This determined and positive but differentiated attitude towards nationalism made Friedlaender almost an outsider in post-war Germany.

As far as I can see, contemporaries' assessments of nationalism and national thinking have not moderated over time. In his book on the German question published in 1948 Gerhard Ritter reflected upon 'German neo-nationalism'.[29] He used the same long chapter, almost unchanged, in the revised second edition of the book, which appeared in 1962.[30] In this chapter Ritter continued the story of German nationalism into the time of the Weimar Republic. In 1948, however, he had avoided discussing the problem of nationalism in post-war Germany. But at that time his judgement on nationalism was unequivocal. Nationalism, wrote Ritter,

> is never and nowhere the expression of a peaceful and secure national consciousness. On the contrary, it arises out of a national consciousness that is touchy, somehow startled, and driven to worry or indignation. The

27. Ibid., p. 36.
28. Ibid., p. 37.
29. G. Ritter, *Europa und die deutsche Frage: Betrachtungen über die geschichtliche Eigenart des deutschen Staatsdenkens* (Munich, 1948), pp. 55–150.
30. Ritter, *Das deutsche Problem: Grundfragen deutschen Staatslebens gestern und heute* (Munich, 1962), pp. 55–146.

more shrilly it expresses itself, the more likely it is that in the final analysis there is an inner insecurity behind it.[31]

In both editions of his book Ritter defines nationalism as 'a political national consciousness, exaggerated in its bias, and raised to the level of presumption'.[32] But we have already suggested that Ritter's attitude towards nationalism was fundamentally ambivalent. In his expanded 'conclusion' of 1962, he writes: 'Because it was misused for the most dreadful acts of violence, nationalism has rightly fallen into disrepute.' He then continues:

> But was it not also the symptom of a strong, unbroken vitality? If this desire for recognition had been directed towards sensible goals, it need not have had a destructive effect.[33]

Among the early Federal Republic's leading politicians, the Christian Democratic (CDU) Chancellor, Konrad Adenauer, often addressed the problem of nationalism. In most cases, official visits to other European countries provided the occasion for his comments. Thus early in 1949 in Berne, Adenauer expressed the opinion that there were only relatively few 'supporters of nationalism of the type propagated by Hitler' in Germany. However, he believed that a reawakening of national feeling was noticeable in the western half of the divided country. On this occasion Adenauer used the same argument which Gerhard Ritter had put forward in 1946:[34] 'One can only welcome the reawakening of a healthy national feeling that does not stray from the right paths, for a people that no longer possesses a national feeling has lost itself.'[35] One year later, when the political status of the Saar district was at issue,[36] Adenauer feared the revival of nationalist movements among the German people.[37] When 'one section of the Germans' resisted the Schuman Plan which was to be the first important step towards closer economic union in Europe Adenauer interpreted this in 1951 as evidence of the difficulty 'of liberating this section of the Germans from the nationalistic thinking they have so far

31. Ritter, *Europa und die deutsche Frage*, pp. 55–6.

32. Ibid., p. 55.

33. Ritter, 'Schlußbetrachtung: Hitler und das Deutschland von heute', in Ritter, *Das deutsche Problem*, p. 204.

34. See above, p. 161.

35. Speech in Berne, 23 March 1949, in K. Adenauer, *Erinnerungen 1945–1953*, vol. 1 (Stuttgart, 1965, 2nd edn, 1973), p. 188.

36. The Saar district was occupied by the French who gave it a special status within their zone of occupation. French policy aimed at separating it from the rest of Germany.

37. Adenauer, *Erinnerungen*, vol. 1, p. 307.

38. Ibid., p. 467.

been pursuing'.[38] In the same year, 1951, he declared on a visit to London that 'the overwhelming majority of the German people have outgrown nationalism'.[39] In his memoirs Adenauer unequivocally called nationalism the 'cancerous sore of Europe',[40] and in April 1958 he described himself to a high-ranking Soviet visitor as 'a pronounced opponent of nationalism'.[41] In 1955 he agreed with the President of the European Union that the Germans had to come to see the desired reunification of their country as a pan-European and not as a national problem. A German 'nationalism of reunification' would result in the political isolation of Germany in Europe.[42]

Adenauer, an opponent of Hitler and co-founder of the conservative CDU, was only too well aware that any signs of a new German nationalism would cause deep anxiety abroad. Nationalist movements in the new Federal Republic, which was more or less the creation of the Western powers, would be observed with suspicion, and impede the consolidation of the young state. It is true that after 1945 the German policy of the Allies, and their public opinion at home, long reflected a deep mistrust of Germany. A memorandum which the British foreign secretary Anthony Eden transmitted to his colleagues in the War Cabinet at the beginning of 1945 is entirely typical of the attitude of the Allies. In this 'study of the German mentality and its possible development in the future',[43] the danger of a revival of National Socialism after the foreseeable defeat of Germany was rated as slight – unlike the threat of a continuing German nationalism. 'It would be superficial to regard Hitlerism as likely to remain a menace of the same order as German nationalism and German militarism. These two evils may unite again under a new totalitarian cloak.'[44] The memorandum continued on a warning note:

> The mere resentment of defeat and disarmament, quite apart from the final political, economic and territorial settlement imposed upon her, will be enough no doubt to inflame nationalist and militarist feelings in Germany... It is, however, a fact, simple and unoriginal but inescapable, that Germany's mental reaction to defeat will be determined, in the long run, not by the mere fact of defeat, but by the settlement it leads to. It will be determined most of all by the territorial settlement, and by such

39. Ibid., p. 501.
40. Ibid., p. 425.
41. Adenauer, *Erinnerungen 1955–1959*, vol. 3 (Stuttgart, 1967), p. 383.
42. Ibid., p. 252.
43. Thus Anthony Eden in his introductory remark (Public Record Office, London, FO 371/46791/C 150, W. P. (45) 18: German Reactions to Defeat, p. 1).
44. Ibid., p. 5.

possible accompanying burdens as the wholesale transfer of populations from ceded areas.

The memorandum argued that Germany's territorial losses and the accompanying expulsions of Germans from the areas where they had lived for centuries would place a heavy burden on any post-war European order from the start.

> To exacerbate Germany's feelings of nationalism and militarism by inflicting on her very extensive territorial losses, which she will regard as unjust and intolerable and to which she will never become resigned, would gravely diminish any hope there may be that Germany might eventually become reconciled to the settlement of Europe, and co-operate in its maintenance.[45]

Sir Robert Vansittart's well-known view that there was a deep-seated flaw in the German 'national character' seems to have been widely held right across the political spectrum in wartime Britain and immediately after the close of hostilities in the European theatre of war.[46] It undoubtedly influenced much of Britain's policy-making towards occupied Germany and may help to explain British mistrust of early anti-fascist and democratic associations in post-war Germany. Any political activities by Germans encountered the British suspicion that under the guise of 'democratic' groupings some potent nationalist movement might re-emerge and threaten the security of the occupying forces.[47] As the Labour leader and future British prime minister, Clement   Attlee, put it rather simplistically in the summer of 1944:

> It was an illusion to imagine that there was a normal Germany to which one could return. There had been no normal Germany for fifty years or more, except one governed by a centralised and militaristic machine.[48]

The historian A.J.P. Taylor was only expressing the mood of the time when he drew the following rather sweeping conclusion in his widely read book, published in July 1945, *The Course of German History*:

45. Ibid., p. 6.
46. A.M. Birke, 'Geschichtsauffassung und Deutschlandbild im Foreign Office Research Department', in B. J. Wendt (ed.) *Das britische Deutschlandbild im Wandel des 19. und 20. Jahrhunderts* (Bochum, 1984), pp. 171–97. H. Fromm, *Deutschland in der öffentlichen Kriegszieldiskussion Großbritanniens 1939–1945* (Frankfurt and Berne, 1982).
47. See A. Glees, *Exile Politics during the Second World War: The German Social Democrats in Britain* (Oxford, 1982), esp. pp. 124–44. F. Pingel, 'Verborgener Nazismus unter demokratischem Gewand? – Ein Beitrag zum Deutschlandbild im Wandel (Britische Besatzungszone 1945/46)', in Wendt (ed.) *Das britische Deutschlandbild*, pp. 198–218.
48. Quoted in L. Kettenacker, 'Großbritannien und die zukünftige Kontrolle Deutschlands', in J. Foschepoth and R. Steininger (eds) *Die britische Deutschland- und Besatzungspolitik 1945–1949* (Paderborn, 1985), p. 37.

The history of the Germans is a history of extremes. It contains everything except moderation, and in the course of a thousand years the Germans have experienced everything except normality...One looks in vain in their history for a *juste milieu,* for common sense – the two qualities which have distinguished France and England. Nothing is normal in German history except violent oscillations.[49]

Thus it is hardly surprising that as an occupying power, Britain, for example, closely observed real or alleged manifestations of nationalism in post-war Germany. The mood of the German people and their political attitudes were attentively monitored. But on the whole, the information about nationalist activities which the Public Opinion Research Office collected, or which is contained in consular reports to the Military Government in Germany, is of limited use. It is impressionistic and often highly speculative, and suggests that there was no question of a survival or revival of German nationalism after the surrender. The Allies' fears in this respect, therefore, were exaggerated, perhaps even unfounded.

For example, a British intelligence report from Berlin, dated July 1945, contains the following statement:

The prevalent mental attitude, where it is not one of dumb indifference, is one of complete cynicism. They [the Germans] have learnt at last how disastrously wrong their own propaganda was.[50]

Three months later, little had changed in the attitude of the German people. 'With regard to politics', we read in a report from the end of October 1945,

there is still a general apathy among the mass of Germans. All four parties are by way of starting new drives to combat this, but they all admit that they have so far not touched the great masses of the nation.[51]

The Allies had expected that in occupying Germany they would have to contend with far more hostile acts by Germans against the occupying forces than in fact occurred. But at the end of 1945 the situation was summed up thus: 'We could not expect the Germans to be so

49. A.J.P. Taylor, *The Course of German History: A Survey of the Development of German History since 1815* (repr. London, 1976), p. 1.
50. Public Record Office, London [=PRO], FO 1005/1706: HQ British Troops Berlin, Intelligence Summary no. 1, 8 July 1945.
51. PRO, FO 1005/1727: HQ British Troops Berlin, Political Intelligence Report no. 15, 27 October 1945. The report refers to the newly founded political parties: the Social Democrats, the Liberals, the Christian Democrats and the Communists.

devoid of national feeling as to accept being occupied with complacency or even with resignation.'[52] The shock of Germany's collapse and fear of an uncertain future together had the effect of paralysing the German population.

Occasionally opinion polls, an instrument for the analysis of political attitudes hitherto unknown in Germany and imported by the Anglo-Saxon occupiers, produced unsettling results. In the summer of 1947 a sample of 350 people in Hamburg was asked: 'Has the dictatorial method of Government advantages over a democratic form?' More than half of the people asked (57.5 per cent) replied in the affirmative, with 19.1 per cent of the sample justifying their reply by saying that in the present crisis, strict organisation and planning were necessary.[53] In September of the same year, a British poll of 6,000 Germans of both sexes produced a result which, from the point of view of the occupying powers, was even more depressing. The survey asked whether National Socialism was a bad idea, or a good idea badly carried out, with the result that about 50 per cent of those interviewed thought that Nazism was a good idea badly carried out.[54]

The reliability and value of such opinion polls may be questioned, especially as other observations from the British side contradict their findings. Thus, for example, a consular report from Bremen sent to the Political Division of the Military Government at the end of 1948 suggests that

> the Germans are beginning to gain confidence at least in their local
> democratic institutions...and feel that democracy cannot be imposed by
> dictatorial methods. It would be a mistake, even a contradiction to
> describe this tendency as nationalistic, though in an entirely different sense
> nationalism has always been strong in Bremen, and has been more vocal
> of late amongst the Right Wing parties...The press and responsible
> opinion has uttered frequent warning against nationalist temptations and
> there has been more than a hint that not only the USSR but even the
> Western allies...may have encouraged nationalist manifestations in support
> of their Machiavellian ends.[55]

52. PRO, FO 1005/1700: CCG (BE), Intelligence Review no. 1, 12 December 1945.

53. PRO, FO 1014/190: CCG (BE), Reaction Report for June 1947 from Information Control Hamburg.

54. PRO, FO 1056/130: Morale Report no. 111A. See also an American report of September 1946 in A.J. Merritt and R.L. Merritt (eds) *Public Opinion in Occupied Germany: The OMGUS Surveys, 1945–1949* (Urbana, Ill., 1970), pp. 103–6.

55. PRO, FO 1049/1782: Political and General Report on Land Bremen for December Quarter 1948 to CCG (BE) Political Division, Berlin, p. 3.

However, just a few weeks later, a morale report by the Public Opinion Research Office pointed out that

> increasing anti-British sentiments and a revival of German nationalist feeling are reported on all sides, perhaps because it has become fashionable to recognize these symptoms which have, in fact, always been there. Such sentiments are now expressed with increasing confidence.[56]

II

How could the danger of a revival of aggressive nationalism in Germany be banished? How could a 'post-national' Germany be created – a Germany that, after the dreadful events of the period from 1933 to 1945, wanted to be accepted back into the family of nations? Looking back, the Bavarian politician Franz Josef Strauß, who was highly influential in shaping the history of the Federal Republic from the start, wrote: 'In 1945 and later...we asked ourselves: what is to happen now? Does this Germany have a future at all?'[57] The philosopher Karl Jaspers later reminded his readers of the major task which the Germans had faced after the end of the Third Reich:

> From 1945 the question was: will a German state now be born out of a change in political consciousness among statesmen and population? Or will it be an external order, without a source in the hearts and minds of the people, without a new political mentality?[58]

Many answers were given to this question in the immediate post-war period, especially by those Germans who gradually assumed political responsibility and, under the supervision of the occupying powers, attempted to lay the foundations for a democratic society in Germany. Although these answers differed in detail, they can in fact be reduced to a few guidelines which were intended to shape the future Germany. All sides in the Western zones, politicians as well as journalists, agreed that the unity of the German state should be preserved, that a federal constitution should be the objective, and that Germany's internal order should be based on the values of Western democracy. In its relations with its western neighbours Germany should aim for closer economic

---

56. PRO, FO 1056/131: CCG (BE), Public Opinion Research Office, German Morale Report no. 29, 1–31 January 1949, p. 1.

57. F. J. Strauß, *Die Erinnerungen* (Berlin, 1989), p. 60.

58. Jaspers, *Wohin treibt die Bundesrepublik?*, p. 67.

and political co-operation. In fact, these ideas had long been discussed by the Anglo-Saxon powers. They were now accepted in more or less modified form by the Germans. For example, the British Foreign Office memorandum of early 1945 cited above had predicted a revival of particularist feelings, which favoured a federal structure for Germany. It had also mentioned the incorporation of Germany into a new European order.[59]

The ideas put forward by the Americans and the British, later joined, only reluctantly, by the French, fell on fertile soil among the Germans after the surrender, if only because they seemed to point a way to the future and to provide a guarantee against the return of nationalism. The 'right to unity', much cited in internal German debates after 1945, was explicitly described as a desire that had nothing to do with nationalism, but a great deal to do with human rights. 'I reject any suggestion that this legal claim is nationalistic', wrote the journalist Ernst Friedlaender in 1947. 'Nationalism is nothing but unjustified national egoism. Someone who has been robbed and does not relinquish his property is no more an egoist than we are nationalists because we do not give up the right to our homeland.'[60] In his memoirs, the liberal politician Reinhold Maier reported on the beginnings of political life in Württemberg, in which he was actively involved. He remembered that some of his speeches had been received in silence. 'But when I came to the part about the German fatherland, the faces of my listeners lightened for a minute, and their workmen's hands relaxed into softer or louder applause.'[61]

Although Maier was very much a regional politician, he still clung to German unity. At the same time, however, he advocated a federal Germany, in which 'powerful *Bundesländer* would be members of a united Germany'.[62] Wilhelm Röpke wanted to go further than Maier. He suggested that the rebuilding of the state in Germany should be preceded by decentralisation, to be achieved by the dissolution of the Bismarckian Empire and the weakening of Prussia. He called for the buried tradition of the old German states to be resuscitated:

That means that the Rhineland, Westphalia, Hanover, Hesse,
Schleswig-Holstein, and the rest, must acquire the rank of independent

59. PRO, FO 371/46791/C 150, W.P. (45) 18: German Reactions to Defeat, p. 2 and p. 6.

60. E. Friedlaender, 'Der deutsche Standpunkt, 27 February 1947,' in Frei and Friedlaender (eds) *Ernst Friedlaender*, p. 98.

61. R. Maier, *Ein Grundstein wird gelegt. Die Jahre 1945–1947* (Tübingen, 1964), pp. 212–13.

62. Ibid., p. 162.

German States...This is the very cure that corresponds to our detailed diagnosis of the German malady. Germany must regain her character of a 'nation of nations', and return to the good traditions from which, three generations ago, she departed to her undoing.[63]

Germany's recovery, he claimed, depended essentially

on this *Einheitsdeutscher* – who is simply the *Bismarckdeutscher* with his dangerous mentality – giving place once more to the true type of the Bavarian, Hanoverian, Rhinelander, or Württemberger.[64]

Röpke believed that conditions in Germany favoured confederalism, for

Munich, thank Heaven, is still Bavarian, Hamburg is still itself, Cologne is still Rhenish, and we can only congratulate ourselves if they are determined to remain so.[65]

In Röpke's view the aim of Germany's political transformation was 'the constitution of a genuine German *confederation*'.[66]

Unlike Röpke, however, the new political parties in their first statements unequivocally advocated a federal rather than a confederal structure for the new German state. The platform of the Christian Democratic Party in the Rhineland and in Westphalia, published in September 1945, states simply: 'The form of state appropriate to the German people is the *Reich* as a federal state.'[67] In 1946 the Bavarian Christian-Social Union called for a political structure of Germany 'on a federal basis'.[68] The Social Democrats wanted the same thing:

The German republic of the future should be built on *Länder,* which do not see their highest purpose in their own existence, but which regard themselves only as the building blocks of a higher national order.[69]

The Liberals, finally, in February 1946 were working with guidelines which stated:

This state is to be built upon the broadest foundations, starting from the bottom. At the lowest level the *Gemeinden* are to administer their own affairs independently; above them the *Kreise* should do the same; and, at a

---

63. Röpke, *The German Question*, p. 186.
64. Ibid., p. 190.
65. Ibid.
66. Ibid., p. 207.
67. Printed in T. Stammen (ed.) *Einigkeit und Recht und Freiheit: Westdeutsche Innen-politik 1945–1955* (Munich, 1965), p. 87.
68. Ibid., p. 99. See also Strauß, *Erinnerungen*, p. 100.
69. Political Guidelines of the SPD, May 1946, in Stammen (ed.) *Einigkeit*, p. 124. Also C. Schmid, *Erinnerungen* (Berne, 1979), p. 293.

higher level, the *Länder*. The limits of autonomy are to be set by the *Reich*. The *Reich* alone directs and makes policy.[70]

In March 1946 Reinhold Maier, who in the meantime had become minister president of Württemberg-Baden, explained: 'We know what we are aiming for – namely, a federation with considerable powers for the centre, but without an emasculation of the *Länder*.[71] Attempts by conservative circles in Bavaria to turn their *Land* into an autonomous state and to return to a constitutional monarchy under the House of Wittelsbach remained a rather curious episode without wider significance.[72] Opinion polls conducted in 1947 and 1948 revealed that the overwhelming majority of Germans in the Western occupation zones wanted a unified state on a federal basis.[73]

Just as they agreed on the organisation of Germany as a federal state, the major parties and their leading representatives were also largely unanimous on Germany's commitment to Europe after 1945. It is well known that for Konrad Adenauer, Germany's integration into the West was the highest priority. After his first visit to Bonn in November 1949, the US secretary of state Dean Acheson summed up his impressions of Adenauer thus:

> I was struck by the imagination and wisdom of his approach. His great concern was to integrate Germany completely into Western Europe. Indeed, he gave this end priority over reunification of unhappily divided Germany.[74]

Four years earlier, in October 1945, Adenauer had already spoken out in favour of creating a German federal state to consist of the Western occupation zones. The economy of the West German area, he suggested, should be closely linked with those of France and Belgium, 'in order to create common economic interests'.[75] Adenauer also wanted the Netherlands, Luxemburg, and if possible, Britain, to be involved in this association.[76] Thus the origins of the later European Coal and

70. Stammen (ed.) *Einigkeit*, p. 108.

71. Quoted in K.-J. Matz, *Reinhold Maier (1889–1971: Eine politische Biographie* (Düsseldorf, 1989), p. 309.

72. See Walter Dorn's notes of February 1946: W. Dorn, *Inspektionsreisen in der US-Zone: Notizen, Denkschriften und Erinnerungen aus dem Nachlaß*, ed. L. Niethammer (Stuttgart, 1973). Also Strauß, *Erinnerungen*, pp. 99–100.

73. E. Noelle and E.P. Neumann, *Jahrbuch der öffentlichen Meinung 1947–1955* (Allensbach, 1975 3rd edn), p. 145.

74. D. Acheson, *Present at the Creation: My Years in the State Department* (London, 1969), p. 340.

75. Adenauer, *Erinnerungen 1945–1953*, vol. 1, p. 35.

76. Enclosure with a letter by Adenauer to the Lord Mayor of Duisburg, 31 October 1945, in H.P. Mensing (ed.) *Adenauer: Briefe 1945–1947* (Berlin, 1983), p. 130.

Steel Community and the European Common Market, which Adenauer was to help found, are already visible here in 1945.

The leader of the other major party in post-war Germany, Kurt
Schumacher of the SPD, also strongly supported German integration
into Europe. The SPD's programme of 5 October 1945, which was
largely composed by Schumacher, states that the SPD

> is aware that in order to achieve vital European economic unity both
> Germany and the world need to create adequate political forms. As
> Montesquieu once said: 'Europe is simply a nation which is made up of
> several nations.'[77]

In June 1946 Schumacher wrote:

> Social democracy does not want a new, integral Germany as a new
> nationalism. It wants to see Germany as part of a new European
> confederation from the start…Today something that has always been true has
> become clear, namely that national and international are not opposites…The
> greatest enemy of the nation is not the international idea, but nationalism.[78]

A few weeks previously Schumacher had stated:

> A new Germany must not be a nationalistic Germany. It must fit into the
> framework of European needs right from the start. As far as we are
> concerned, we Germans are prepared to give up several potential aspects
> of future sovereignty in favour of this new Europe. But we ask the same
> of the other European countries.[79]

As a public opinion poll held by the British Military Government in
April 1948, for example, showed, the German people strongly supported a policy of European integration.[80]

III

The rejection of national categories by most Germans after the turning-point of 1945, the distance they wanted to keep to such matters

---

77. Stammen (ed.) *Einigkeit*, p. 117.

78. K. Schumacher, 'Die Sozialdemokratie im Kampf (June 1946)', in Schumacher, *Nach dem Zusammenbruch. Gedanken über Demokratie und Sozialismus* (Hamburg, 1948), p. 162.

79. Schumacher, 'Deutschland braucht den Sozialismus (March 1946)', in ibid., pp. 133–4.

80. PRO, FO 1012/818, CCG (BE), Public Opinion Research Office, Information and Statistics, Report no. 7: German Views on Marshall Plan, United Nations, Western Union and Bizonia, 23 June 1948, p. 1.

and the aversion they felt for them are vividly reflected in their attitudes towards national symbols. The choice of a 'national anthem' after the establishment of the Federal Republic is a graphic example. The bitter realisation that their national feelings had been misused by a criminal regime profoundly affected the national consciousness of the Germans. After 1945 they could no longer have a naive national feeling such as that which had been characteristic of the nineteenth century. An uncomplicated relationship with nationalism was no longer possible for them. It has recently been claimed that the lack of a well-developed German national feeling is 'an anomaly requiring explanation' in a European context.[81] Undoubtedly, recent German history and the thorough discreditation of national values since the collapse of the Third Reich provide some of the explanation.

Insecurity about national symbols, discontinuities in their use, and doubts about their general validity are, in fact, nothing new in the history of Germany since the creation of a national state in 1871.[82] After the experience of National Socialism, however, the national symbols which had been in general use until then had become almost devoid of any meaning. The creation of new symbols and their acceptance by the German people was therefore a protracted process. When the Federal Republic of Germany was founded in 1949, agreement was most easily reached about a flag for the new state. Without a great deal of discussion in the Parliamentary Council, the black, red and gold flag of the 1848–9 revolution and the Weimar Republic was accepted as the *Bundesflagge* (Art. 22 of the Basic Law). In October 1949 the constitution of the other German state created out of the ruins of the Third Reich declared that black, red and gold were also the 'colours of the German Democratic Republic'. Since the wars of liberation against Napoleon in the early nineteenth century these colours had symbolised the democratic tradition in German history.

The choice of a national anthem for the Federal Republic, a tradition which the politicians wanted to retain, proved to be much more difficult.[83] In the process, the fact that the German state had not had an official national anthem at all until 1922 was forgotten. After Bismarck established the Reich the main contenders were 'The Watch on

81. Thus H. Mommsen, 'Nationalismus und Nationalstaatsgedanke in Deutschland', *Journal Geschichte* 6 (1990), p. 47.

82. See the pioneering study by T. Schieder, *Das Deutsche Kaiserreich von 1871 als Nationalstaat* (Cologne and Opladen, 1961). Also E. Fehrenbach, 'Über die Bedeutung der politischen Symbole im Nationalstaat', *Historische Zeitschrift* 213 (1971), pp. 296–357.

83. For the long debate on a German national day see H. Hattenhauer, *Deutsche Nationalsymbole: Zeichen und Bedeutung* (Munich, 1984), pp. 129–35.

the Rhine' ('*Die Wacht am Rhein*'), and the Prussian royal anthem, which had been adopted as the imperial anthem, '*Heil Dir im Siegerkranz*', sung to the same tune as 'God save the Queen'. Not until the end of the nineteenth century did Hoffmann von Fallersleben's 'Song of Germany', set to a melody by Joseph Haydn, become popular.[84] And not until 1922, that is under the Weimar Republic, was the 'Song of Germany' (*Deutschlandlied*) declared the official German national anthem by the President of the Reich, Friedrich Ebert.[85] During the Third Reich, it was largely discredited by the fact that it was mostly sung together with the *Horst-Wessel-Lied*, the party song of the National Socialists. In the Control Council Law no. 154 of July 1945 the Allies prohibited the singing not only of Nazi songs but also of 'German anthems' in general, in order 'to prevent...the continuation and revival of military instruction'.[86]

At the end of 1949, as Allied policy for Germany changed, this prohibition was lifted and discussion of the problem of a German national anthem began almost immediately in the new Federal Republic. After all, it was argued, the Federal Republic was one state among other states, all of which clung to their national symbols, and the new German state could not simply ignore that. In September 1951 an opinion poll was held in the Federal Republic of Germany, and 73 per cent of those asked were in favour of the reintroduction of the 'Song of Germany' as a national anthem; 30 per cent of them voted for the third verse, which begins with the lines 'Unity and Right and Freedom/For the German Fatherland', whereas only 25 per cent favoured the better-known first verse ('*Deutschland, Deutschland über alles*').[87] Only a year earlier there had been a scandal when Adenauer, the Federal Chancellor, had called for the third verse of the 'Song of Germany' to be sung at the end of a large political meeting in Berlin.

84. Schieder, *Das Deutsche Kaiserreich, p. 75.*

85. H. Tümmler, '*Deutschland, Deutschland über alles': Zur Geschichte und Problematik unserer Nationalhymne* (Cologne and Vienna, 1979). Hattenhauer, *Nationalsymbole*, pp. 59–61. U. Mader, 'Wie das "Deutschlandlied" 1922 Nationalhymne wurde', *Zeitschrift für Geschichtswissenschaft* 38 (1990), pp. 1,088–100. According to Mader the British government played a role when the decision on the German national anthem was made. In June 1920 it had asked the German government 'what the German national anthem was at the present time'. The foreign minister Walter Simons suggested in the *Reichstag* 'to give a simple and honest answer to the British government: at the moment the German people has no national anthem'. He then gave a number of reasons to explain this curious fact (p. 1,091).

86. See O. Busch, *125 Jahre – 'Deutschland, Deutschland über alles'* (Munich, 1967), p. 26.

87. Noelle and Neumann, *Jahrbuch*, p. 159.

On that occasion the Western Commandants in Berlin had pointedly remained seated, while prominent Social Democratic politicians had left the assembly hall.[88] In the public debate of 1951 and 1952, a national anthem was often declared superfluous, and frequent calls were made for it to be replaced by a supranational European anthem.[89] The Federal President at the time, Theodor Heuss, publicly declared himself against using even the third verse of the old 'Song of Germany' as a national anthem because in his opinion 'the profound turning-point in the history of our people and our state calls for new symbols'. He wanted to avoid restoring nineteenth-century political ideas and movements.[90]

But from 1950 on it was clear that the majority of the West German people saw the third verse of the 'Song of Germany' as their national anthem.[91] Theodor Heuss's attempts to popularise a completely new German anthem had had little success. Against this background Konrad Adenauer finally prevailed against Heuss's misgivings. As the result of an exchange of correspondence between Adenauer and Heuss in April and May 1952, published in the Federal Government's official Bulletin, the third verse of the 'Song of Germany' was accepted as the national anthem of the Federal Republic of Germany. Some contemporaries saw this – perhaps correctly – as the symptom of an unintended, and fundamentally undesired, national restoration. But the rather bureaucratic and unsentimental way in which a decision had been arrived at about the necessity for, and opportunity to introduce, an official national anthem, can equally be seen as something else. It can be seen as a symptom of the political culture and mentality of a German people that had emerged, purified, from the excesses of nationalism.

SUGGESTIONS FOR FURTHER READING

M. Balfour, *West Germany: A Contemporary History* (London, 1982).
D. Botting, *In the Ruins of the Reich* (London, 1985).

88. M. Overesch, 'Grenzen der Erneuerung: Die bundesdeutsche Nationalhymne', *Journal Geschichte* 1 (1988), p. 12. Tümmler, '*Deutschland*', p. 17.

89. Overesch, 'Grenzen der Erneuerung', p. 14.

90. Heuss to Adenauer, 2 May 1952, in *Bulletin des Presse- und Informationsamtes der Bundesregierung* 51/6 May 1952, p. 537.

91. Overesch, 'Grenzen der Erneuerung', pp. 16–17.

R. Dahrendorf, *Society and Democracy in Germany* (London, 1968).

R. Ebsworth, *Restoring Democracy in Germany: The British Contribution* (London, 1960).

A. Hearnden (ed.) *The British in Germany: Educational Reconstruction after 1945* (London, 1978).

L.E. Jones and K. Jarausch (eds) *In Search of a Liberal Germany: Studies in the History of German Liberalism from 1789 to the Present* (New York, Oxford and Munich, 1990).

A. Mann, *Comeback: Germany 1945-1952* (London, 1980).

B. Marshall, *The Origins of Post-War German Politics* (London, 1988).

T. Sharp, *The Wartime Alliance and the Zonal Division of Germany* (Oxford, 1975).

I.D. Turner (ed.) *Reconstruction in Post-War Germany: British Occupation Policy and the Western Zones, 1945–1955* (Oxford, 1989).

H.A. Turner, *The Two Germanies since 1945* (New Haven, Conn., 1987)

R. Willett, *The Americanisation of Germany, 1945–1949* (London, 1989).

CHAPTER TEN

Nation, state and political culture in divided Germany 1945–90

Mary Fulbrook

The excesses of German nationalism under Adolf Hitler achieved the destruction of the German Reich: the severance of the recently united Austria (since 1938), the loss of eastern territories of Prussia to Poland and the Soviet Union, and the division of what remained into two separate states, divided from one another by an almost impermeable 'Iron Curtain' which also served to divide the post-war world. With the expulsion of millions of ethnic Germans from their former homes in the east, and the imposition of radically new political systems and ideologies in the newly created states, the chances for the long-term success of post-war arrangements might at first sight have seemed slim. Yet for over forty years the reduction and division of Germany appeared to have provided the basis for an almost unprecedented period of political stability in central Europe: surviving longer than the Weimar Republic and the Third Reich put together, the two Germanies developed into model instances of their respective socio-political types. It took major upheavals originating elsewhere in the eastern Europe of the later 1980s to inaugurate a revolution in East Germany which finally brought down the Communist regime and placed the issue of German unity back on the serious political agenda in 1989–90.

What role did perceptions or new definitions of national identity play in the political dynamics of the two Germanies? How far did the imposition of new political forms actually serve to transform patterns of political culture among Germans, East and West? And what have been the implications of changing patterns of political culture for the relative stability of the two Germanies over forty years, and for the dramatic developments of 1989–90, which have, with astonishing speed, sealed the effective end of the post-war period?

'NATIONAL IDENTITIES' IN A DIVIDED NATION

The issue of identity has plagued post-war Germans, East and West. Neither state, at the time of foundation, was considered to be permanent; there was therefore the outstanding question of the survival of a transcending German nation, which would ultimately at some time be reunified. On the other hand, both states – perhaps the West more than the East – did in fact demote national unity in favour of integration and stabilisation in their respective blocs. Thus new forms of 'national myth' had to be developed, which both retained the links with the past – representing the present as the only legitimate successor state – and yet defined the particular part of the divided present in distinctive terms, to legitimise the partial state as representative of the whole. This process was further confused by issues concerning the immediate Nazi past: the explanation of its location in the longer sweep of German history, the degrees of responsibility and guilt for the Holocaust, the extent to which the successor states had made clean breaks with the discredited past, or were burdened by continuities or inadequate overcoming and mastering of the past. To some extent, both Germanies had difficulty with developing new forms of national pride precisely because of the Third Reich, and sought different paths of escape from this problem: whether through attempted submersion of German nationalism in wider western European integration (in the West), or by historical simplification and disavowal of responsibility (in the East).

Such processes of attempted legitimation and self-definition took place under very different political constraints and within different social and intellectual contexts in each of the two Germanies. In the German Democratic Republic (GDR), views of the past and present were very much state-sponsored (or at least self- and state-censored) varying with the degrees of relative liberalisation at different times in the GDR's history. In the Federal Republic of Germany (FRG), debate has been much freer, a greater diversity of views more evident, and questions of national identity have been hotly contested political terrain.

In the FRG, during the 1950s there was a degree of 'collective amnesia', combined with widespread efforts to escape a compromised past by seeking submergence in a transcendent, European identity. From the early 1960s interpretations of German history took on a particularly heated and political significance. From the Fischer controversy over German responsibility for the First World War onwards, the West German historical profession has been characterised by considerable diversity and sharply stated differences of approach. 'New orthodoxies' in such fields as social history, the history of everyday life, and feminist history have arisen to challenge previously dominant approaches. There has also been a proliferation of interest in regional and local history, which has spread beyond the bounds of the historical profession as lay members of history workshops have explored forgotten aspects of the immediate environment.

The political significance of historical interpretations in West Germany was revealed to an extraordinary degree in the so-called *Historikerstreit* (dispute among the historians) of the mid- and later 1980s. Simplifying what has been an extremely muddy debate, characterised by vitriolic accusations, misquotations and misrepresentations, one may broadly summarise the essential underlying thrust as follows. A number of largely conservative historians sought to relativise the crimes of the Nazi past by attempting to locate them within a wider context. In part this was a context of comparison with other evils, arguing that as Germans were not uniquely evil, therefore they had no need to be uniquely ashamed of their national identity. In part, Nazi acts were seen as responses to the crimes of others, as in Ernst Nolte's arguments linking Hitler's policies to Stalin's crimes. In response, a range of critics of this new conservative revisionism sought to show how little supporting evidence there was for many of the (frequently rather vaguely phrased) hypotheses, and also what were the political and moral implications of these new ways of whitewashing, justifying or relativising the past.[1] There was a close connection between this debate – carried out not only in learned journals and books, but also in the national press and public debate – and the new conservatism of West Germany under Chancellor Kohl, given heightened significance in the run-up to the 1987 elections. We shall turn to the question of the impact or popular importance of national identity in a moment.

In rather different ways, the role of history and historical consciousness had political significance in the GDR too. In particular, a twofold process can be observed in the period after *Ostpolitik* (the policy of seeking agreements with the GDR and other Eastern European states pursued by the FRG). On the one hand, there was a conscious effort

---

1. For balanced introductions to the debates in English see R.J. Evans, *In Hitler's Shadow: West German Historians and the Attempt to Escape from the Nazi Past* (London, 1989); C. Maier, *The Unmasterable Past: History, Holocaust and German National Identity* (Cambridge, Mass, 1988); and the section on the *Historikerstreit* in *German History*, 6/1 (1988). For a flavour of biased political diatribe masquerading as 'academic' argument, from a right-wing point of view, see D. Bark and D. Gress, *A History of West Germany*, vol. 2, *Democracy and its Discontents* (Oxford, 1989), pp. 415–44.

in the early years of the Honecker regime to establish a form of cultural *Abgrenzung* (demarcation), separating a distinctive GDR identity from the wider German identity which would underline common links with the West. This was essentially an attempt at a psychological and cultural distancing from the West at a time when physical contacts and communications between the two states had been made easier. Thus, in the 1974 revision of the GDR constitution, references to 'German' were replaced wherever possible by 'GDR'. (Some curious anomalies were allowed to remain, such as the rather startling *Deutsche Reichsbahn* on the somewhat geriatric East German trains.) On the other hand, particularly from the late 1970s and early 1980s, there was a marked change in official GDR views of German history. The *whole* of German history was now terrain to be appropriated by the GDR, with a distinction being made between 'traditions' and 'historical legacies' or 'inheritances' (*Tradition* and *Erbe*), such that only certain aspects were viewed as 'progressive' and to be built upon. The resurrection or re-evaluation of previously demoted historical figures – Luther, Frederick the Great, Bismarck – and of phases and elements of German history (notably that of Prussia), provided evidence of a new attempt to anchor the German people in a form of nationalist legitimacy or pride in their national identity. This carried with it the risk of emphasising a common German-ness with the West – particularly when parallel exhibitions and celebrations (for example, of Berlin and of Luther) were mounted in competition over common anniversaries.[2]

Officially in the 1950s and 1960s both states were formally committed to reunification. The FRG, in the Hallstein Doctrine, refused even to recognise the legitimacy of a separate state in what it continued to call 'the Zone'. After *Ostpolitik* there was essentially agreement to differ. The GDR adopted a class theory of the nation which argued for the development of two different nations in the two Germanies, while the FRG view was that there were 'two German states in one German nation'. Notwithstanding official views, it is clear that the relationship between the two Germanies was quite distinctive. The GDR recognised the value and importance of its special relationship with its richer twin, despite its assertions of separateness, while the FRG increasingly paid only (rather embarrassed) lip-service to the notion of re-unification. Nor were the dynamics of the relationship between the two Germanies always just a mirror of those between the two super-powers, as the rapprochement between the two Germanies

---

2. I have discussed these issues at greater length in M. Fulbrook, 'From *Volksgemeinschaft* to divided nation', *Historical Research* 62/148 (1989), pp. 193–213, where further references can be obtained.

in the early to mid–1980s at a time of increased tension between the two super-powers illustrates. Whatever the debates over partial identities, some concept of a wider whole and common bonds remained clearly alive – even with Erich Honecker when he returned in 1987 to visit his homeland in the Saar.

Thus in neither Germany, it may be suggested, was there an entirely successful resolution of the problem of promoting a partial national identity as well as sustaining wider notions of being 'German'. Let us now turn to the issue of whether, in practice, the two Germanies had in fact been developing rather distinctive profiles of popular political culture, whatever the official views of national identity.

DIVERGING PATTERNS OF POLITICAL CULTURE

More important than official views or public debates in shaping popular patterns of political orientation have been the actual political structures of the two Germanies in the period 1949 to 1989. Living in different environments, subjected to different pressures and constraints, perceiving different opportunities and harbouring different aspirations, people in the two Germanies *did* in fact develop rather different sorts of political culture in the period up to 1989. There might be some common German identity in theory; but in practice, what one can observe is an actual growing apart, which, if the division had been sustained for another couple of generations, might have made the two Germanies as 'foreign' to each other, or as convinced of their differentness and separate identities, as – over a very long historical period – do the German-speaking Swiss, or, over a more recent historical period, the Austrians. Not only outward appearances, so noticeable in November 1989 as East Germans streamed across to stare in amazement at the consumer goods of the West after the opening of the Berlin Wall (BMWs and Mercedes versus Trabants and Wartburgs, fashionable affluence versus blue jeans and denim or black leather jackets), but also modes of behaviour, attitudes, patterns of 'being-in-the-world', developed in different ways in the two Germanies.

Such differences are extraordinarily difficult to define, to identify and to explain. Here only a preliminary periodisation and characterisation can be suggested. Clearly, there is not even a simple, homogenous base-line from which the development of the differences can be traced. In what were the Soviet and Western Zones of occupied Germany after the defeat of the Third Reich, there were a wide range of political and cultural traditions and attitudes. These were further complicated by post-war population movements, and by the coming to terms with new post-war conditions. Whatever the degree to which German society had or had not been permeated by any 'Nazi' ideology (itself a difficult question to answer), it is clear that there was only a minority of die-hard Nazis after 1945.[3] While a minority of democratic Germans were politically active in the occupation period – contributing to the foundation or resurrection of German political parties, the re-emergence of intellectual and cultural life – probably the most prevalent preoccupation of a majority of Germans at this time was sheer material survival, amid the ruins and rubble. (This view is borne out by Peter Alter's chapter in this book.) A very widespread attitude was a determination to keep out of politics, for fear of 'getting one's fingers burnt'.[4]

After the foundation of the two Germanies, developing differences can be observed. In the West, attitudes more favourable to democracy correlated with the economic successes of Adenauer's Germany. While in the mid-1950s, many Germans still assented to authoritarian, monarchist and even pro-Hitler statements in opinion surveys (such as agreeing with the assertion that Hitler would have been one of the greatest statesmen ever, had it not been for the war), by the early 1960s more democratic sentiments were expressed by greater proportions of the population. Political scientists at this time suggested there was an increasing pragmatic support for democracy, with a sense – in contrast to the association of economic chaos with democracy in the Weimar Republic – that now the 'system worked'. The later 1960s were characterised by increased polarisation of varieties of political culture, with hostility between an emerging new left and what were viewed as materialistic, bourgeois *Spießbürger* who refused to come to terms with the Nazi past. The importance of generational conflict, which in Germany took on a particularly acute and

3. On popular opinion in the Third Reich, see the by now classic studies by I. Kershaw, *Popular Opinion and Political Dissent in the Third Reich* (Oxford, 1983) and *The 'Hitler Myth': Image and Reality in the Third Reich* (Oxford, 1987). For the immediate post-war period see Chapter 9 by Peter Alter in this volume.

4. There is as yet no full account of the transformation of popular political opinions after the war. These comments are based on a reading of the reports of the Military Government (such as the OMGUS attitude surveys), the post-war press (such as the *Süddeutsche Zeitung*, one of the first German newspapers to be licensed in the American zone, the early editions of which provide interesting insights into the attempted reconstruction of democracy) and of a range of auto-biographical material located in the Institut für Zeitgeschichte, Munich.

pointed form in confronting 'the sins of the fathers', should not be under-estimated. This polarisation in many ways continued through the 1970s and 1980s. However, extremist views – left and right – were held only by minority groups (even if these minorities committed acts of terrorism or staged demonstrations and agitated in ways affecting large numbers of people). The broadest spectrum was encompassed by citizens assenting to the procedures of parliamentary democracy, with a marked development of citizen participation in democratic processes compared with earlier decades.[5]

The pattern of development was different in the GDR. In the 1950s there were many who, in grumbling fashion, either tried to come to terms with their new circumstances or left for the economically more attractive West. Among the politically active, those whose commitments were at odds with the new hard-line Marxist-Leninist orthodoxy of SED leader Walter Ulbricht were systematically purged: already in the merger of the KPD and SPD to form the SED in 1946, then again after the SED became a 'party of a new type' (following Moscow) in 1948; then after the uprising of June 1953, and again in 1956 and 1958 there were purges of those whose more humanistic approaches (for a 'Third Way' form of democratic socialism, for example) were not in line with Ulbricht's fairly Stalinist views. In the 1960s, some political scientists – notably P.C. Ludz – perceived the development of more positive appoaches to the regime. Particularly under the New Economic System (1963–70), and with the new status accorded to technical experts, there was, on this view, the development of a more career-oriented achievement society, in which people sought to make the best of a seemingly unalterable situation. The building of the Berlin Wall, closing the last means of exit to the West, in 1961, obviously also contributed to this reorientation. While the economy was recentralised under Honecker from 1971, the focus on consumer satisfaction and the improvement of living conditions through social policy measures (for example, on housing, or maternity provisions), as well as the increased ease of contacts with the West after *Ostpolitik*, contributed to a continuation of this process of learning to live with the regime. Dissenting intellectuals, such as Havemann and Bahro, were relative easily isolated (through house arrest or exile

5. For a lucid summary of such developments see D. P. Conradt, *The German Polity* (London, 1986, 3rd edn); for earlier analyses, S. Verba, 'Germany: the remaking of political culture', in L. Pye and S. Verba, *Political Culture and Political Development* (Princeton, NJ, 1965). For intriguing details of opinions and attitudes on different issues over the years, see the volumes edited by E. Noelle and E.P. Neumann, *Jahrbücher der öffentlichen Meinung* (Allensbach: Verlag für Demoskopie, series).

to the West) and did not gain mass followings. Even the widespread protests about the expulsion of the subversive singer Wolf Biermann in 1976 had as a consequence little more than increased disaffection (and loss of party membership) for many writers, with increased numbers choosing to leave for the West in the later 1970s.[6]

What was particularly interesting about developments in the GDR was the formation of what Günter Gaus called a 'niche society', a retreatist culture characterised by a double life: conformity in public, authenticity in private. This retreatism was in many ways similar to the adaptations to living with an intolerant and intrusive regime which many people developed in Nazi Germany.[7] Clearly there were many differences between the degrees and modes of intolerance of the Third Reich and the GDR, as well as their intrinsic aims and ideals. The GDR was obviously far more humanitarian in at least some of its aspirations – towards emancipation and equality – even if in practice this seemed, under the circumstances of bureaucratic state socialism, to have entailed an unacceptable repression of liberty. Leaving aside these wider questions, what is of interest here is that the retreatist mode of political orientation actually helped to stabilise the East German regime over twenty-five years or so (from the early 1960s to the mid-1980s). Combined with the relative isolation of dissent – and the ease of exporting awkward individuals to the West – the prevalence of the retreatist mode, in combination with at least a minimum of material satisfaction, resulted in a degree of domestic political stability.

From the late 1970s, and especially from the mid-1980s, qualitatively new forms of political orientation developed, in ways which have yet to be fully explored by western analysts. An important turning-point came with the Church–state agreement of 1978, in which the role of the Church as the only autonomous social institution in the GDR was officially recognised. It now became possible, under the wing of the Church, for wide-ranging discussions to take place about alternatives to the prevailing orthodox views. In the early 1980s, the Protestant churches became important as an umbrella for the emergence and development of unofficial peace initiatives, which differed from the official, state-sponsored peace movement in that they op-

6. See for example P.C. Ludz, *The German Democratic Republic from the Sixties to the Seventies* (Harvard Centre for International Affairs, Occasional Paper no. 26, November 1970); R. Woods, *Opposition in the GDR under Honecker, 1971–1985* (London, 1986).

7. G. Gaus, *Wo Deutschland liegt* (Munich, 1986). I have developed at greater length a theory of the relationship between intrusive states and retreatist forms of political culture in my article 'The state and the transformation of political legitimacy in East and West Germany since 1945', *Comparative Studies in Society and History*, 29/2 (1987), pp. 211–44.

posed Warsaw Pact as well as NATO nuclear missiles. From the mid-1980s, these dissenting groups proliferated in two important respects. They became more numerous, and began to organise outside the protective framework of the Church, and they began to deal, in a specialised fashion, with an increasing range of issues, concerning themselves not only with peace, but also with human rights and environmental questions. These groups formed the background to the emergence, in the late summer of 1989, of new parties and organisations – notably the New Forum – which, for the first time in the history of East German dissent, sought official status and concerned themselves with the whole gamut of problems with which governments have to deal, including the reorganisation of the economy and the political system itself. On the evidence of some of these activists, who had been brought up in the authoritarian system designed to produce conformists, it was extremely difficult to learn how to be democratic, to speak and debate freely, to tolerate differences of opinion, and to pressurise for change in a peaceful manner. The role of the Protestant churches should not be underestimated in helping to shape the distinctive characteristics of secular dissent in the late 1980s.[8]

While recognising the crucial importance of such developments, it must be observed that such activities and orientations were characteristic of only a minority of East Germans. Private grumbling combined with public conformity remained the most predominant political orientation for most, even in the summer of 1989. We shall come back to developments in the revolutionary autumn in a moment.

THE IMPLICATIONS OF NATIONAL IDENTITY AND POLITICAL CULTURE FOR REGIME STABILITY AND CHANGE

Patterns of popular political culture are but one element among many in explaining stability and change in different types of regime. Popular support for a regime may not be as central to stability in practice as is often assumed. Political passivity and indifference may be as important

8. These developments have yet to be fully explored. My comments here are based on discussions with some of those involved, both among East German dissenters and Westerners who worked with them.

in making certain developments possible, as opposition may be in deflecting other developments. There is as yet no definitive interpretation of either the causes or consequences of patterns of political culture: frequently, cultural elements are taken as givens in any historical explanation. Here, some suggestions may be made concerning the location of the developments sketched above in a wider framework for interpreting the dynamics of the two Germanies in the various stages of their history.

Division and consolidation of the new regimes

First of all, it can be suggested that notions of a German nation transcending the divided states played very little role in political developments – and particularly the consolidation of division – in the early period. Even before the foundation of the two states, German politicians in the Soviet and Western Zones were cooperating with their respective occupying powers in the processes of socio-economic separation and eventually political division. (A particular example might be the Munich conference of German *Land* Prime Ministers in June 1947, when there was clearly no will to reach agreement among the Germans, or to compromise to a greater degree in the interests of unity than the respective occupying powers were prepared to do.) In the early 1950s Adenauer's determined policies of western integration took precedence over any prospect of unity, even when reunification was quite possibly negotiable in the spring of 1952. Although Adenauer's actions were certainly in line with the policies of the Western Allies, they were not determined by the latter; it was his own decision – supported by the Americans and British – not to take Stalin's first note seriously.[9] In June 1953 the West Germans were content merely to observe the East German uprising, rather than intervene to aid their East German brethren: again, stabilisation of the status quo was preferred to any riskier strategy. The same might be said of the Berlin crisis at the time of the building of the Berlin Wall in August 1961. National unity was effectively jettisoned by the West German political leadership in favour of the benefits brought by stability, economic growth, and incorporation in the western part of a divided world. In the East, it might be said that there was less leeway for independent

9. See particularly R. Steininger, 'Germany after 1945: divided and integrated or united and neutral?', *German History* 7/1 (1989), pp. 5–18, for a discussion of early 'missed opportunities'.

decision-making on the foreign policy front: East German Communists were clearly more at the behest of Moscow than West German politicians were of the Western powers. Nevertheless, given the fact that East German Communist leaders would certainly lose their own political position of dominance in a united Germany, they had very little reason to be interested in the effective dissolution of their state in a united democratic Germany.

Nor, it might be suggested, did popular notions of national identity, or patterns of political orientation to the new regimes, play much of a role in their initial rather successful consolidation. Sheer growing affluence in the period of the 'economic miracle' played the greatest role in bringing West Germans around to supporting the idea of democracy in principle. Other factors too were important in the early phase of West German democracy. These included Adenauer's policy of incorporating former Nazis – including many in high places – in the new regime, thus avoiding a potential breeding ground of serious opposition. Anti-Communism in the era of the Cold War was also a useful transitional ideology. The reconstruction of western Europe more broadly – in the context of the Marshall Plan, the birth of the European Economic Community, and the security framework of NATO – also served to integrate and stabilise the new West Germany in a new international framework. These 'external' factors, along with the material successes of the early years as well as the at least pragmatic commitment of various economic, intellectual and moral elites to West German democracy (in sharp contrast to elite attacks on Weimar democracy), together help explain the early consolidation of the new regime in the West.

While East Germany certainly did not experience the spectacular economic successes of the West – and indeed suffered considerably, from reparations, from reorientation towards a less developed set of economies in Eastern Europe, and from the loss of skilled labour in the flood of refugees to the West in the 1950s – it too experienced a certain qualified consolidation in the early period. Most notably, Ulbricht, whose position up to 1953 had been by no means unassailable, was able to confirm his own hold on power and remove those who held less hard-line views from positions of influence in the SED. The relative discipline and uniformity of official views in the SED proved to be a major factor in its subsequent hold on power over the next three decades. More important than any assent to the new East German regime on the part of the masses were at this time the threat of coercion, the difficulty of alternative options, the amnesty for former small Nazis, and the still possible escape route to the West – as well as the hope that the division was impermanent, and would not long remain. From August 1961, the option of attempted escape was too risky for all but a handful.

The 'established' phase

One could perhaps denote the period from the early 1960s to the late 1980s as the 'established' phase in the history of divided Germany. During this period, the prospect of reunification appeared increasingly remote, the nature of a divided post-war world, under the respective spheres of influence of the two super-powers, increasingly 'normal'. Division appeared to have given Germans a stability never achieved in a united German nation–state; and, in the longest period of peace experienced in Europe in the twentieth century, division seemed to many (particularly West Germans!) an acceptable price to pay. Neither Germany was without domestic tensions; yet each, in different ways, appeared to be a system intrinsically capable of reproduction and development, rather than one which – like the Third Reich – was inherently destructive and self-destructive, or building up internal tensions inevitably leading to a revolutionary conflagration. Given the ultimate demise of the GDR with the revolution of 1989 this point is worth reiterating: had it not been for wider changes in the Eastern European context, the collapse of the East German Communist state from internal tensions alone would have been exceedingly unlikely.

West German democracy was not without its difficulties during this period. Right-wing extremism was constantly viewed with anxiety, from the *Land* electoral successes of the NPD in the later 1960s to the rise of the Republicans and their local election triumphs in Berlin and Frankfurt in 1989. Racism, largely directed against the foreign worker (*Gastarbeiter*) population, provoked concern. The terrorism of the Red Army Faction was a continuing, at times major, if intermittent, problem from the early 1970s. State measures to deal with extremism, encroaching arguably on to the legitimate bounds of democratic debate (such as the *Berufsverbot* implied by the 1972 Decree Concerning Radicals whereby political considerations would influence appointments in the public service sector), contributed to the polarisation between Left and Right (and to some extent between younger and older generations) evident from the late 1960s. The rise of citizens' initiatives and pressure group politics – over environmental and peace questions, and particular local issues – as well as the challenge mounted to established political parties by the emergence of the Greens on to the national political scene, have been viewed by some as thorns in the flesh of 'sensible' democracy.[10] The established political parties suffered from scandals (such as the Flick affair) and accusations of bribery and corruption (for example, in the bitterly contested and narrow votes ratifying Brandt's *Ostpolitik*, and in the related 1972 election campaign). Perhaps a less obviously problematic, but in some ways serious, aspect of the functioning of West German democracy was the role of the chameleon FDP, rarely gaining over one in ten votes (and sometimes little over the one in twenty necessary to gain representation in the Bundestag) but able nearly always to determine the balance of power and political complexion of the government. On each occasion where there was a major change at national level – 1966, 1969, 1982 – it was the FDP which determined the switch.

More broadly – as adumbrated above in connection with views of its past – West Germany continued to suffer from a perceived identity crisis: not only the contested question of 'coming to terms with the past' (particularly the Nazi past), but also the question of its role in the present, was problematic. This was summed up in the phrase, coined already in the 1960s, of being an 'economic giant but a political dwarf'; it was also connected with certain difficulties in Germany's relationship particularly with its erstwhile enemy and victor, then saviour and protector, the USA. To some extent, influential elements in the FRG sought to overcome both aspects of the problem by reasserting pride in being German while at the same time attempting to subsume West German identity in a wider, and increasingly integrated, European identity. (This focus on European integration continued to be put forward as the supposed solution to fears of a resurgent greater German nationalism with the events of 1989–90.) If one wants a key clue to West Germany's stability in the 'established' phase, however, it can still be summarised in two words: economic performance. Clearly this is not the place to embark on a major review of West German history in this period, but it may be said briefly that West Germany rode the economic troubles of the 1970s and 1980s remarkably smoothly (in contrast, for example, to a declining Britain); and that without the continued and widespread affluence of West Germans, their political history would probably have been very different.

How does one explain the rather different – but in many respects more surprising – relative political stability of the GDR in the quarter-

10. Evaluations of later West German democracy differ remarkably: for contrasting views, see Conradt, op.cit., and Bark and Gress, op.cit.

century from the early 1960s to the later 1980s? It seems to me that four factors in East German regime stability are of major importance; and that, again perhaps oddly, issues of national identity and popular political orientation in the end played a greater role in the demise of this non-democratic state than they did in any political developments in its democratic twin in the West.

The key factors explaining both the relatively long-lived stability of the GDR and also in the end – in their transformation – its final collapse, have to do with the international situation; the cohesion of elites; the incorporation and defusing of dissent; and the (minimal) satisfaction of material needs. Here, we shall deal with the established phase; the next section will consider the end of the post-war era and the revolution of 1989.

While the Cold War continued, the Soviet Union could never contemplate a serious breaking of ranks among Warsaw Pact countries, and would intervene to suppress any domestic developments which seemed to threaten Soviet interests. This is the key difference between all earlier unsuccessful uprisings in Eastern European countries (1953, 1956, 1968, 1980–81) and the revolutions of 1989. The existence of Communist regimes in Eastern Europe was, at the most basic level, predicated on the latent or manifest coercion of the Soviet Union.

Second, if one turns to domestic features contributing to regime stability, a key factor has to do with elites. The political elite, the SED, was for a long time a more disciplined and at least publicly united party than were other Eastern European Communist parties at certain times (the Czechs in 1968 under Dubcek, the Poles in 1980–81 when faced with the challenge of Solidarity). This East German Communist authoritarianism and discipline clearly require further exploration. Other elite groups were, for a series of different reasons, in large measure either coopted (the technical intelligentsia) or their challenge as potential counter-elites deflected (for example, the cultural intelligentsia). A partial exception became the Protestant churches, a question to which we shall return.

Third – and related to the cohesion or cooption of elites – an important factor in the relative lack of domestic sources of political instability in the GDR from the early 1960s to the mid-1980s was the fact that dissent was relatively successfully incorporated, defused – or exiled to the West. Alone among East European states, the GDR had a western twin which automatically recognised rights of citizenship for those who had fled or been exiled from the East. This proved a useful safety valve from the point of view of the East German regime: dissenting groups lost their articulate and active leaders, or critical writers tired of censorship and self-censorship left to become submerged in the wider seas of intellectual dissent in the West. Even with the emergence of the unofficial peace initiatives in the early 1980s, members of the Protestant church leadership – concerned to protect the delicate balance of Church–state relations, and to pressurise gradually for change – to some degree stepped in to moderate the actions of dissenters and to contain oppositional activity within certain bounds (as in, for example, the ending of the 'Swords into ploughshares' armband campaign).[11]

Finally, there is the issue of East German economic performance. Quite obviously, East Germans were aware of the enormously greater affluence of West Germans, and this was a potent and particular source of grievance – again, in contrast to places like Poland or Hungary, which did not have a living example of what they might have experienced had political conditions been different. On the other hand, however, the East German economy had the best performance among Eastern Bloc countries, and although choice was severely limited and quality low by Western standards, there was not actual *want* or acute food shortages, as in Poland at different times. For all its shortcomings and inefficiencies (not to mention low health and safety standards and high levels of pollution), the East German economy did actually work – until its collapse with the opening of the borders in 1989. Thus, for the East German masses, there was not the basis for food riots – which, in Poland at different times, combined with the dissent of the intellectuals to produce more revolutionary domestic situations. While the external and elite elements in the situation appeared unassailable – while the USSR controlled its empire, and the domination of the SED was asserted with confidence – material dissatisfaction alone would not suffice to produce a revolutionary situation. The masses might grumble; but they would not rise in a hopeless revolt simply because the choice in East German greengrocers was between cabbages and more cabbages, while West Germans ate bananas, peaches and grapes.

11. For the view of the Church as a moderating or stabilising influence in the early 1980s, see M. Fulbrook, 'Co-option and commitment: aspects of the relations between church and state in the GDR', *Social History* 12 (1987), pp. 73–91. Clearly things changed somewhat in the later 1980s when the delicate balance of the earlier 1980s was changed with the proliferation of dissenting groups outside the Church, the diversification of opinion within the Church – and within the SED – and with a changed external context (with hopes for reforms along Gorbachev's lines).

The 1989 revolution

From the mid-1980s all the four factors just identified began to change, in different ways. Most important for bringing about changes in the German situation were the changes in Soviet policy under Gorbachev. With domestic economic and political difficulties, and the introduction and promotion of reforms which had reverberations for democratising and liberalising currents in other Eastern European states, Gorbachev presided over the new non-interventionism in Eastern Europe. In Soviet spokesman Gennady Gerasimov's disarming phrase, the new approach to Eastern Europe was characterised by the 'Sinatra doctrine' of 'letting them do it their way'. This was the essential precondition for the fundamental political changes which took place in Poland, and particularly Hungary – where the dismantling of the Iron Curtain between Hungary and Austria provided the location for the refugee crisis of the summer of 1989. The flood of East German refugees over this border to the West was the precipitating factor in the East German domestic political crisis, which, it may be added already, would not have advanced very far if the USSR had not permitted it to continue and, indeed, encouraged change.

Second, there was the crisis among the East German domestic elites. Already from the mid-1980s, the SED had been losing its monolithic profile. This partly had to do with the fact that Honecker was ageing, and there was a succession question in the air; this was overlain by the context of discussions of *glasnost* and *perestroika*. Thus while many pointed to Egon Krenz as the likely crown prince, *aficionados* mentioned the name of an obscure, but more liberal, potential leader of the SED waiting in the provincial wings: Hans Modrow. The resistance of the old-guard leadership to the Soviet reforms had fostered more open debates and shifting of positions – and less disciplined conformity in the certainties of the party line – among the wider SED membership, with greater differences emerging between grass-roots and activists, between local and central leaderships, than had been seen since the 1950s. These uncertainties were to play a key role in the way the peaceful revolution was to unfold.

Third, given the new and more hopeful conditions, dissent had been proliferating and emerging into organised opposition already over some years before 1989. From the mid-1980s onwards, groups had been organising *outside* the bounds of the Church, discussing human rights and environmental issues as well as peace initiatives. These took advantage of the situation of regime crisis in the late summer of 1989 to argue for the need for change *within* the GDR, to transform it into a place were people would want to stay and work for a better future.

Finally, there is the issue of mass discontent. Clearly this was the major factor behind the refugee crisis: people wanted to cross while the going was good, abandoning home and possessions in search of better conditions in the West. But it was not the *cause* of the revolution, first, in that it was a *result* of the wider changes in Eastern Europe (and specifically, the dismantling of the Iron Curtain on the Austro-Hungarian border), and second, in that the masses played a minimal role in the very early phases of the actual revolution in East Germany itself. It was brave and committed dissenters who dared to march around Leipzig in the early days, before the turning-point of 9 October when the use of force to suppress the revolution was officially renounced. The details of this turning-point are themselves interesting: it was a local decision, not even ratified by local party leaders, which in the course of the evening received backing from Berlin (in the person of Krenz) which determined the calling-off of the troops. Once it was clear – a rather faltering process, with different patterns in different localities – that demonstrating would not result in mass bloodshed, more and more people came out on the streets to proclaim '*Wir sind das Volk*' ('We are the people').

If ever a 'GDR national identity' existed (though not the one for which the regime had been striving for over forty years), it was between 9 October and 9 November 1989. For a month, a tremulous solidarity of a wondering people forced concession after concession from a regime which attempted to salvage what it could from the situation by a 'last revolution from above'. The final concession – when it was clearly no longer possible to try to imprison the entire East German population under a form of national house arrest – proved the undoing both of the Communist regime and the fragile and short-lived GDR national identity. The opening of the Berlin Wall on 9 November was equivalent to the opening of floodgates; and with the westwards stampede, the East German economy and state entered the chaotic period of effective collapse. The simple replacement of one word in the slogans of the autumn symbolised the deflection of the revolution: '*Wir sind das Volk*' became '*Wir sind ein Volk*'. A transcending national identity was claimed, to preside over the abandonment of the past and to express the desperate hope to acquire overnight the life-style of the West. It was, essentially, the vote for the Deutschmark, as fast as possible, which then determined the right-wing outcome of the March 1990 elections.

The end of a divided nation

What did the dramatic developments of 1989–90 reveal about the national identity or diverging identities of the Germans in the two Germanies? The picture is a complex and multi-faceted one. In the first place – as at all times in German history – there was no one uncontested conception of what made up a 'German national identity'. This has been, perhaps, the sole consistent feature of the changing history of Germans in central Europe since the beginnings of notions of the German nation in the early Middle Ages, and is traced in the various other chapters in this book. So the difficulties in redefining a united Germany's role in the radically changed conditions of late twentieth-century Europe, after the end of the Cold War, are but a new variant on an old, ever-changing theme.

What are the distinctive features of this new stage of an old problem? The importance of being German – if one can put it that way – for many Germans in 1989–90 lay in the economic strength of the FRG. Notwithstanding the emotions aroused among the West as well as East German people by the breaching of the Berlin Wall, and the long-standing obligations, officially recognised and adhered to, on the part of the West German leaders towards the East Germans, as well as the continuing ties of family and friendship between East and West, the degree of divergence between the two Germanies during forty years of separation should not be underestimated.

In all manner of spheres, assumptions and orientations to life were revealed as being different in East and West: many aspects are only surfacing to consciousness with the realisation of changes occurring or likely to occur with unification. For example, the taken-for-granted reliance on generous maternity provisions and almost universally available child-care facilities for East German mothers, who assume that it is abnormal *not* to work, stands in some contrast to the patchy, largely private nature of West German provision for pre-school children and the rather different considerations concerning the combination of work and family in the West. Whatever one's views on the 'double burden' rather than 'emancipation' of women in East Germany (where the traditional division of labour in the household remained largely resistant to social policies affecting the non-private sphere), there was clearly a considerable divergence of attitudes on the gender front. More diffuse and difficult to specify are differences in what one might call degrees of individualism. By and large, East Germans did *not* have to take autonomous decisions, or be aggressive, competitive and thrusting on the market-place; they *did* have to learn to obey and carry out decisions taken above. Adapting to the conditions of market capitalism – with not only the benefits of affluence when all goes well, but also the risks of unemployment, homelessness and squalor amid plenty – would clearly prove to be problematic for many. Learning to think independently, and have the courage to articulate one's own view even when contradicted by others – and often to agree amicably to differ – would also be something of a problem for those affected by East German authoritarian education and socialisation processes. Although in the winter of 1989–90, on experiencing for themselves the apparent consumers' paradise of the West, many East Germans felt bitterly that they had lost or wasted forty years, and would now have to jettison overnight all the sacrifices of the past which had in the end been for nothing, others felt that under an effective West German takeover much of value in GDR life would be lost. This was particularly felt among those – many of them Christians – who had spearheaded the early stages of the peaceful revolution of the autumn, hoping to be able to build a 'Third Way' form of democratic, humanistic socialism. To collapse into crass materialism appeared to these a profoundly depressing denouement to the revolution.

In other respects, currents previously suppressed now found a – not always welcome – voice. This was true of right-wing extremism in the GDR, fomented to some extent by West German Republicans in the winter of 1989–90, although it had existed before. Anti-Semitic acts such as the desecration of Jewish graves (including those of Helene Weigel and her non-Jewish husband, Bertolt Brecht), as well as racist attacks on foreigners in the GDR, increased after the relaxing of police control and political repression of such acts. Problematic, too, would be a 'coming-to-terms', under democratic auspices and conditions of free debate, not only with the previously inadequately confronted Nazi past, but also the compromises and complicities of life in the Stasi-state. 'De-stasification' was already beginning to take on parallels with the denazification of the post-war period; and the grumbles were being heard again of the *Bonzen* (roughly, bigwigs) remaining in position, benefiting from new circumstances as they had from the old. A post-revolutionary period of uncertainty and insecurity was beginning to pave the way for a new wave – a double wave – of coming to terms with two sets of compromised pasts.

Developments in West Germany were in some respects simpler; but West Germany did not remain intrinsically unaffected by the East German changes. There, too, new currents arose or were made manifest by the changing situation. There were new social prejudices in a period of increased pressure on housing and jobs, when the West German economic miracle appeared threatened by the incorporation of growing numbers of emigrating East Germans, or by the rises in taxes and interest rates to accommodate the merger of the two economies. Moreover, uncertainties on the role – and even the boundaries, while Kohl played to the far-right gallery in prevaricating on Poland's western border – of the new united Germany allowed the reassertion of revisionist voices which not so long before had seemed essentially anachronistic. To a much greater degree than in the East, young West Germans had taken little interest in their twin state, and many had barely regarded it as much more than an entity related only by the dimmest of historical ties. (There was scarcely the same acute thirst among Westerners to travel to, and experience the deprivations of, the East as there was among young East Germans to make the opposite journey to the West. Nor were many, if any, young West Germans tempted to watch the monotonous fare of East German television night after night, in the same way as East Germans avidly watched the Western media.) While the victory in the East German national elections of the political forces supported by the West German conservative parties ensured that West German political and economic arrangements would in the main be taken over to a new Germany, that new united Germany would still be a different entity than the partial state, the Federal Republic had been; and West Germans would have to accommodate themselves and adapt to the new circumstances, although in different ways and from different base-lines than their Eastern brethren.

CONCLUSIONS

For four decades, the democratic and Communist states established in the western and eastern parts of a divided nation were more successful – in their own, rather different terms – than were their historical predecessors, from imperial Germany through the Weimar Republic to the Third Reich. This success is perhaps particularly surprising for two reasons: first, neither state was an intrinsically 'legitimate' nation-state, but rather an impermanent entity in a divided nation; and second, the new political forms which were imposed did not, at least initially, represent the outcome of indigenous political orientations. It has often been said that a major problem of the Weimar Republic was that it was a 'Republic without republicans'. Even more might such a comment be made about the two post-war German states at the time of their foundation: a Communist state with precious few Communists, and a democratic state with probably less than a majority of democrats in any deep-rooted sense.

Neither state succeeded entirely in finding a satisfactory solution to the problem of 'national identity', whether at an all-German level or at the level of the partial state. All-German notions played little role in the early stages of division and consolidation of the two states. With *Ostpolitik*, West German aid to East Germany – in recognition of its common bonds with East German citizens and desire to improve their material and human circumstances – paradoxically helped to sustain division through bolstering the East German regime. That does not mean that the GDR would have collapsed earlier without such aid. Material distress alone does not lead to revolution and the crucial external preconditions for such revolution were absent until the late 1980s.

At the level of partial 'national identities', the attempted construction of different East and West German identities must also be viewed with some qualification. Official propagations of a 'GDR national identity' were probably never swallowed wholesale by more than a minority of the population, although this might – had 1989 not intervened – have changed eventually with the passage of generations. There were certain bases for (limited) pride in the GDR's modest economic achievements compared to its Eastern European neighbours, and these comparisons might have displaced those made with the richer West Germany if the division of Europe had continued – but this is to speculate. In the West at least a number of highly articulate intellectuals continued to suffer from explicit identity crises, and attempts to proclaim any universally valid notion of national identity remained intrinsically contentious and politically divisive.

Despite all this, however, the two Germanies *did* begin to develop distinctively different profiles or patterns of political orientation. In the West, a combination of external factors and domestic economic success contributed to the early establishment of democracy. As a *result* – not a precondition – of the consolidation of democratic political structures, more democratic forms of political orientation spread among greater proportions of the populace. A predominance of monarchist and authoritarian sympathies prevalent in the 1950s gave way to pragmatic assent to democracy by the early 1960s; by the late 1960s, this had become support for democracy in principle. Once the transformation of most West Germans from 'fair-weather' to 'principled' democrats had taken place, the economic and political troubles of the 1970s (economic recession, oil crises, terrorism) could more easily be weathered. By the 1980s, there were widespread moves for more participatory, and not purely representative, democracy, which arose at a time of new challenges on the international military and environmental fronts. With the passage of generations, and the changing of issues, the West Germans of the late 1980s were not the same sorts of people as those of the 1940s, whatever the mythology of popular folklore among Germany's former enemies, such as Britain, which began to be expressed over the issue of German unity in the winter of 1989–90.

In the East, a combination of coercion and attempted indoctrination were important in the early phase of establishment. From 1961, a widespread retreatism into a 'niche society', combined with the isolation, defusing or exiling of dissent, for two decades or more contributed to the maintenance of a modicum of domestic stability. In the 1980s dissenting voices developed into more active, organised opposition groups. Interestingly, the early stages of the 1989 revolution revealed just what new forms of political culture had emerged among a minority in the GDR: that minority, typified by New Forum in the early autumn, that was in favour of a form of democratic socialism rather than capitalist democracy as in the West. In the event, when the majority – who had until 1989 led quiet political lives in the retreatist mode – took the opportunity to go West (both before and even more after the opening of the Berlin Wall), the economic collapse of the GDR took away the material conditions for any such experiment in democratic socialism to be attempted.

It was the Cold War which divided Germany; it was the end of the Cold War which removed the conditions sustaining division. Within each of the two Germanies, it was the support or co-option, in different ways, of a range of elite groups which determined the relative domestic stability of each partial state over the forty years of division. When a regime crisis, in the context of changed external circumstances, precipitated the loss of elite control in East Germany, then active opposition could take advantage of the situation to initiate major forces for change. Finally, with the emergence of the masses on to the political scene – expressing the simple desire for a better standard of living and an end to repression – the final basis for the existence of a separate East German state was removed.

While the parameters of the current situation are relatively clear, there are still many uncertainties on the form, social and economic profile, and particularly military alliance of any future united Germany.

We may end with a few wider ruminations. In a very simple sense, a 'German nation-state' has never really existed, given the complicated ethnic boundaries of central Europe and the existence of German minorities outside wherever 'Germany' happened to be at any given time, while non-German groups lived within 'Germany'. So in some respects the unification of Germany is simply another variant of the centuries-old game of redrawing the boundaries of 'Germany' in central Europe and redefining – or constructing – an identity for what lay inside.

There are nevertheless some interesting new features to the current situation. These have to do with the changed structural location of the state in the late twentieth-century with respect to both supra-national and sub-national levels. There is, on the one hand, the set of movements 'upwards', integrating European states into wider economic and political decision-making networks – most notably, with the moves for enhanced significance for the European Community and wider European integration. On the other hand, there is a simultaneous set of movements in almost the opposite direction: the resurgence of local nationalisms in multi-national states (such as in the former USSR) or of regional and local identities in nation-states. *Heimat* and local particularism are attaining new significance in a period of trans- or supra-national entities. Clearly, with the ending of the Cold War and the collapse of the Soviet Empire in Eastern Europe, the 1990s constitute a major historical watershed. The era of European nation-states which began in the early nineteenth century may be nearing a significant end. The task of the historian is to explain the past, not predict the future; but no doubt the land in the centre of Europe will continue to play a central role in European history. Perhaps Germans' difficulties with concepts of national identity, and the arguable irrelevance of these concepts to patterns of political stability and change, represent a helpful corrective to the virulent consequences of earlier views of the role of the German nation.

SUGGESTIONS FOR FURTHER READING

See the following for introductions to the history of the two Germanies:
M. Balfour, *West Germany: An Introductory History* (London, 1982).

V. Berghahn, *Modern Germany* (Cambridge, 1987, 2nd edn).

D. Childs, *The GDR: Moscow's German Ally* (London, 1983).

M. McCauley, *The GDR since 1945* (London, 1983).

G. Smith, W. Paterson and P. Merkl (eds), *Developments in West German Politics* (London, 1989).

H.A. Turner, *The Two Germanies since 1945* (New Haven, Conn, 1987).

My own views are developed at greater length in M. Fulbrook, *Germany 1918–1990: The Divided Nation* (London, 1991).

CHAPTER ELEVEN

Germany in Europe: the German question as burden and as opportunity

Wolf Gruner

PRELIMINARY REMARKS

'In the year 1990 the future of Europe appears more open than at any time since the end of the Second World War.'[1]

So began the new book on Germany and her neighbours by the former Chancellor of the Federal Republic of Germany, Helmut Schmidt. This is an appropriate judgement of the historical crossroads at which we now find ourselves, bringing with it both risks and opportunities.

In the 1990s one can envisage two possible lines of development. In the first the changes in Eastern Europe could lead to the re-emergence of nationalism and of a Europe of nation-states in a new form. This development would stop or at least delay the policies of European integration being pursued in Western Europe. In the second the democratisation of Eastern Europe, the introduction of market economies, and the reunification of Germany could all promote the integration process by locking Germany more closely into a network of European connections, and thereby accelerating and even completing the tasks of integration. European states would give up or at least reduce their political freedom in favour of a pan-European structure. At the end of this path there would come a day of the kind described by Lothar Späth in his recent book *1992: The Dream of Europe*:

Church bells peal throughout Europe. They ring in the new millennium *and* a new epoch in European history. In the park in front of the European Parliament in Strasbourg people sing and dance and celebrate. They link arms and wave European flags. The treaties setting up a United

1. H. Schmidt, *Die Deutschen und ihre Nachbarn* (Berlin, 1990), p. 12.

States of Europe (Vereinigten Staaten von Europa; Les Etats Unis de l'Europe) come into force on 1 January 2000. There is a ceremony in which the first European President, the former Prime Minister of Luxemburg (until 31 December 1999) is sworn in by the President of the European Parliament.[2]

The unity of Europe which had broken apart in the medieval period is restored on a new basis which transcends the nation-state. The centuries-old dream of unifying Europe, of the creation of a single European nation, has become a reality.

Most Germans wish to see this second path followed, the one that leads to European unity.

However, we are not nearly there. The path to a United States of Europe, to a European federal state will be steep and stony, but nevertheless it could be travelled. Germany, reunited on 3 October 1990, must play the leading role in this process, and not only for historic reasons. The authors of the Basic Law, the constitution of the Federal Republic, set out the moral obligation.

> The German People…animated by the resolve to preserve their national and political unity and to serve the peace of the world as an equal partner in a united Europe…have enacted…this Basic Law.[3]

The creation of a united Europe remains after German reunification a constitutional commitment, only now it applies to *all* Germans. In the treaty establishing German unity there is a reference to the obligation '…by means of German unity to contribute to the unification of Europe and the creation of a peaceful order in Europe'.[4] A united Germany should be an integral part of this greater Europe, a pillar in the new European building. Germany will take its place in the common European home to which medieval popes swore allegiance.

The chances of European unity are not too bad because Europeans have little choice but to follow this path and to persevere in it despite all the dangers. However, there are many basic problems which will have to be confronted.

1. What would be the constitutional forms of a new European polity: a federal state, a federation of states, a Europe of sovereign states, or of groups of such states, a Europe of nations or a Europe of regions?

---

2. L. Späth, *1992: Der Traum von Europa* (Stuttgart, 1989), pp. 9–24. This is not a quotation but a summary of the points made by Späth in this part of his book.

3. *The Basic Law for the Federal Republic of Germany*, 23 May 1949, Preamble.

4. *Vertrag zwischen der Bundesrepublik Deutschland und der Deutschen Demokratischen Republik über die Herstellung der Einheit Deutschlands: Einigungsvertrag*, dated 31 August 1990, Presse und Informationsamt der Bundesregierung, *Bulletin* no. 104 (6 September 1990), pp. 877–1,120 (877).

2. Can the peoples of Europe free themselves of the burdens of the past
    and bring the process of European integration to its conclusion? Is it
    true that one can find no historical justification for such integration be-
    cause the history of Europe reveals inveterate hostility to integration?[5]
3. The German question has always been a European question, since long
    before 1939 and at least since the eighteenth century. Will reunification
    settle that question once and for all or will it for both historical and new
    reasons turn out to be an obstacle in the way of European unification?
4. Which role can and should the new German state play in Europe?
5. How European is our thinking and feeling? Are convinced Germans also
    committed Europeans? Or are they rational Europeans, Europeans by de-
    fault because lacking in national identity? Do Germans lack a sense of
    Europe as a cultural and spiritual reality, not just as the consequence of
    successful political and economic integration?

These are the questions and problems which press upon us. As an
historian it is not possible to invent a formula for German and European unity. It is possible, however, to sketch out the German dimensions of European history and the European dimensions of German
history and to bring to light ideas about a common Europe which
have been concealed under the categories imposed by the nation–state.
This will be both necessary and valuable in the promotion of a European historical perspective and an understanding of what Europe
means. Historical knowledge is an important element in forming the
'future of history' (Sheehan). Sheehan suggested that it was time to put
aside the idea that the foundation of a united Germany in 1871 was
somehow the central event in modern German history. Rather one
should

> acknowledge that the present period has a legitimacy of its own, a
> legitimacy which comes not from its relationship to the old Reich, but
> from its place within a broader and deeper historical tradition. The
> German present is not a postscript to the imperial past; it is a new chapter
> in a much older story.[6]

Recovering a sense of the fullness of German history beyond its relationship to the founding of modern Germany brings home to us such
issues as the federal tradition in German statehood and how this fitted
into a broader European setting, it leads us to question that idea of a
continuity which runs from Arminius through Luther, Frederick the
Great and Bismarck to Hitler, and enables us to re-evaluate German
history.

5. See R.W Foerster, *Europa: Geschichte einer politischen Idee* (Munich, 1967), p. 156.
6. J. Sheehan, 'What is German history?', *Journal of Modern History* 53 (1981), pp.
1–23 (23). See now Sheehan, *German History 1770–1866* (Oxford, 1990).

What Sheehan says about Geman history can also be said about European history. The European present also has to be linked to a re-evaluated European history. It cannot be reduced to the links between the nation-states; it must be seen as something more than the sum of these national histories. We should seek to go beyond such propaganda. If we take off our national spectacles, be they tinted German, Czech, British, Russian, French, Dutch, Polish, Italian or Hungarian, new perspectives open up to us which can help us move beyond the nation-state, can promote new ideas and can bring us closer to the goal of European unity in all its complexity. There needs to be a concern with 'Europe as reality and as task'[7] in order to link past, present and future.

In what follows I wish to select three elements from European history. Closer consideration of these elements can help us understand the situation in which Europe and Germany find themselves now.

1. The first element is the tension between the national and the European idea since the breakdown of the unity of Christendom.
2. The second element is the European dimension of the German question, or the German problem as it has often been termed by Germany's neighbours. The German problem has been and remains of great concern to those neighbours.
3. The third element is to consider the issues of European unity and the German question in relation to the process of western integration since 1945.

I will conclude with a consideration of what it will mean for Europe, for states both inside and outside the EC, and for the European unity process now that a united Germany is a member of the EC.

THE IDEAS OF THE NATION-STATE AND OF EUROPEAN UNITY

Geographically the core area of Europe is fairly clearly defined. This allows, despite the variety of landscapes and of national, cultural, linguistic, religious and political histories, a certain element of unity to

7. *Europa als Wirklichkeit und Aufgabe* is the title of a reader intended for the final class of primary school in Hamburg from the year 1954. The book contains documents concerned with European history and culture.

persist.[8] This sense of common European links and traditions which developed over centuries was obscured in the period in which the nation–state and national attitudes came to be dominant. This has also affected historical study which

> came to be placed clearly and completely within the framework of the nation and of the national homeland, rather like a child put into a tight jacket in order to prevent freedom of movement.[9]

A survey of lecture courses given at German and other European universities, as well as the history curricula of schools, makes it clear that this tight jacket is still worn. The central point of reference is national and generally the history of the nation dominates. This is an obstacle to the promotion of any sense of historical community at a European level. If we wish to develop a European identity, without denying the significance of the regional and the national, then we must try to develop European perspectives.[10] We need to explore the reasons for the development of nationalism and the nation–state in Europe and also see how the idea of Europe has evolved along with that development.

One feature of modern European history is the close connections between the formation of the nation–state, the principle of sovereignty, the concern with security and the concept of a balance of power. These in turn are related to a certain idea of Europe. At first there seems to be no connection between that idea and the concept of the balance of power. Yet that concept, especially in terms of a European balance of power implies an understanding of the ties that bind the continent together.[11]

One can find the origins of the ideas of both the nation–state and of Europe in the medieval period. The sharpening conflict between Empire and Papacy for pre–eminence in Christendom destroyed the unity and universalism of the Christian West. Christendom had embraced equally all the various European lands. The dynastic nation–state idea contributed to its disintegration. Special interests displaced unity. Tensions between the territories of the various European peoples took on increasingly a dynastic–national character. That in turn promoted a

8. See D. Hay, *Europe: The Emergence of an Idea* (Edinburgh, 1967, 2nd edn); O. Halecki, *The Limits and Divisions of European History*, (London, 1950); P. Wolff, *The Awakening of Europe* (Harmondsworth, 1987).

9. Leonard Reinisch, in his preface to Reinisch (ed.) *Die Europäer und ihre Geschichte. Epochen und Gestalten im Urteil der Nationen* (Munich, 1961), p. vi.

10. S. de Madariaga, *Portrait of Europe* (London, 1952), preface.

11. Cf. W. Gruner, 'Deutschland und das europäische Gleichgewicht seit dem 18 Jahrhundert', in Gruner, *Gleichgewicht in Geschichte und Gegenwart* (Hamburg, 1989), pp. 60–133.

desire to win back the lost unity. With the emergence of nation-states from the early modern period and their dogmatic insistence on the need for national sovereignty, such a European idea seemed increasingly utopian and idealistic.

There is not space here to consider in detail the tension between the European and the nation-state ideas.[12] My main concern is to indicate that early plans for the restoration of European unity – and until the eighteenth century Christendom was the central point of reference in such plans – contain elements which continue to figure in plans for European Union in the twentieth century. Thinkers with whom such ideas are associated include Dante Aligheri, Pierre du Bois and Georg von Podiebrad, and in the seventeenth and eighteenth centuries, Emeric Crucé, the Duke of Sully and the Abbot de St Pierre.[13]

Podiebrad's *Treaty for a League of States* (*Vertrag zu einem Staatenbund*) (dated 1462/63) takes as its point of departure the emergence of nations within Europe. His plan failed, but it influenced later plans. The members of the league should accept a limitation upon the sovereignty of the individual states, decisions taken by a majority of states, a court of arbitration, a Supreme Court, a league army and executive authority.

There were various motives behind attempts at European unity since the fifteenth century apart from the wish to overcome national barriers. We encounter such plans especially at times of political and economic crisis. They are frequently presented as a way of ensuring perpetual peace and contributing towards prosperity. The authors of such plans came from widely differing backgrounds. It is often difficult to establish their contemporary and later significance. As with the national movements from the late eighteenth century they increasingly recruited from intellectual and political-social elites who were involved in politics. However, unlike the national movements of the nineteenth century, the European movement did not acquire a popular basis.

In its early stages the nation-state was seen in dynastic terms, but this changed with the French Revolution, which also spread the national idea throughout Europe. Into the twentieth century nationalism, the nation-state, and the national character of politics have come to shape an increasingly wider and international political order.[14] The

12. See W. Gruner, 'Probleme und Aspekte der europäischen Einigung bis zu den Römischen Verträgen', in A. Schomaker *et al.* (eds) *Plädoyer für Europa. Beiträge zur Europäischen Einigung* (Hamburg, 1989), pp. 11–62.

13. Cf. F.H. Hinsley, *Power and the Pursuit of Peace* (Cambridge, 1967).

14. This conjunction of nationalism with increasing international ties led Theodor Schieder to refer to the nineteenth century as an 'age of antinomies'. T. Schieder, 'Europa im Zeitalter der Nationalstaaten und Europäische Weltpolitik bis zum Ersten Weltkrieg', in *Handbuch der Europäischen Geschichte*, vol. 6 (Stuttgart, 1968), pp. 3ff.

idea that the nation–state was the only thinkable way in which a world of nations could be organised became a dominating dogma. Plans for European unity, grounded in motives other than that of power politics, were disparaged as utopian.

Despite their differences one can see common elements in the various ideas about European unity, even if combined in different ways. The intellectual forerunners go back to the fifteenth century, but they have been forgotten by historians in the grip of a national approach towards the past. Among these elements there are recurrent references to certain institutions which also appear in ideas about European Union today. These include European assemblies, a council of states, a parliament, courts, an army, and an agency to enforce compliance with a European treaty upon offending states. Almost all these plans have a federalist character which is situated somewhere between the notions of a league of states and a federal state. In addition to the various institutions which have been constructed since the European Community for Coal and Steel in 1952, these constitutional proposals for some kind of United States of Europe can provide us with some guidance. Germans can also usefully draw upon their own federalist tradition. After the Second World War Paul Claudel saw in partitioned Germany a way 'to bring together rather than to divide the peoples of Europe'.[15] Germany lies at the centre of Europe and its geography makes it a central focus of European concerns. How Germany is organised politically is crucial to any European order, especially since the political nation, described by Ortega y Gasset as 'the obstacle to any creative historical movement'[16] has been at the centre of German political action. The relationship of Germany to Europe has been an important component, both in the past and today, of the German question.

---

15. Paul Claudel, quoted in R. Weizsäcker, 'Die Deutschen und ihre Identität', talk given on 8 June 1985 in Düsseldorf to the twenty-first assembly of the Evangelical Church, Presse und Informationsamt der Bundesregierung, *Bulletin*, 64 (12) June 1985, pp. 537–44 (544).

16. J. Ortega y Gasset, *Der Aufstand der Massen* (orig. 1930; Reinbek bei Hamburg, 1961), p. 136.

THE HISTORICAL AND EUROPEAN DIMENSIONS OF THE GERMAN QUESTION

The Germans, now once again in a single state, have an important role to play in the process of European unification. Germany is made up of what was the most Eastern part of Western Europe and the most western part of eastern Europe. Germany has no great power profile which could stand in the way of pragmatic policy-making. This provides Germany with a 'second chance' to shape the European order in the twentieth century.[17] Much depends upon whether the emphasis is upon a German Europe or a European Germany. The first would involve a renewed drive for hegemony over the rest of Europe. Some of Germany's neighbours have expressed anxiety that this could be the direction taken by the reunified Germany. To avoid these anxieties, and the dangers associated with such a direction, it is the second policy which must be pursued. To achieve this we must aim to be Europeans, though without ceasing to be Germans, and also Rhinelanders, Bavarians, Saxons, Mecklenburgers, and so on. How is this to be done?

Partly it requires historical understanding. Such understanding is important to any sense of identity. The President of the Federal Republic, Richard von Weizsäcker, has stressed this in various speeches to his countrymen in recent years:

> If a people do not know how they stand in relation to their past, then it is easy for them to be led astray in the present, for they have an identity problem.[18]

Perhaps this is why so much has been written and said recently about the question of identity in Germany. Germans cannot escape from their history; the burden of that history remains with them today.

The German question has always had a European dimension and has never been only a German concern. Following the creation of an atomic balance of power between the super-powers by the end of the 1950s and then the erection of the Berlin Wall, the German question no longer seemed as important as before. It seemed that the construction of two Germanies, especially when the Federal Republic signed treaties both with the German Democratic Republic and other Eastern European states, had settled the German question for the foreseeable

17. The point was made by the historian Fritz Stern, who also pointed out that Germany wasted her first chance, and history does not normally provide second ones.

18. Weizsäcker, op. cit., p. 539.

future. The German question did surface again with the conflicts arising out of the NATO 'double-track' decision[19] and the discussions
about neutralism which that decision stimulated. However, although
this created some anxieties, both within Germany and among her
neighbours, it did not really call into question the stability of the two-
Germany arrangement. For younger people in the Federal Republic
the German question seemed dead. Even on the eve of the events
which would lead to the collapse of the German Democratic Republic
there was talk of altering the references in the Basic Law to German
unity. The GDR was regarded as a foreign and distant land. Eastern
Europe was ignored. The term 'Germany' came to mean 'West Germany', and 'Europe' meant 'Western Europe'. Germans had come to
forget the close links there were and always will be between the German problem and the process of European unification.

The long-serving Italian ambassador to the Federal Republic of
Germany said the following in a talk given in 1986:

> The European solution of the German question, indeed the European
> vision of those who founded the Federal Republic, began with a lesson
> that was drawn from German history. This was to see the European idea
> as a negation of that German history. The Europe of the future would be
> an 'answer' to history. But one must move towards new and positive
> decisions if the mistakes of the past are to be avoided and a universal and
> eternal peace secured.[20]

Another Italian, the journalist Luigi Barzini, also considered this question:

> The unification of Europe without Germany would be impossible and
> pointless, but with Germany would entail the acceptance, for all members,
> of the German problem.[21]

He concluded that the issue of European unity must wait until the
German question had been solved.

> One must be content with what there is, for the time being anyway. The
> future is in the laps of the gods. It will probably be decided, once again,
> by Germany's decisions. And Germany is, as it always was, a mutable,

---

19. The term used to describe the policy of installing intermediate-range nuclear
missiles in Western Europe, including the Federal Republic of Germany, while continuing to negotiate on arms control agreements with the USSR.
20. L.V.G. Ferraris, 'Betrachtungen zur deutschen Geschichte', talk given on 2 October 1986 in Berlin, MS, p. 15.
21. L. Barzini, *The Europeans* (Harmondsworth, 1983), p. 266.

Proteus–like, unpredictable country, particularly dangerous when it is unhappy.[22]

What is it that gives the German question such priority? To understand this one needs some definition of the term 'German question', though this has varied greatly from one observer to another.[23] There are at least two levels on which to approach the subject: a national-German and a European-international one. Both have a strong historical dimension which one can see determining policy-making in the Second World War and which continues to influence policy-making today.

This became vividly apparent in the political reactions and public comment which accompanied the process of German reunification in 1989–90. Statements by various European politicians and newspaper cartoons bear witness to this. Germany's neighbours have very mixed feelings about the end of German partition.

In the winter of 1990 the *Los Angeles Times* and the *Economist* commissioned a poll of opinions among Germany's neighbours concerning reunification. The headline for the article describing the findings of the poll was 'They like it and they fear it'.[24] There was joy at the way in which the citizens of the GDR had thrown off Communist rule in a peaceful revolution coupled with anxiety and insecurity triggered by the spectacle of popular support for reunification among Germans.

Historically the European–international dimension has also played an important part in the German question, and this cannot be neglected in the present situation. Kurt Schuemacher's insistence that 'one could not see the German question only from a German angle... that there was no German question which was not simultaneously a European question', is a view that has long been accepted.[25]

To make progress we need to introduce further differentiation. In terms of period there are shifts in the nature of the German problem from the Peace of Westphalia of 1648, since the French Revolution, and since the Second World War. One also needs to distinguish between themes of power politics, security interests, European unity, political ideologies, and the principle of the self-determination of peoples.

The different perspective of Germans and their neighbours can be seen in the way Germans use the term 'German question' whereas

22. Ibid., p. 267 (concluding sentence of the book).

23. For different ways of defining the question see W.D. Gruner, *Die deutsche Frage: Ein Problem der europäischen Geschichte seit 1800* (Munich, 1985), p. 15ff.

24. *The Economist*, 27 January 1990, pp. 29f.

25. K. Schuemacher, *Reden – Schriften – Korrespondenzen 1945–1952* (Bonn and Berlin, 1985), p. 382.

their neighbours prefer the term 'German problem'. They are aware of the problems raised since the middle of the nineteenth century in central Europe, problems which sometimes Germans seem to have forgotten. These problems were of European significance up to 1914 and came to take on an even broader, global importance after 1918.

There are six levels on which one can approach this problem: the geographical situation of Germany in the centre of Europe; the economic, political and military potential of Germany; the population question; the political and constitutional arrangements of Germany; the issue of security and balance of power in Europe; the image of Germany.

It is impossible to consider these in detail in a short essay.[26] Here I will focus upon the last issue – the image of Germany. In many ways this connects the other elements. It is a certain image of Germany which unsettles some of Germany's neighbours. Apart from support for national self-determination for Germans there is the fear that the old German Adam will re-emerge.

One can see this in the interview with the British minister Nicholas Ridley that was published in the *Spectator*, in which questions such as whether Germany was planning to take over Europe or to establish a 'Deutschmark Zone' were raised, and which led to his resignation.[27] One can also see it in the leaking of a Chequers memorandum of 25 March 1990 from Margaret Thatcher's private secretary, Charles Powell. In *The Times* the Irish historian and journalist Conor Cruse O'Brien warned of a

> pan-German entity, commanding the full allegiance of German
> nationalists, and constituting a focus for national pride... In the new
> proud, united Germany, the nationalists will proclaim the Fourth Reich,
> for while the term *Reich* is associated with victory and periods of German
> ascendancy, that of *Republik* is associated with defeat and the ascendancy
> of alien values. I would expect a reunited Germany to bring back the
> black-white-red flag of the Hohenzollerns, and possibly a Hohenzollern
> Kaiser to go with it.[28]

26. Gruner, op.cit., pp. 11ff; Gruner, *Bündische Formen der Staatlichkeit in Geschichte und Gegenwart* (Duderstadt, 1990), pp. 29ff.

27. 'Saying the unsayable', *Spectator*, 14 July 1990, p. 8.

28. Conor Cruse O'Brien, 'Beware a Reich resurgent', *The Times*, 31 October 1989, p. 18. A version of this article, which appeared in German translation in *Die Welt* on 4 November 1989 under the title 'Wenn Nationalisten das Vierte Reich ausrufen', left out the last sentence quoted above, though without indicating the omission. O'Brien was mistaken about the question of flags. The flag of Prussia used to be black and white. Red and white were the colours of the old Empire. The flag of imperial Germany was a combination of both. Thus the national colours of Germany before 1918 were black, white and red.

There was a similar argument by the Spaniard Heleno Saña who lives in Germany and experienced as a child the attacks by the German air squadron 'Legion Condor'. For him

> the Germans are again on the march. Suddenly their restless activity
> threatens the status quo in Europe. We non-Germans must be ready for a
> new Teutonic offensive. Certainly this time it will not take the form of
> tanks and artillery fire, but ultimately the aim is the same: to expand the
> power of the Germans at the cost of smaller and economically weaker
> countries.[29]

Saña believes that the coming down of the Berlin Wall removed the restraints upon Germany. He was disturbed by the 'sight of the masses'. He saw this

> demonstration of mass exhibitionism which Europe has seldom
> experienced since the end of the war. And it will not be the last one.
> Bear in mind that these are not any crowds, but crowds of a special
> quality, made-in-Germany crowds, more gifted than just about any other
> to act and react as a mass, always ready to organise, to shout, to wave flags
> and posters, to shout slogans, to follow orders blindly, to march forward
> and to attack. In the future Europe must reckon with such a crowd, for it
> is already on the march in the Fourth Reich.[30]

These expressions could be easily multiplied from the last twenty years. They show how a certain image of Germany shapes people's views about how the peoples of Europe can live together. We cannot really reduce our picture of others to just a few key words, but it is what happens. We must also remember that such national stereotypes, particularly images of the alien, have a functional role to play.

This image of Germany has changed historically. Until the mid-nineteenth century the dominant image of the German lands (rather than Germany) was quite positive. The emphasis was upon the romantic, emotional German who loved singing and drinking and who, with his rich cultural and religious traditions, had made a major contribution to European culture. However, from the time of the foundation of the Second Empire in 1870–72 the picture began to change in negative ways. Thus the Frenchman Paul de Saint-Victor wrote in 1870:

> We do not go any more into the idyllic German forests. His
> *vergiss-mein-nicht* (forget-me-nots) are spattered with blood.[31]

29. H. Saña, *Das Vierte Reich: Deutschlands später Sieg* (Hamburg, 1990), p. 22.
30. Ibid., p. 25.
31. P. de Saint-Victor, *Barbares et Bandites* (Paris, 1971). The German term for forget-me-nots is used in the French original.

The assertion of a British journalist in January 1871 that 'Politically, Prussia is a camp and the Prussian a conscript'[32] indicated another shift of image. Since the late eighteenth century Prussia had been seen as a combination of militarism and effective bureaucracy. Now the image was reduced to that of militarism. Then the image of Prussia was projected upon the image of Germany. This negative image was promoted in the years up to the First World War. With the help of propaganda this image was more firmly established during the First World War. That image of Wilhelmine Germany persists to this day.

Germans themselves contributed to this picture in various ways, through historical writing, speeches, the over-bearing, often aggressive nationalism of the Wilhelmine period, and general boastfulness, as evidenced in statements such as the following.

> [The Germans are]…the people of art and science…. the bearers of human culture….We are the first of all nations, by virtue of our spiritual power, our knowledge, our ability.[33]

> [The Germans regard themselves] as the most gifted cultural nation in the world.[34]

The experience of National Socialist Germany could only seem to confirm this negative image of the German character.

The British historian A.J.P. Taylor expressed the views of many when he gave vent to his mistrust of this German character in a book written in 1944 (first published in 1945), which is still used in the teaching of history:

> The history of the Germans is a history of extremes. It contains everything except moderation, and in the course of a thousand years the Germans have experienced everything except normality. They have dominated Europe, and they have been the helpless victims of the domination of others; they have enjoyed liberties unparalleled in Europe and they have fallen victim to despotism equally without parallel; they have produced the most transcendental philosophers, the most spiritual musicians, and the most ruthless and unscrupulous politicians. 'German' has meant at one moment a being so sentimental, so trusting, so pious, as to be too good for this world; and at another a being so brutal, so unprincipled, so degraded, as to be not fit to live. Both descriptions are true: both types of Germans have existed not only at the same epoch, but

---

32. F. Harrison, 'Bismarckism: or, the policy of blood and iron', *Fortnightly Review*, December 1870, pp 631–49 (641).

33. O. Klopp, *Die deutsche Nation und der rechte deutsche Kaiser* (Freiburg i.Br., 1862), p. 47.

34. A.B. (anon), *Die deutsche Frage* (Hamburg, 1859), p. 30.

in the same person. Only the normal person, not particularly good, not particularly bad, healthy, sane, moderate – he has never set his stamp on German history. Geographically the people of the centre, the Germans have never found a middle way of life, either in their thought or least of all in their politics.[35]

One could find many similar estimations from the period of the Second World War in British, French and American archives, in pamphlets and publications of all kinds. More positive, discriminating and well-meant critical judgements are rare, although among those with power and in the media there always could be found some voices who condemned this wholesale indictment of the whole German people.

One critic of this dominant image of the Germans thought it possible 'that the Germans have been saddled by a divine Providence with a double dose of original sin'. He complained that in this image one always encounters Fichte and Hegel, never Kant and Humboldt. A scientific method which could provide reliable evidence on what was typical for a people needed to be developed. Until then it must remain open whether

> Fichte's nationalism and Hegel's aggressiveness are more typically German than Kant's belief in a firm international order and Humboldt's belief in the state as the servant rather than the master of its citizens.[36]

A passage from a British memorandum written almost exactly forty-five years before the meeting of the 'experts' at Chequers very clearly reflects the widespread view of Germans which even today a democratic Germany must confront. Here the view was expressed that National Socialism was

> just an extreme manifestation of the German character. [The German submissiveness and 'double personality'] causes the transfer of allegiance from the discarded leader to the conqueror, with admiration for his power and success. The German therefore now obeys the conqueror and will do so as long as the latter acts in the way the German is accustomed to. He becomes most humble, submissive, indifferent and apathetic, and is quite content to see his country occupied... he is prepared to leave everything to the occupying powers; it is the job of the conquerors to run Germany and to solve her problems, he has no ideas on the subject and no contribution to make; all he wants is order, work and bread. But if the conqueror in turn fails and does not make good his promises... the German will in time turn away from the conqueror, and will again listen

---

35. A.J.P. Taylor, *The Course of German History* (orig. 1945; London, 1971), p. 1.
36. J.C. Maxwell Garnett and H.F. Koeppler, *A Lasting Peace with Some Chapters on the Basis of German Co-operation* (London and New York, 1940), p. 279.

to some new self-proclaimed saviour of the German Volk and will follow him as before.[37]

Even when recent polls of neighbouring countries have shown, with the exception of Poland, support for German reunification, nevertheless one also encounters this image of the 'ugly' (*häßlich*) German. This is especially true at times of crisis. I can only list some of the crises since 1945 which have brought these opinions back to the surface.

The conflicts in the 1950s concerning German rearmament; the treaties with East European countries; the first meeting between Willy Brandt and Stolph in Erfurt in 1970; the increased cooperation between the Federal Republic and the GDR; the debates on the 'double-track' decision of NATO and the discussions of neutralism; the emergence of the Greens and the Republikaner as political forces; and finally the dynamic and momentum of the reunification process, coupled with a fear of Germany going it alone.

Concern at developments since November 1989 was aroused both by the speed at which events have moved and also by the way in which Germans have gone about reunification. For example, an adviser on foreign affairs to the former French prime minister Chirac remarked critically in an article in *Newsweek* that

> the Germans these days resent any restraint from outside. Understandably they feel that the German unification process is *their* business, as Chancellor Kohl's 10-point plan made clear. They feel that they do not have to consult anybody, nor give any additional 'conditions' or 'guarantees' to anyone....I am also disturbed by mounting evidence of a new German assertiveness – some say outright arrogance – which translates at times into a neglect of others' legitimate concerns.[38]

There were fears that the romantic Germans, wanderers within the world, could also explore new options which would take Germany out of the Western alliance – a new Rapallo, or Tauroggen, or Hitler–Stalin pact.

This image of Germany also plays a part in the approach to security questions. It is reasoned from historical experience that a single and powerful Germany placed in the centre of Europe automatically will be a security risk, and that Germany will not be bound by treaties and agreements if these do not suit her interests. The view was expressed

37. Public Record Office London (PRO), FO 371/16864, *The German Character*, 1 March 1945.

38. Pierre Lellouche, 'Frenchmen and Germans: the relationship between the two allies is turning increasingly sour at the very time it is needed most', *Newsweek*, 12 February 1990, p. 4.

in a British memorandum drawn up shortly after the outbreak of the Second World War.

> Germany has shown that if she is sufficiently strong, no treaties or undertakings will deter her from taking by force anything that she may happen to want. Therefore security in Europe is only possible if Germany is not strong enough to act in this way.[39]

This belief played a central role in post-war policy towards Germany and Europe. It was felt that even the dismemberment of Prussia (not the whole of Germany) and the construction of a federal state, although creating a better foundation for a stable and functioning democracy in Germany, would not offer a lasting security to Germany's neighbours.[40] Only with the partition of Germany in 1948–9, a policy which it had been difficult for the Allies to pursue openly or explicitly, did a satisfactory solution seem to have been found. Each of the states could become a 'star pupil' within their respective blocs. Reunification was promised, but one hoped that the promise would never be put into practice. Until 9 November 1989 the watchword was 'Security before the right of self-determination'.

THE GERMAN QUESTION AND EUROPEAN WEST INTEGRATION

In post–war discussions of European questions the term 'integration' became a key idea. It represented a political conception which bound together an image of Germany with views about how to handle security questions, and how the German state should be organised. In relation to Germany integration could be seen negatively, in terms of containing West Germany, or positively, in terms of admitting West Germany as a equal in a community of states.

One can see this from a particular example. From the late 1940s the tensions between the two power blocs led to the idea of rearming West Germany. There was opposition to this not only from within Germany but also from Germany's neighbours, who feared that rearmament would also strengthen West German economically and help lay the basis for a renewed phase of aggression.

39. PRO, FO 371/24370, 'Postwar Security', 12 March 1940.
40. Cf. PRO, FO 371/39080, 'Confederation, Federation and Decentralisation of the German State, and the Dismemberment of Prussia', November 1944.

In connection with the tying in of West Germany to a more tightly organised community of West European states, there were disagreements about the form of economic, political and military integration. The possibility of German reunification constantly played a role in these disagreements. The plan of the French prime minister Pleven in 1950 to establish a European army, the treaties for a European Defence Community, and the question of West Germany's entry into NATO all set off heated debates over the issue of military integration between the Federal Republic and her neighbours. One can see this in the responses of two of Germany's smaller neighbours, Belgium and Denmark, both of which had been occupied by Germany during the Second World War.

In November 1951 the party congress of the Belgian socialists supported the idea of a European army but, by a large majority, opposed the rearmament of West Germany. The fear was that in the event of German reunification the defence forces of the remainder of Western Europe would be too weak. German rearmarment posed a threat to democracy and world peace. Some of the speakers in the debate recalled the Nazi–Soviet pact of 1939, the Treaty of Rapallo, the Convention of Tauroggen, and warned against over-hasty moves towards European unity. The potential German threat meant that there should be no move towards European Federation which did not include Britain. Only a few delegates, like Paul Henri Spaack, saw in the formation of a European Federation an opportunity to solve the German question. In relation to Germany he advocated a policy of 'bold trust' (*Politik des kühnen Vertrauens*), that is taking Germany in as an equal member of such a federation. If this did not happen, but instead the fears of revanchism determined policy, then the West would repeat the mistakes it had made after 1918. The West had denied to a friendly, democratic Weimar Republic what it later gave to Hitler.

Spaack saw the only way forward in the full integration of West Germany into a European Federation. Only this could overcome the anxiety of the German threat. Without Germany Spaack believed there was no chance of a strong Europe developing which could assert itself as an equal partner against the two super-powers. Furthermore, Spaack, as a citizen of a small country, was convinced that the age of the sovereign nation-state in Europe was coming to an end.

Around the same time there was also a debate on security matters in the Danish parliament, the *Folketing*. Fears were expressed about the dangers that Europe and the world might face if democracy were to fail in a rearmed Germany and the military were to take power. It would be preferable to neutralise Germany and to control the German problem in this way. The Danish foreign minister argued against the view that an unarmed, neutral Germany would contribute towards security, peace and a reduction of tension in Europe. On the contrary, a country with 60 million people at the heart of Europe which had become a military vacuum would be a threat to peace.

The debates since the 1950s on security arrangements which would bind a reunited Germany into a European order have been constantly accompanied by the theme of neutralism and neutrality. Even during the Second World War the question of the political organisation of Germany was connected to the task of reducing the German threat to security. Although it is the case that today the majority of Germans have no desire to see a strong, centralised German state, it is necessary for Germans to appreciate these fears of a reunited Germany on the part of her neighbours. For them the unitary German state makes possible the concentration of all the resources of Germany into one pair of hands, as it did in the Wilhelmine period and under Hitler. What is more, a 'Fourth Reich' would be economically much more powerful than its predecessors.

It also should be borne in mind that most other European states have little experience of a federal state system. The point is often forgotten or neglected that federalism has been the traditional form of German state organisation rather than the unitary, unified state. German statehood has developed historically and in the present within a tension between the centralised state and the federal principle. Examples of the latter are the Hansa-Bund, the Holy Roman Empire of the German Nation, the German Confederation of 1815, its successor the North German Confederation, and the Federal Republic. The idea of the normal German state as the Prusso-German power state has pushed these other traditions into the background.

German historical writing, following upon a national movement oriented towards a unitary and powerful nation-state and rejecting federalist ideas, has helped contribute to the contemporary European image of what German unity might mean. A federalist state permits an evolutionary development which mixes together different kinds of statehood. It allows of formations from confederations to leagues of states to a federal state with numerous intermediate stages. This process can be halted or broken at any time. In the development towards a united state of Europe Germans can use their federal historical tradition to good effect and can link it to the West European unifying developments and institutions since 1945. German deputies, for example, were involved in the working out of constitutional proposals for the European Parliament and some submitted their own constitutional schemes.

With Altiero Spinelli as its secretary (Spinelli had already outlined proposals for a European Federation during the Second World War) the Institutional Committee (established 1981) of the first directly elected European Parliament, submitted in 1984 a draft treaty for a European Union. This was accepted by the Parliament on 14 February 1984. This envisaged a two-chamber system within a federal state structure, and aimed for a balance of institutions which does not yet exist. Since then German deputies have outlined proposals for European Union which draw more strongly upon the constitutional model of the Federal Republic of Germany.

Will German unification, welcomed by the European Parliament, accelerate the process of European unification? Will it turn the constitutional ideas of the European Parliament more quickly into reality?

A UNITED GERMANY AS PART OF A UNITED STATES OF EUROPE

In this section I wish to see what credible arguments one can put forward about the role of a united Germany in Europe. It is my view that most Germans see the future in European rather than German terms. 'From Germany to Europe' is the one sensible maxim of German policy, not the resurrection of older plans, such as those developed during the Second World War, of a united Europe organised through German power.

The changes in Eastern Europe and the dissolution of the two political blocs have ended the unnatural divisions of both Germany and Europe. They open up new perspectives for a unification of the continent based on what has already happened in Western Europe. They also demand new pan-European thinking, a vision of Europe, the use of the imagination. Those who work for a united Europe must always remember that they are a link in a tradition which goes back a long way and which in this century is associated with names such as Briand, Stresemann, Churchill, Monnet and Spinelli. These men 'provide us with examples that it is not pointless to try to work out a new conception of the future of Europe'.[41]

41. H. Schmidt, op.cit., pp. 562f.

There are, in my view, two key guidelines for the path to a European nation. Already in 1930 Ortega y Gasset wrote that

> Nationalisms are dead-ends... They lead nowhere. Only the decision to make one nation out of the various groups of people in the world can reinvigorate Europe. Our continent will win back its self-belief and, as a consequence of setting itself a great task, put its own house in order.[42]

The experiences of the Second World War turned Jean Monnet into a convinced European and architect of the Iron and Steel Community. When the European Community was established he wrote

> The 'Common Market' is not a static creation; it is a new and dynamic phase in the development of our civilisation. The essential characteristic of this new phase is that nations have now begun to accept that their problems are joint problems and cannot be settled by national measures only.[43]

However, the Europe of nation-states has not yet been superseded. The process of European integration has stagnated. In the light of this, Monnet, in his memoirs, insisted on the need to push on unceasingly for a United States of Europe. There was no alternative. This was a path on which there could be no turning back.

> As our provinces learnt yesterday, so must our nations learn today, to live together under common rules and under common, freely devised institutions, if they wish to make progress and master their own fate. The sovereign nations of the past are no longer the units within which the problems of the present can be solved. And the community [that is the EC] is only one stage on the path to a form of world organisation in the future.[44]

Today we need new concepts for the building of the common house of Europe, for the future organisational forms of Europe, which go beyond fine speeches without serious commitment.

For example, Poland, Hungary and Czechoslovakia already formally meet the requirements set out by the draft treaty of the European Parliament for membership of a European Union. They are no longer 'peoples' democracies' but have turned themselves into pluralist democracies along Western lines which form governments by means of democratic and free elections. This also fulfils a central requirement for membership of the EC. Article 2 of the draft treaty on European Union declares:

42. Gasset, op.cit., p. 136.
43. J. Monnet, 'Introduction', in R. Mayne (ed.) *The Community of Europe: Past, Present and Future* (New York, 1963), p. 5.
44. J. Monnet, *Erinnerungen eines Europäers* (Munich, 1980), p. 662.

Every democratic European state can apply for membership of the Union.[45]

However, an immediate entry of these states, even if formally justified, given the simultaneous intensification of efforts at political integration in Western Europe can serve the interests neither of Western Europe nor of the aspirants of Eastern Europe. The new Europe must leave open a place for the USSR in the European house. Besides the EC states, the states of east-central and south-eastern Europe and the USSR, there are states which do not belong to the military alliances, for example the EFTA member states, the European signatories to the Conference on Security and Cooperation in Europe, and those states which are merely members of the Council of Europe. All these states and groups of states must find a place in the Europe of the future. The Council of Europe, which since 1949 has stimulated changes in the political landscape of Western Europe, can play an important part in the changes within Europe. In a transitional phase the Council of Europe and its institutions could serve as a way of tying together all European states and groups of states.

On the basis of geography and its special European position Germany, deliberately but not arrogantly, must take on a constructive and creative responsibility for the growing together of Europe, though without presenting itself as the 'master' of this process. If Germany is to do this, to take the second chance in the twentieth century in a European sense, and not, as an anxious Europe fears, to reverse a lost war by other means into a victory, with Germany the master from Atlantic to Pacific, then it must act for a Europe beyond that of nation-states. Germans must renounce state egoism and attempts at hegemony. They must oppose the nationalist rhetoric of a minority and demonstrate that a democratic Germany will also be a European Germany. Germany, once more a sovereign state since 3 October 1990, must take up once again its centuries-long tradition of European peacemaker. If a united Europe is to develop, Germany must place its potential in the service of the common European interest. Other Europeans hope that this will furnish a welcome and reconciling conclusion to the German question.

The path to a united Europe, as for a united Germany, will take the federalist form. The discussions in the nineteenth century and after 1945 of a German constitution with 'narrower' and 'wider' federations can be

45. 'Entwurf eines Vertrages zur Gründung der Europäischen Union', printed in R. Bieber and J. Schwarze (eds) *Verfassungsentwicklung in der Europäischen Gemeinschaft* (Baden-Baden, 1984), pp. 95–128 (97).

of use in the construction of a European constitution. This could be related to the necessary transitional phase – one of a two-speed Europe – when a narrower political union of the EC states concerned with creating a single internal market, must coexist with a broader band of states beyond the EC.

It was only as recently as 1989 and early 1990 that such a model of a narrower and a wider federation seemed appropriate to the process of German unification. Now it offers a perspective for a growing together of the various parts of Europe in a fairly smooth fashion. Germany must take on responsibility for such a policy if it is serious about its European calling and wishes to be understood as a European Germany.

The aim of all Germans today must be, precisely because of the historical and European dimensions of the German question, to make the new, democratic and federal Germany into a stabilising element within Europe, positively pursuing first Western European and then pan-European integration and acting as a catalyst for the realisation of the long European dream. This must include a pan-European security order which must reach across the Atlantic and the whole of Europe and bind together the two super-powers of the USA and the USSR.

The Germans must show their European neighbours and partners, through the policies pursued, that the historically understandable fears of a united Germany are groundless, that a democratic Germany does not close itself to its history, but has learnt from that history and re-nounces that old Germany which still preoccupies others. Only in this way can a new image of Germany and a new understanding of Germany emerge from the shadows of the past. What is also important is the cultivation of a European consciousness.

Salvador de Madariaga noted in 1952 in his portrait of Europe:

> 'Fiat Europe' will not be possible until Europeans cease to trumpet the age-old war cries of their tribes, scantily covered over by nationalist historians with the fig-leaf of academic history. Europe must think its history anew and experience it afresh as what it really is, as European history.[46]

As Europeans we must all take responsibility for the construction of a genuinely European history, for the 'future of history'. Graf Ferraris referred to an important step in this work when he demanded:

> If German history…is once again to be fitted harmoniously into the history of Europe, then Europeans must be conscious of their history and must cease, in common with Germans, to be prisoners of the recent and dramatic past. That past is indeed dramatic, but it is also short.[47]

46. Madariaga, op.cit., p. 9.
47. Ferraris, op.cit., p. 16.

Today the chance is offered to Germans and to all Europeans to seize the opportunity that is offered and to find unity.

SUGGESTIONS FOR FURTHER READING:

Luigi Barzini, *The Europeans* (Harmondsworth, 1983).

David Calleo, *The German Problem Reconsidered. Germany and the World Order, 1870 to the Present* (Cambridge, 1980).

Jean-Baptiste Duroselle, *Europe. A History of its Peoples* (London, 1991).

John Gillingham, *Coal, Steel, and the Rebirth of Europe 1945–1955. The Germans and French from Ruhr Conflict to Economic Community* (Cambridge, 1991).

Wolf D. Gruner, *Die deutsche Frage – ein Problem der europäischen Geschichte seit 1800* (Munich, 1985); new enlarged edition 1992 (Series Piper Aktuell).

Wolf D. Gruner, *Deutschland mitten in Europa* (Hamburg, 1991).

Wolf D. Gruner, 'European Integration and the German Question,' in Brian Nelson, David Roberts, Walter Veit (eds), *The European Community in the 1990s. Economics, Politics, Defence* (Oxford, 1992).

Wolf D. Gruner, 'The Impact of the Reconstruction of Central Europe in 1814–15 on the System of Peace in the 19th Century,' in A.P. van Goudoever (ed.), *The Great Peace Congresses. Proceedings of the Conference. Utrecht August 16–17, 1991* (Utrecht, 1991).

Wolfram Hanrieder, *Germany, America, Europe: Forty Years of German Foreign Policy* (New Haven, 1989).

Olov Riste (ed.), *Western Security, The Formative Years. European and Atlantic Defence 1947–1953* (New York, 1985).

John K. Sowden, *The German Question 1945–1973* (London, 1975).

Richard H. Ullman, *Securing Europe* (Princeton, 1991).

Derek W. Urwin, *The Community of Europe. A History of European Integration since 1945* (London and New York, 1991).

Dirk Verheyen, *The German Question. A Cultural, Historical, and Geopolitical Exploration* (Boulder, 1991).

Dirk Verheyen and Christian Soe (eds), *The Germans and their Neighbors* (Boulder, 1992).

Nils H. Wessell (ed), *The New Europe. Revolution in East-West Relations* (New York, 1991).

CHAPTER TWELVE

Conclusion: nationalism and German reunification

John Breuilly

The historian is no better equipped to predict than anyone else; studying the past only makes one aware of how uncertain is the future. However, it is worth trying to relate the themes of the changes and significance in the role of political nationality in modern German history to the present and immediate future.

What role did nationality play in the 'revolution' of 1989–90? To understand that we need first to remind ourselves of the speed with which changes took place. At the beginning of 1989 Erich Honecker was still in power and insisting that the Berlin Wall would remain 'as long as the conditions leading to its erection have not changed, it will still be standing in 50 and even in 100 years' time'.

The events which developed rapidly from mid-1989 can be broken down into three elements: the impact of changes in Eastern Europe, especially the USSR, upon East Germany; the shifts of political power and mood in East Germany; the policies pursued by the West, especially West Germany, in response to events in East Germany. In turn, political action in East Germany can be divided into those involving the power-holders, the political opposition, and large numbers of previously politically uninvolved who sought to leave East Germany from September 1989 and took to the streets from October.

By mid-1989 the USSR faced many internal problems and it was increasingly clear that it would not intervene in the affairs of Warsaw Pact countries in order to sustain existing Communist regimes. In July at a Warsaw Pact meeting in Bucharest this position was made explicit, and the countries rejected the Brezhnev doctrine which had legitimated such intervention in Czechoslovakia in 1968. The satellite states of Eastern Europe were on their own. Already a number had embarked on major political and economic reforms, leaving East Germany behind in this respect. One reform was to remove border controls between Hungary and Austria. For many East Germans, Hungary had been important as a holiday resort and a place where one could escape some of the rigours of their own situation. Such possibilities had in turn been an important element in the way the East German government had sought to make life more attractive for its own citizens, without abandoning its basic economic and political policies.

Now Hungary came to serve as an escape route to the West as well, and many East Germans flooded into the country, and into the missions of the Federal Republic of Germany in Budapest as well as Prague and East Berlin. By August the situation was sufficiently serious for the West German government to reach agreement with the Hungarian and Austrian governments for tens of thousands of East Germans to cross into the Federal Republic. By early September the Hungarian government had decided it could no longer restrict the exit of East Germans, and announced the complete opening of its borders. Some 50,000 East Germans travelled by this route to West Germany.

This touched off an internal crisis in East Germany. Opposition groups now came into the open politically in early September, with the formation of the New Forum, and within a couple of weeks the first protest demonstrations had started in Leipzig. East Germans continued to vote with their feet, and various agreements were struck to allow them to move from other East European countries to West Germany. The East German government was faced with the dilemma of allowing this to continue or to seal its borders with the rest of Eastern Europe.

The obvious response was to pursue political reform in order to remove the pressure both of political opposition and mass emigration. It was clear that the USSR favoured this course. Gorbachev visited East Germany in early October on the occasion of the fortieth anniversary of the regime. He made this clear and also distanced himself from Honecker, encouraging other elements within the country's political elite to remove Honecker and embark on a reformist course. Within a fortnight Honecker had gone, and was replaced by Egon Krenz.

Political change also continued apace in other Eastern European countries. There were mass demonstrations in Czechoslovakia and on 23 October Hungary declared itself a multi-party republic. In early November the GDR revoked its border controls with Czechoslovakia. Thousands more East Germans escaped to West Germany by this route. Between 8 and 10 November a new Politburo was elected for the GDR. The dramatic change came on 9 November, when the GDR government finally decided it could hold the line no longer against mass pressure to emigrate and declared the Berlin Wall open.

So far in the crisis the West German government had only acted in its role of welcoming anyone who wished to leave East Germany and making arrangements to enable such movement. 'Nationality' played a role only in the sense that it was the 'two states, one nation' doctrine which underpinned that commitment, and also that awareness of this commitment had long encouraged East Germans to compare their situation with that of West Germany and to look to West Germany as a refuge, even as a 'home'.

At this moment, however, Chancellor Kohl moved on the other 'national' element of West German policy, namely the commitment to reunification. On 28 November he presented to the *Bundestag* a ten-point programme for overcoming the division of Germany and of Europe. He placed that programme firmly within a commitment to NATO and the European Community, insisting that it was those alliances whose firmness at times of crisis had helped bring about change in the east. He also argued that good relations with East Germany, especially allowing so many cross-border visits, had helped maintain a sense of national unity. But now was the time to move decisively to end the division in Germany.

First, there needed to be emergency aid to assist the many East Germans coming into West Germany. Also communications with East Germany needed improving. West Germany could help East Germany if she introduced democratic political reforms and economic reforms that would move the country towards a market economy. There could be more treaty arrangements with East Germany, and one could even consider the establishment of confederal relationships, but only once a democratic government had been established in East Germany. Interestingly Kohl appealed here to German history, pointing out that political structures had most usually taken a federal or a confederal form. However, he also insisted that these developments must take place within a European context and Kohl's next points concerned agreements with the USSR, further integration and extension of the European Community, and arms reductions and controls undertaken by the Conference on Security and Cooperation and the various arms limitation talks. Finally, Kohl reiterated the commitment to German reunification.

Kohl had moved the debate from issues of refugees and internal crisis to one of fundamental political and economic reform which would press East Germany towards democracy and a market economy and open up the prospects for reunification, but set within a broader European context. Yet even Kohl had as yet no inkling of the speed with which events would move in East Germany, assuming that there would be for some time a credible government with which to make agreements and exert pressure. For a short period this seemed to be the case as the GDR, with Hans Modrow as prime minister, introduced various reforms and negotiated treaties and agreements with West Germany.

However, these agreements and the reforms undertaken in the GDR actually hastened its demise. Political reform led to the formation of political parties in readiness for elections to the *Volkskammer* which were to be held in March 1990. Bringing down the Berlin Wall reduced the rate of emigration to West Germany, but now allowed a steady loss of population which created severe economic problems. That, along with the exposure of a frail economy to Western competition and the collapse of Comecon trading patterns, meant that the idea of reforming the GDR economy with a gradual move to market economics had to be given up in favour of the idea of West Germany taking responsibility for all of Germany.

In both cases what mattered was in effect a West German intervention. The attractions of her economy and the right of all Germans to move undermined the GDR economy. One can see this at a number of critical points. For example, in the early demonstrations of late September/early October in Leipzig, one of the major slogans had been '*Wir bleiben hier!*' ('We are staying here!'). This was a rejection of emigration as the solution to problems. It was also a commitment to the idea of an internal renewal within the GDR. However, the removal of the Berlin Wall now made emigration easier. What is more, the policy of the West German government to give every East German visitor 100 Marks to spend in the West helped reinforce the sense of common deprivation in the East and the attractions of a rapid integration into West Germany. The size and number of the demonstrations increased (there was now much less danger involved in participation), the social basis extended downwards. Another popular slogan in the early demonstrations had been '*Wir sind das Volk!*' ('We are the people!'). This was not only a commitment to democratic reform but also an indignant repudiation of the governmental propaganda which had presented the demonstrators as an irresponsible and self-interested mob. Now the slogan became '*Wir sind ein Volk!*' ('We are one nation!'). Never have the multiple meanings of the word *Volk*, combined with a shift from the definite to the indefinite article, reflected so profound a change in mood and purpose. What is more, the new GDR government gave some support to this commitment to unification, with Modrow's emotional statement that there was but a single German fatherland.

This rapidly increasing mass commitment to joining the West, along with the sheer political and economic bankruptcy which was made clear in the early months of 1990, pushed events on rapidly. West German political parties, in particular the CDU, effectively took over the campaign of its East German counterpart for the March 1990 elections. The GDR CDU obtained a majority of seats with other conservative political groupings in a coalition calling itself the 'Alliance for Germany'. This led in turn to the formation of a new government with a CDU (East) prime minister, Lothar de Maizière, committed to German unity.

At the same time Kohl was removing the international obstacles to unity. He tied the USA and the European Community into this process by getting their agreement to his unity policy and to measures to integrate the GDR when this was achieved. In February he visited Moscow to agree on the steps to unification with Gorbachev, who made it clear that he did not oppose this in principle and that there would be no Soviet military action to halt such a process. This led on to talks (known as the Four plus Two talks) between the wartime Allies and the two German governments.

By May a treaty between the two Germanies establishing monetary, economic and social union was signed. This came into effect in July. In August treaties on all-German elections and unification were signed, and were ratified by the two German parliaments through September. The old *Länder*, which the GDR had abolished in 1954, were restored. This made possible, on 3 October, the unification of the GDR with the Federal Republic by means of Article 23 of the Basic Law of 1949 which permitted accession by individual *Länder*. In the same period final agreement was reached with the USSR on the united Germany choosing to be a member of NATO and a timetable for the phased withdrawal of Soviet troops from GDR territory. Finally, on 2 December the first all-German elections to the *Bundestag* were held, resulting in a victory for the CDU/CSU/FDP coalition. Interestingly, the electorate did not reward Kohl and his own party for his policies. The arguments of the FDP leader Genscher, who took much credit as foreign minister for the unification process, that it would be dangerous to have a simple CDU/CSU majority were heeded. The FDP did particularly well in GDR territories. By now the SPD reservations about rapid unification, as expressed in the campaign of their Chancellor candidate, Oscar Lafontaine, had become a clear vote loser.

In retrospect one can see that by the end of 1989 the major factors at work were the policy of the West German government and popular opinion in East Germany. Kohl's decisive shift of policy from November 1989 had made it clear to the East German population that rapid change was to be encouraged. For the bulk of East Germans rapid change meant moving closer to West Germany rather than pursuing a course of reform within an independent state. This undercut the position of the existing political opposition as well as the government in East Germany. Lacking any other political elites, the key political forces became in effect subsidiaries of West German parties.

It is clear that in many respects Kohl moved ahead of public opinion in West Germany. Opinion polls in early 1990 point to scepticism about moving too rapidly towards unification, above all for fear of the extra burdens it would place upon West Germany. The SPD built its own political line around those reservations. Its Chancellor candidate, Oscar Lafontaine, identified himself with that policy and went on to contest the December election on that basis. In early 1990, in East Germany as well as West Germany, there had been widespread fear that over-rapid unification could prove painful. In the euphoria created by the collapse of the East German political and economic system and the removal of international obstacles to rapid unification, these doubts and fears were temporarily forgotten.

Three things above all had undermined these doubts in the short-term, or at least prevented them from slowing down the path to reunification. First, the speed of collapse of the East German political and economic system meant that there was little alternative but for the West German government to make the running. Second, the monetary union of July 1990, on the unrealistic conversion rate of 1:1 (with some exceptions for certain kinds of savings) provided a temporary glow of satisfaction – giving East Germans a sudden surge of purchasing power and increasing demand for goods from West Germany. Coupled with Kohl's assurance that unification would be economically painless, something people were only too anxious to believe, this enabled the third element to play its part. The latent sense of national identity, that it was 'natural' for there to be a single German state, could now come to the surface, unhindered by all the political and economic considerations which had relegated the idea of unification to the realm of fantasy. All this helped Kohl and his coalition to a decisive election victory in December.

In all this, therefore, nationality mattered decisively. It underpinned the West German commitment to accepting citizens of East Germany, and that in turn shaped the way East Germans acted. Emigration to the 'better Germany' rather than political dissent began the internal crisis and the popular vote for the Deutschmark and integration with West Germany brought the crisis to an end. The commitment to unity meant that it was the intervention of West German political forces which resolved that crisis rather than internal political opposition, either from within the SED or from among the emergent opposition movements. In other East European countries change was brought about by shifts within the political elite (Hungary), by the rise in political dissent and opposition (Czechoslovakia), by the development of mass oppositions (Poland), or by some combination of these (Romania). The national dimension to the German situation gave the internal crisis a different character and meant it was very quickly resolved by means of unification. Reformist Communism, political dissent, and mass politicisation were all undercut by a West German takeover before they had been able to become politically significant.

Yet that option of radical change by means of rapid unification emerged as a practical one only some time after the crisis had begun. It was not nationalism as a determined politics of unification which mattered, so much as nationality as a latent sense of identity which underpinned the political obligations of the Federal Republic to GDR citizens and gave focus to a 'fixation' with the West among the population of East Germany. For many years East Germans could be visited by relatives from the West, could watch German television, and in some cases could visit West Germany. In this way the 'national' and the 'West' were fused, as a model and as an objective. This was counterposed to the bankruptcy of the GDR. For example, people watched West German television not only because it revealed to them lives they could only dream of (in a way West Germans watching *Dynasty* and *Dallas* were doing the same), but also because so much of GDR television output had nothing to offer, be it attractive fantasy or an engagement with the real problems of its viewers.[1] It was not only the Deutschmark payments and the lure of Western consumerism that attracted people to the West but also the knowledge of the bankruptcy of their own economy. In this double way, West Germany served as a focus for most people's hopes. Once it became clear that the East German government could no longer maintain control, this fixation swept all before it.

Perhaps the only really puzzling feature of the whole event is why

1. The point has been interestingly made that, where GDR television did engage in that way (and where its successors still do) – in the field of drama rather than news or current affair programmes – then such programmes have secured much larger viewing figures than other programmes. How far this will continue when a greater diet of Western programmes becomes available is another matter. See P. Hoff, 'Continuity and change: television in the GDR from autumn 1989 to summer 1990', *German History: The Journal of the German History Society* 9/2 (1991), pp. 184–96.

the Kohl government decided to exploit this fixation to the maximum when so many in West Germany had been reserved about too precipitous a policy. Partly this seems to be due to the problem of the unexpectedly rapid collapse of control in the GDR: if the Federal Republic had to assume responsibility, better to do so swiftly and completely. Partly it could be seen in terms of electoral calculation: to be able to go into elections as the man who reunified Germany. Kohl had been doing badly in opinion polls and reunification certainly did rejuvenate him and his party. Partly it could be seen as exploiting a brief opportunity. One could never be sure at what point the USSR might harden its position,[2] or indeed whether various of Germany's allies would start indicating serious reservations about the process. Partly it could be seen in terms of economic pressures. At the beginning West German business seems to have been sanguine about the impact of reunification. Few anticipated the subsequent difficulties and many could see rich pickings. But above all I would plump for the simplest explanation. For decades German conservatives had tried to combine the apparently contradictory − full integration into the West with the reunification of the nation-state. Suddenly in late 1989 this appeared possible. They had no desire to see a reformed GDR perhaps insist on different kinds of German–German relations; maybe to try to uncouple the Federal Republic from its strong Western orientation. In this sense, therefore, the specifically conservative view of national unification in the Federal Republic also played a key role in the events of 1989–90. Nevertheless, that particular policy worked only on the basis of a much broader support for unification which flowed from the underlying sense of national identity.

The character of unification and the role of nationality in unification was, therefore, very different from 1871. It was very much *re*-unification, in the sense of a commitment to the idea of a nation-state which had in some sense already existed. Strictly speaking, of course, it was unification because it brought together two states which had never previously been connected to each other, but this sense of a pre-existing nation-state made it appear as reunification. It was also above all a popular idea, and not so much a nationalist idea as a route for East Germans to an imagined world of prosperity and freedom. Obviously there was a good deal of truth in this idea, but there were also unrealistic expectations which actual reunification would be bound to expose.

2. I write these words on 21 August, just after the collapse of the coup against Gorbachev. During the short time of the coup Kohl argued that an event of that kind justified his pursuit of rapid unification.

At first the idea seemed to have few drawbacks. In the euphoria of 1989–90 it was the German component of a dawning of freedom in the Eastern Bloc countries. And in this case it did appear that many of the difficulties of the transition to that freedom would be carried on the strong back of West Germany. Indeed, at first all the talk was of how much stronger the accession of the GDR territories would make Germany. Few critics saw this in territorial terms – the fears associated with the Germany of 1871 or 1914 or 1938–9 – but rather in terms of economic domination. It was only the critical intelligentsia – both of West and East Germany – who condemned this as Deutschmark patriotism. Otherwise, the only reservations concerned the pacing and modalities of the change. The *Bundesbank*, for example, warned against rapid monetary unification on an unrealistic exchange rate.

Events since December 1990 have rather altered this mood. The 1:1 convertibility of the Mark has proved a grave error. Hopes that money wage levels would stay unchanged in the former GDR, thereby compensating for lower productivity rates, proved false. Economists now consider that even the productivity differences understate the relative inefficiency of the GDR economy in relation to the West. Measured in terms of the purchasing power of GDR products to West German products in international markets, a conversion of 4:1 would have been realistic, as a few economists argued at the time. However, the effect on East German living standards made such a rate unacceptable. The 1:1 rate rendered much of GDR economic activity hopelessly uncompetitive at a stroke. Coupled with the loss of Comecon markets, a lack of access to USSR natural resources, and the insistence of the USSR on trading for the hard currency of dollars, the result has been catastrophic.

A few figures tell the grim story more effectively than words. GDR gross national product fell some 20 per cent in 1990, with industrial output down 50 per cent. Comecon trade has been cut to one-third of its earlier level. From an 'official' zero rate of unemployment, by the end of March 1990 there were over 800,000 jobless and some 2 million people working short-time, much of that subsidised by the German government. (This support has now been extended to December 1991.) Some economists think unemployment could go up to 2 million with another 0.5 million on short-time working. Another 2 million people (usually the younger and more energetic and more skilled) have moved west out of former GDR territory, and 20,000 still leave every month. In a total population of around 17 million, these represent serious losses to the total labour force of the former GDR territory and to its economy.

All this reveals just how weak and uncompetitive most of the GDR economy had become, probably weaker relatively in 1990 than it had been ten years earlier, thanks to a precipitate fall in capital investment, itself partly due to an attempt by the GDR regime to legitimise itself by bolstering consumption and social benefits.

The West German economy faces very different problems. There was a huge 'demand shock' as East Germans used their savings to purchase hitherto unavailable goods, especially as such purchasing power was inflated by the favourable convertibility rate. The result was inflationary pressure, over-employment, and a push on wage rates. Another result was a switch away from production for export to production for domestic consumption (though, of course, what had originally been counted as exports to the GDR now became a component of domestic consumption). Germany's traditional balance of payments surplus was wiped out in a single year. There was pressure on public finance – for example paying social security and retraining programmes in the former GDR which also led to government borrowing. The effect was to raise interest rates and to put pressure on the Deutschmark.

The way the contrasting economic difficulties combined has also been unfortunate. German trade unions, concerned about lower wage levels in the East undercutting the rates of most of their members in the West, have pressed for national wage rates with East German earnings rising to that of their West German counterparts. The effect can only be to increase inflationary pressures, reduce resources for capital investment, increase unemployment and closures in East Germany, and sustain or increase the flight to the West. However, that in turn will put pressure on housing and job markets and create further tensions.

The situation has not been helped by the doctrinaire economic policies which at first accompanied the reunification process. The collapse of Communism has been seen as automatically indicating the superiority of the free market system. The German government at first wanted to see as rapid a transition to market economics as possible. The *Treuhand* concern which took over all former state enterprise in the GDR saw its task primarily as one of privatisation. The market would take care of everything and 'intervention' would only slow down and possibly even undermine the rapid transition which was so necessary. This also had the attraction of appearing to avoid the need for higher taxes to finance any interventionist policy.

In recent months the German government appears to have seen the error of its ways. *Treuhand* increasingly sees its role as restructuring as much as of privatisation. The necessity to raise taxes has finally been recognised. Policies to encourage investment in infrastructure (e.g through loans to local government) are being adopted. But much more remains to be done. Perhaps the biggest bullet to bite might be the idea of a labour subsidy to former GDR areas to enable employers to keep their work force but at competitive wages. But a measure of that kind would cost an enormous amount, and meets the problems of unpopularity in western Germany as well as going against the general philosophy of the government.

Indeed it is the immensity of the reconstruction task and its unpopularity in western Germany which now (August 1991) dominates public opinion. It appears that the government has no clear idea any more of just how much reconstruction will cost and how it is to be financed.[3] There is also fear that this might undermine the lead Germany has taken in European affairs. For example, the issue of monetary union in the European Community has been tied very firmly to notions of 'economic convergence'. Germany realises more strongly than ever the consequences of monetary union with 'backward' areas. What is more, it will be difficult for the German government to press a policy of monetary restraint upon a future European bank, if it itself is being more spendthrift in terms of borrowing and printing money. The government has made it clear that an early casualty of its over-extension will be aid to Eastern European countries. Yet at the same time, it is the economic weight of the European Community which appears to offer the one slim chance of preventing the break-up of Yugoslavia. It is also argued that only Western aid will prevent even worse crises erupting in the USSR. (This argument will surely increase in weight since the unsuccessful coup in August 1991.) Germany is more acutely aware of the dangers posed to itself by such crises; yet at present seems to be less capable than a year ago of taking the lead in responding in a positive and preventive way.

Pessimism is not confined to the German economy and European developments. East Germans in many walks of life are finding reunification a bitter experience. In the universities and academies there are closures of politically suspect institutions and a scrutiny of the political and intellectual credentials of those who remain. There is, in my view, no alternative to such a policy – one cannot allow corrupt propagandists and party hacks to continue to teach and enjoy academic privileges. However, individual cases are never simply black or white; and so far as academic credentials are concerned the blame lies less with the individual than with the limited opportunities and resources avail-

---

3. *Der Spiegel*, 1 July 1991: feature article 'Steuer-Opfer für den Osten: Wieviel noch?'

able to scientists, social scientists and other academics in the GDR. This problem of accommodating to West German standards is repeated in every sector of skilled employment.

At the same time resentment and a sense of superiority can be discerned among West Germans. There is resentment at having to pay to help East Germans. There is also an increasing awareness that living in two very different societies and states has created very different people. At times East Germans are talked about in ways which in other countries would be regarded as racist. 'Nationality' as a latent sense of identity inherited from the existence of a nation-state between 1871 and 1945, as a commitment of the Federal Republic to the GDR, and as a fixation upon the Federal Republic shared by many GDR citizens is turning out to be something very different from 'nationality' as actual habits and values and ways of living together.

My own feeling, however, is that much of this pessimism is as unrealistic as the optimism was a year ago. Indeed, one exaggerated mood has followed in reaction to the disillusionment of the first. In economic terms surely the most basic point is that the dynamic West German economy which had an ageing population has suddenly acquired access to a younger population. Not only that but also this population is itself German and is well-disciplined and quite well-schooled at least up to secondary level. Indeed it has recently been asserted that young East Germans are better equipped in basic literacy than their West German counterparts. When one considers the problems Germany faced in 1945 and compares them to the problems that it confronts now, and when one thinks that the most basic components of economic success in developed economies are technology and what in economic jargon is known as 'human capital' – then the pessimism appears misplaced. There will be problems in the short term, but provided a sensible policy of infrastructural investment is followed in the GDR areas, I would think these will be overcome within a decade.

The same will then apply to the 'problem' of cultural tensions and 'national identity'. German intellectuals, and less understandably, intellectuals from Britain, constantly agonise over an alleged problem of 'national identity' in Germany. But what the historical evidence suggests, as analysed in this book, is that there is no problem. 'National identity' does not develop as a consequence of deliberate propaganda and governmental policy, or as a product of historians and others who betray their vocation as social scientists to engage in myth-making. National identity develops at two levels – institutional and cultural. Institutionally it develops by people learning the same 'habits' – of voting, joining organisations, using the courts, dealing with the police, paying taxes, etc. Culturally, in modern industrial societies, it develops through the construction of a 'standard national culture'.

So far as the first is concerned, the majority of Germans have now learnt thoroughly the 'habits' of the Federal Republic of Germany. In terms of 'institutional loyalty', in certain respects it might appear that the Federal Republic is more stable than the United Kingdom. In the United Kingdom there is one part of the country – Ulster – where institutional loyalty has not really established itself. Partly as cause, partly as consequence of that, Ulster actually has different institutions from the rest of the UK. If one takes willing tax-paying as a measure of institutional consent, then the poll tax, especially in Scotland and many inner cities, reveals far less institutional loyalty than anything in Germany.

At a cultural level, a recent opinion poll showed that even most whites, let alone non-whites, believed Britain to be a racist society. (It might be said that this also applies to German attitudes towards foreign workers, but unlike the United Kingdom or France, large numbers of these ethnic minorities do not possess citizenship rights in the state so this is politically, although not of course morally, a less important problem.) No doubt there is a difficult learning process to be gone through in Germany – not only by East Germans who must come to terms with living in an 'open society', but also one hopes by West Germans who will see that the optimal solution to problems is not always just to adopt the existing West German approach. But the population is ethnically homogeneous and shares in the major components of a 'standard national culture'. I cannot see that the remaining problems of integrating East and West Germans are somehow more difficult tasks than those faced by other developed industrial societies. In many ways a strong economy and a well-accepted set of economic and political institutions makes the task a lot easier.

The Federal Republic by 1989 had developed into one successful democratic and industrial society among others. Unification – based on the acceptance of the nation-state of 1871–1945 (less certain eastern territories) as the 'normal' political unit – in one sense was not unique either. *Everyone*, German and non-German, sees the nation-state as normal. It is indeed this perception of the nation-state as natural that gives it its power as a political idea. What history should do is make us aware of how novel and in many ways strange is this idea. The assumption that the German nation-state is a natural entity is largely the product of the modern German nation-state, just as French identity and British identity are products of their nation-states. Before that state was created, conceptions of nationality were less central and served many different, often conflicting purposes. After that state was created, internal and external tensions meant that there were competing forms of nationalism, but underlying this there did develop a more latent, 'natural' sense of national identity. The same happened in other countries with stable political institutions, fairly successful economies, and mass cultural institutions. One can assume that such a sense of identity will continue to exist, now modifying itself as it incorporates GDR territory and citizens.

At the same time, the character of recent German history has meant that Germans are less politically committed to the idea of the nation-state as a hard concentration of sovereignty. Federalism has been more important in a much more recently unified country than in the longer-existing unitary nation-states of Britain, France and Spain. At the same time over-assertive nationalism was discredited and destroyed by the Third Reich. Ideas of incorporation into larger international blocs do not disturb Germans in the way they do many British people. I would not see this policy of European integration as some cunning German route to indirect domination (now that the direct route has been discredited). It is not even uniquely German: inhabitants of countries which were occupied by Germany between 1939 and 1945 are also well aware of the limitations and fragility of nation-states. It is not an 'escape' from national identity – with the implication that identity is a matter of deliberate choice rather than a set of habits which develop over time. Rather it is a part of the way German habits have developed since 1945.

That does not mean the Europeanism of Germans is 'right' and the hostility of many British people to such Europeanism is 'wrong'. It may be if Germany does prove economically successful in the medium-term she will dominate integrated European institutions, and that may cause problems in other parts of Europe. But in part the dispute is based upon the way national identity has been developed within different kinds of nation-states. In a way the British state is as many of its politicians see it – very centralised, with inseparable links between executive and legislature, with little idea of the rule of law as entrenched in written constitutions. Equally the German state is not like that, but more federalised, with a written constitution, and a matter of fact acceptance of the idea that different powers can be located in different places. In other words, different kinds of states promote, by the habits their institutions inculcate, different kinds of national identity. To understand Germany today, and to understand its relationship with Europe, requires us to understand how different and changing conceptions of nationality have developed. We need to see national identity neither as a deliberate and special belief nor as part of the natural order of things, but as a central component of modernity, closely bound up with the way modern states have developed. I hope this book has made something of that clear for the case of Germany.

SUGGESTIONS FOR FURTHER READING

The events considered in this conclusion are too recent and unfinished to have yet given rise to much in the way of historical analysis. I have mainly relied on British and German newspapers and periodicals. The German government has published some useful chronologies and collections of documents such as *Umbruch in Europa: Die Ereignisse im 2. Halbjahr 1989. Eine Dokumentation* (Bonn, 1990). There is a large amount of material being published in German but little, if anything, has yet filtered through into English.

Index